"Patricia Fletcher's book *Classically Speaking* is a compendium of everything there is to know about how words are formed when speaking Neutral American, Classical American and Standard British, both using IPA and in detailed description of lip, tongue and jaw positioning. She explains figures of speech, rhythms of speech and speech inflections and offers hundreds of practice texts from one-liners to tongue twisters to poems and speeches. THE SERIOUS STUDENT WILL FIND EVERYTHING HERE TO EXPAND AND ENRICH HIS OR HER AWARENESS AND EXPERTISE IN SPEECH, DIALECTS AND TEXT INTERPRETATION. Ms. Fletcher is a brilliant and sensitive teacher - her knowledge is faithfully represented in these pages."

Kristin Linklater
Founder, Linklater Voice

"I consider Patricia Fletcher ONE OF THE FOREMOST INSTRUCTORS IN THE FIELD. Through her character-driven speech and dialect work, Pat's care and concern is always on the mantle of originality and creativity. I am enviable of today's graduate students, and I welcome her daily to the classroom in appreciation for this very valuable new textbook for the 21st century actor."

Robert LuPone
Artistic Director, MCC Theatre

"Patricia Fletcher's sensitivity to the sounds, rhythms, and musicality of American speech TUNES THE ACTOR'S EAR TO A WORLD OF DIALECTS, through the use of phonetics, comprehensive audio selections, and an arsenal of quotes from Shakespeare, Chekhov, Ibsen, Strindberg, Shaw, Wilde, Congreve, Poe, Dickens, Melville, Lewis Carroll, and much much more..."

Christopher Martin
Founding Artistic Director, Classic Stage Company

"Patricia Fletcher is a gifted teacher whose work reflects a unique understanding of speech as a 'character' choice. *Classically Speaking* is amazingly thorough and enormously 'user-friendly'. Whether an experienced actor or beginner, THIS BOOK IS ESSENTIAL."

Nova Thomas
Princeton University, New School University

"Whether you are an actor, voice teacher, or director, *Classically Speaking* by Patricia Fletcher is A TERRIFIC AND COMPREHENSIVE WORKBOOK for language and articulation. This book is an invaluable and well-organized guide in deciding which choices to make to enhance and serve the playing of any text, from the classic to modern repertoire."

Andrea Haring
Columbia University Graduate School of the Arts

"Patricia Fletcher has worked with me for nearly fifteen years, at both the MFA program at Rutgers University and my acting studio in New York, and has done a tremendous service for all of us who are interested in language and classical text. THIS IS A MUST HAVE BOOK."

William Esper
William Esper Acting Studio

CLASSICALLY SPEAKING

DIALECTS FOR ACTORS

NEUTRAL AMERICAN
CLASSICAL AMERICAN
MID-ATLANTIC
STANDARD BRITISH

THIRD EDITION

PATRICIA FLETCHER

CLASSICALLY SPEAKING
e-book version now available

THIRD EDITION

ACCOMPANYING MP3 AUDIO DOWNLOAD

with over 300 selections, including a dozen monologues from Shakespeare, Wilde, Congreve, and Shaw spoken by fourteen professional actors, illustrating all sound changes in Neutral American, Classical American, Mid-Atlantic, and Standard British

available at:

www.patriciafletcher.com
click on: classically speaking-book/audio
type code: clsp3pf

Complete audio books for each individual dialect
scheduled for release in 2013 / 2014
check above website for updates

Acknowledgements

I would like to offer a warm "thank you" to my current and former students for their enthusiasm, dedication, and joy in the spoken word, and for their invaluable feedback. Grateful acknowledgement also, to my colleagues Nancy Mayans and Susan Cameron, and to my sister Susan Lapis, for reading through the manuscript and offering their insightful comments and suggestions, to Sarah Bisman for taking on the daunting task of proofreading, and to Janine Hegarty for her work on the third-edition cover.

I would like, in addition, to thank my teachers of Shakespeare, singing, voice, speech, dialects, and acting, including: Michael Beckett, Linda Benanti, Leigh Dillon, Keeley Eastley, Andrea Haring, Larry Hill, Gordon Jacoby, Raphael Kelly, Dennis Krausnick, Kristin Linklater, Tina Packer, Joe Scott, Roger Hendrick Simon, Bob Smith, Rosemarie Vacca, Daniela Varon, Patrick Michael Wickham, and Walton Wilson, for generously sharing their knowledge and talent.

Special thanks to James Anderson, Susan Cameron, Leigh Dillon, Rebecca Dumaine, Jonathan Fielding, Stephen Hollis, Carman Lacivita, Sybil Lines, Eric Loscheider, Christopher Martin, Nancy Mayans, Evan Mueller, Shane Taylor, and Walton Wilson for their participation in the recording of the audio, Lois Bewley for the drawings, Mark White for *Moose Mirage*, and Allen R. Jones, Director of Education and Technology/New School University, for his invaluable assistance.

I am grateful to William Esper for his support of my work over the years, and to Nova Thomas for her optimism and encouragement in the writing of this book, throughout all its stages of development. I especially thank Christopher Martin, founding Artistic Director of CSC Repertory (Classic Stage Company) in New York, whose direction of the audio and continuous technical, artistic, and moral support helped make *Classically Speaking* a reality.

Lastly, my deepest gratitude goes to my parents Robert and Nina Fletcher, and my wonderful family, without whom nothing would be possible.

"Who the hell wants to hear actors talk?"

Harry Warner, 1927
(On the release of the first talking picture: *The Jazz Singer*)

INTRODUCTION
to the third edition

This third edtition, identical to the second, offers the audio selections as a download and facilitates additional publication in e-book format.

All actors come to the table with the ability to use their pronunciation of English, influenced by their personal heritage or region of origin, to their advantage to portray characters from circumstances or regions of the world similar to their own.

Actors from New Jersey may be able to step straight into *The Sopranos* with no adjustment to their everyday speech. The same is true for Russian immigrants now living in the Brighton Beach section of Brooklyn one hears on *Law and Order* with Slavic-accented English, and the many young actors and actresses who are at ease playing characters with sounds typified by their contemporary pronunciation of "fershURE" or "AHHsome".

But, these same accents and dialects[1] can prove a liability when trying to accurately portray individuals with backgrounds and life experiences uniquely different from one's own. In order to play a *variety* of characters convincingly and believably, actors often need to train and expand their repertoire of skills.

Classically Speaking offers an approach for American actors who wish to explore sound beyond their habitual speech, fine-tune their ability to hear and identify subtle variations in sounds and dialects, and to develop the flexibility and skills necessary to adjust their speech to the particular demands of a wider range of characters and material.

The extensive Neutral American section could also serve advanced speakers of English as a Second Language (**ESL**), as well as English speakers from countries other than the US, including those from Canada, Australia, New Zealand, South Africa, Ireland and Great Britain, among others.

---

[1] The terms 'dialect' and 'accent' are traditionally applied from one's point of view—though the terms are very often used interchangeably. 'Dialect' refers to variations within one's native or first language, while 'accent' refers to variations within one's non-native language. For example, someone with American English as a first language would study a French or Russian accent and a Boston dialect.

Neutral American Speech
(NAS)

Neutral American is the most practical dialect an actor can study. Sometimes referred to as General American, it is spoken without regionalisms that identify an actor's specific point of origin or 'home' sounds. When effectively incorporated, the actor—and therefore the character—is not revealed as explicitly Southern, Mid-Western, or from Boston, New York, Chicago, Tennessee, New Hampshire, Texas, etc. He/she is therefore 'neutral'.

Though very few people actually speak pure Neutral American in their everyday lives, it is commonly used:

* when a particular region of the country is unspecified in the text

* when clear, well-spoken sounds are required, rather than under-articulated speech, or slang

* when actors from various parts of the country need to convincingly play members of the same family

* in classical plays, when more formal classical dialect is not required

* in voiceovers and commercials involving upscale characters, pricey items, or well-articulated spokespersons.

Overall, Neutral American is very useful when attempting to increase one's flexibility and marketability. Many agents prefer their clients to have this dialect in their 'arsenal', and see it as a sign of a well-trained[1] actor. It is the standard against which most dialects and accents are compared in teaching materials for American-English speaking actors.

Rhythm Highlighters

The Neutral American section gives special focus to the Rhythm Highlighters, which address general rhythmic issues for well-spoken American English, before delving into the specific spoken sounds of English in detail. Rhythm Highlighters include: linking words in order to avoid glottal attack,

---

[1] Though vocal production is out of the scope of this text, it is a crucial element in one's training. As a designated Linklater voice teacher, the core of my training and teaching revolves around the methods expressed in Kristin Linklater's *Freeing the Natural Voice*. Actors may also wish to explore the work of many other wonderful voice/singing teachers, including: Roy Hart, Patsy Rodenburg, Cicely Berry, Catherine Fitzmaurice, Nova Thomas, and Keith Buhl, to name a few.

stressed syllables and their relationship to operative or key words, noun/verb variations, the use of weak and strong forms, prefixes, suffixes, syllabic endings, inflection, pause, literary devices, and scansion.

This material is crucial, for rhythmic variations not only promote more intelligible speech, but encourage corresponding changes in pitch, inflection, and musicality necessary for interesting, well-spoken speech choices.

Most importantly, Neutral American rhythms and sounds serve as the foundation for learning the second and third dialects covered in this book: Classical American and Standard British.

Classical American

This dialect offers an intermediate option between well-pronounced Neutral American and Standard British. It builds upon Neutral American, blending additional rhythmic and sound elements, which result in more formal or heightened speech without sounding British to an American ear.

Classical American can be used to indicate well-spoken, non-contemporary speech for plays set in another time or place, or to establish class or character distinctions from Neutral American Speech. It can be used when a language other than English would be spoken by the character, as in the French, Italian and Spanish plays of Molière, Pirandello or Lorca.

Classical American might also be suitably applied to the verse plays of Shakespeare, translations of the Ancient Greeks, or 19th century prose classics of Strindberg, Ibsen, and Chekhov, among others.

As previously noted, no one dialect is capable of fulfilling every requirement, and there are always variables to be considered when determining the appropriate speech or dialect for a particular production. These include:

* What is the director's concept?
* What specific time or place is being represented?
* Are there 'class' distinctions within the play?
* Do any of the characters require foreign accents?
* Do any of the actors speak with accents?
* How much rehearsal time is scheduled?
* How experienced and trained is the cast?

Elements selected for inclusion in the Classical American section are based on conversations with directors, actors, students, and my own experience as an actor, teacher and spectator. A certain degree of flexibility is implied, as choices should offer support for the particular reality being created on stage or screen.

Stage speech known as **Mid-Atlantic** was popular during the mid 20th Century, and is often taught in acting schools and universities. It is almost indistinguishable from Standard British (RP), and many actors, directors, and members of the audience find it objectionable for this reason.

But, if a more British-English sound is desired, if historical characters are being played, or if British and American actors are appearing together in the same production, this dialect could be appropriate, and is covered, *in brief*, at the end of Classical American. [1]

Standard British
(RP)

Standard British is the dialect traditionally spoken by the English upper and upper-middle classes. Also referred to as RP or Received Pronunciation, it is the name given to the speech instruction 'received' by students enrolled in public boarding schools. In an odd twist, public school in Britain is what is referred to in America as private school.

Today, Standard British is often considered too formal, rigid, or old-fashioned, as the contemporary characteristics of upper/upper-middle class speech in Britain have become more flexible and varied. But for period plays, including those of the 19th century Shaw and Wilde, or Restoration playwrights Congreve and Farquhar, among others, the formality and precision of Standard British is certainly appropriate.

It is also beneficial for American actors to know Standard British as a foundation on which to build their study of foreign accents. Many people worldwide who have learned English as a second language have been taught by speakers of Standard British, and this is reflected in their spoken English sounds.

---

[1] For a detailed rendering of Mid-Atlantic dialect, also known as Eastern Standard, see Edith Skinner's *Speak With Distinction.*

Accompanying Downloadable Audio

The complimentary MP3 audio download at www.patriciafletcher.com contains over 300 selections, including a dozen monologues from Shakespeare, Wilde, Congreve, and Shaw spoken by fourteen professional actors, illustrating all sound changes in Neutral American, Classical American, Mid-Atlantic, and Standard British dialects.

International Phonetic Alphabet (IPA)

The brief Overview that follows serves to introduce the International Phonetic Alphabet, and provide enough information on the consonant and vowel sounds to complete the IPA practice material and exercises.

Devised in 1888 by the International Phonetic Association, this system for representing spoken sounds—one symbol per sound—offers a much more reliable method of representing and comparing spoken sounds than alphabetical spelling. Letters of the alphabet in English can present difficulties when one is attempting to decipher, compare, or accurately represent pronunciation. For example, 'a' in the *spelling* of the following words represents seven *different* pronunciations:

father, image, any, cat, sofa, talk, ate

Transcribing, notating, or writing using the International Phonetic Alphabet can help eliminate confusion in pronunciation, as there is one phonetic symbol to represent each sound of spoken English. Thus, seven different symbols would be used to notate the seven sounds represented by the letter 'a' in the words above.

Learning IPA symbols may take some effort, but there is a wonderful pay-off for the professional actor. Neutral American Speech is used as the basis from which other accents and dialects are learned. Sound adjustments necessary in switching from one dialect to another are often written in phonetics. It is also enormously useful to be able to use phonetic markings in one's script in advance of a cold reading or audition, or when researching and studying a role.

It is also possible to transcribe vowel and diphthong sounds with symbols that indicate the length or duration of the sound. Knowledge of the intrinsic lengths of vowels and diphthongs can be extremely useful for actors

6

with English as a second language. Approximating the rhythm of American English is important for increased intelligibility. Duplicating it is crucial for complete neutrality.

Studying the lengths of sounds can also provide a useful tool for actors who habitually swallow or clip their sounds, and/or shy away from expressing themselves through open-throated vowels and diphthongs. Length guidelines are outlined at the end of the Overview, followed by words which have been transcribed in IPA with length markings, transcription practice material, and an answer key. Length guidelines are restated and demonstrated with sample words, in applicable vowel and diphthong chapters. That said: use of length indicators with the IPA symbols is *optional*.

Practice

Dialects covered in *Classically Speaking* are presented in detail for a reason. The English-speaking public is more astute than actors might imagine when it comes to recognizing slight variations in speech sounds. (After all, we have all grown up sounding like the people around us.) So, when making sound adjustments, actors need to be precise and consistent to convince a discerning audience.

This can pose a challenge for actors. Some may begin with speech patterns very close to Neutral, so the need to make adjustments or changes will be small—a 'tweak' to one sound or two may suffice. Others may need to acquire an entirely new 'vocabulary' of sounds in order to possess the skills necessary for playing a wider range of characters and roles. If this describes you, don't worry—actors may have to work to learn your dialect in the future.

If you are going to be successful, you will need to integrate a new set of sound skills, which requires: practice. Think sports—for instance, basketball. More specifically, think about learning to *dribble* a basketball. Beginners can feel awkward and complain of a mechanical lack of freedom, because they need to look at the ball in order to keep from losing it. Even Michael Jordan had to keep his eye on the ball at first.

But practice results in increased muscle memory and skill level. The dribbler begins to be able to scan the court with only partial attention directed toward the ball. Soon, the player can dribble, running full-speed from one end of the court to the other, seemingly unconscious of the basketball itself. Eventually, the player can take (and make!) that shot while being agressively pursued by a member of the opposing team.

The same applies to learning a dialect well enough that it becomes an unconscious part of oneself. Practice, muscle memory, attention to detail, and more practice is required to ensure that the new sounds become an intrinsic part of oneself and therefore, one's character. This will happen with time.

In the meantime. . . practice!

Limited Class Time?

If there is not time to study the Neutral American section in full, I suggest covering the Overview on pages 10-38, the Rhythm Highlighters on pages 48-89, and the following specific **sound checks**, which can be found in the vowel and consonant chapters on the pages listed.

These elements were spotlighted in the previous edition of *Classically Speaking* and, although there are other sounds in Neutral American that might need attention, this 'check list' provides focus if time is short.

All of the individual issues listed below are demonstrated on the audio download and are phonetically marked on the printed Shakespeare monologues, which are included at the end of Neutral American.

Issue	Page
/e/ (g<u>e</u>t) before 'm' or 'n' *Audio 12*	105-111
/æ/ (th<u>a</u>t), relaxed and non-nasal *Audio 13*	112-117
/ɔ/ (<u>a</u>ll) vs. /ɑ/ (f<u>a</u>ther) sounds *Audio 21*	148-156
/aɪ̆/ (m<u>y</u>) before a voiceless consonant *Audio 24*	165-170
/ʊə̆/ (p<u>oor</u>) diphthong *Audio 30*	191-194
/n, d, t, l/ tip of tongue placement *Audio 35*	208-218
Voiceless stop-plosives before a pause or silence *Audio 36A*	221-224
Voiced stop-plosives before a pause or silence *Audio 36B*	225-231
Consonant /r/ and 'dr', 'tr', 'str' combinations *Audio 49A,B,C*	294-302
Shakespeare Monologues *Audio 50, 51, 52*	320-325

OVERVIEW

&

INTERNATIONAL PHONETIC ALPHABET (IPA)

Selections for Recording

The following selections can be recorded at the beginning of study and re-recorded periodically to measure progress.

Rhythm Highlighters:

1. Arthur's amazing agent arranged the appointment.

2. If you have time to spare, become a volunteer.

3. We feel we must contest the results of the contest.

4. I'd like a part in a film, a commercial, and a mini-series.

5. The agency closed its door at the end of the day.

6. This machine takes nickels, dimes, quarters, or silver dollars.

7. They expect to reduce prescription costs before December.

8. What fearless statesman made that important statement?

9. Prudence, the students didn't meet at the center, they couldn't.

Vowels and Diphthongs:

10. I really feel that Neal is ideal for the part.

11. Phil is a little bit exhausted from his trip to the village.

12. Jenny was compelled to delve into the books on the shelves.

13. When apprehended, the criminal pretended to surrender.

14. Sandy and Jan were happy when cast in *As You Like It*.

15. The nervous, surly, underworld character cursed Sherlock.

16. Dr. Tull consulted another physician about his ulcer.

17. Julian, you know the rule. No mint juleps at the school's pool.

18. Wouldn't you rather wear wool in the woods in winter?

19. Olivia O'Neill drew the oasis pictured in the hotel's brochure.

20. Saul became lost in thought while drawing with chalk.

21.   Father commented on the calming effect of the sonatas.

22.   Hail the mailmen, both male and female.

23.   The bright sign shuts off each night, at midnight.

24.   Mr. Doyle prefers oysters broiled, not parboiled.

25.   If you lose your foothold, Joel, grab ahold of that boulder.

26.   Scowling and growling could befoul your reputation.

27.   Oh dear, here comes the peerless financier from Erie.

28.   Are you aware that's an unfair comparison, Gary?

29.   I'm curious, are you sure you're getting health insurance?

30.   Four more reporters poured into the Georgia courtroom.

31.   Arthur and Charlotte have a harmonious relationship.

32.   The fire was completely doused by powerful summer showers.

Consonants:

33.   DAD doesn't talk to DANNY until the end of Act Two.

34.   Tammy tailgated Tommy's truck and took out a tail light.

35.   "Ask the actors where they studied acting," he asked.

36.   We figure that singer has the strongest singing voice.

37.   Jill gave Bill the cold shoulder and felt a little guilty.

38.   Vincent travels to Venice on Friday, November fifth.

39.   What's the earth's length, width and breadth, Mr. Smithy?

40.   Rachel has a fondness for rich chocolate chip snacks.

41.   Pianists need the strongest fingers, wrists, and fists.

42.   We didn't wake up William, Watson—did you?

43.   Yes, yogurt and yellow onions promote youthfulness.

44.   The drunken driver drove into the tractor trailer's trunk.

45.   Go straight. Route sixty-six is obstructed by construction.

46.   She lisps each time she eats six-packs of crispy crisps.

Diagram of the Head
with
Speech Articulators and Related Structures

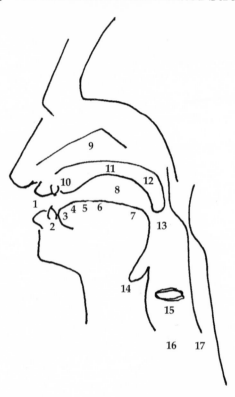

1. lips	10. alveolar ridge
2. teeth	(front of hard palate)
3. tongue tip	11. hard palate
4. tongue blade	12. soft palate
5. tongue front	13. uvula
6. tongue middle	14. epiglottis
7. tongue back	15. vocal folds
8. mouth	16. trachea
9. nasal cavity	17. esophagus

CONSONANT OVERVIEW

The sounds of English can be divided into two major categories: vowels and consonants. They are differentiated by how sound is formed and used. Vowels are formed when an uninterrupted stream of air is released through the mouth. Consonants are formed when the breath is impeded either partially or fully, during the course of its forward release through the mouth or nose. The release is influenced by one or more of the articulators (lips, teeth, tongue, hard palate, soft palate), which come together and result in the formation of a particular consonant.

Clearly spoken consonants and consonant combinations are crucial for understanding the specific spoken word. Open-throated vowels, diphthongs, and triphthongs are especially effective in communicating emotional content.

I understand a fury in your words,
But not the words.

(Othello: IV, ii, 32)

Consonant sounds are either voiced or voiceless. Voiced consonants require vocal fold vibration. Many have a 'partner' sound that is made precisely the same way but without vibration of the vocal folds. This results in a voiceless or whispered sound. These pairs of sounds are called cognates. For example, the voiced and voiceless sounds 'd' and 't' form a cognate pair.

Voiced consonant endings are an important element in clear verbal communication. Vocal fold vibration needs to be maintained through the end of a word that finishes with a voiced consonant, or the voiceless partner may be inadvertently spoken instead. For example, energetically speak the word 'feed'. If you heard yourself say 'feet' instead of 'feed', then voicing was not maintained through the end of the word, and voiceless 't' was spoken instead of 'd'.

Final consonant voicing also influences the length of the preceding vowel sound and therefore affects the rhythm of the word. Energetically speak the words 'feet' *and* 'feed'. Be sure to voice the 'd' ending. Notice how the vowel sound is longer when it precedes the voiced consonant 'd' in the word 'feed' than when it precedes voiceless 't' in the word 'feet'.

So, if the director or the audience cannot understand you, clarify your intentions *and* your voiced endings.

Some accents—German, for example—use the voiceless 'partner' sound instead of the voiced, in certain instances. It can be beneficial to know voiced and voiceless partners before beginning accent study.

Consonants are generally divided into four distinct groups, according to the manner in which the air is modified and the place where it is modified during the course of sound production. These sound categories are listed below and summarized in the chart on page 17.

Stop-Plosives

/t d/　/p b/　/k g/
(tot did)　(pop bib)　(cap gap)

When forming these sounds, the outgoing air is always completely stopped between two articulators, which initiates a build-up of air pressure. The stop element of /t d/ is formed by pressing the tip of the tongue against the alveolar or gum ridge, just behind the upper teeth. The stop element of /p b/ sounds is formed by enlivened contact between the upper and lower lips (referred to as bi-labial) and the stop of /k g/ is formed by energized contact between the back of the tongue and the front of the soft palate or velum. Air is then either exploded or not, depending on the sound that follows the plosive.

If voiceless plosives are followed directly by another *consonant*, then only the stop element is articulated, notated in IPA by / ˌ / following the /tˌ pˌ kˌ/. The following words are marked for demonstration.

Stop only:　　　　tˌrim　　pˌlay　　kˌlutˌz　　thatˌ man

If voiceless plosives are followed directly by a *pause, silence, vowel,* or *diphthong*, then stop and aspiration elements are articulated, notated by / ʰ / after the /tʰ pʰ kʰ/.

Stop, then aspirate:　　　tʰoo　　pʰeekʰ　pʰipʰe　aftʰer workʰ

Voiced partners are not phonetically marked for aspiration in IPA with either / ʰ / or / ˌ /, though the criteria for articulating the stop, or the stop and plosive, is identical. See pages 221-231 for more detail.

Continuants

When speaking continuants, the articulators maintain their position throughout the duration of the sound. Continuants are divided into three sub-groups: nasal, lateral, and fricative, and offer a wonderful contrast in rhythm with the stop-plosives. See pages 232-247 for more detail.

nasal continuants

/ m /   / n /   / ŋ /
(mom)   (on)   (sing)

The articulators maintain their position when speaking these three sounds, which are released out the nose. All three are voiced and have no voiceless partners. See pages 232-247 for more detail.

lateral continuant

/ l / (lily)

This voiced continuant sound is the only consonant sound in Neutral American that releases laterally, over the sides of the tongue. See pages 248-254 for more detail.

fricative continuants

/ f v /   / θ ð /
(leaf leave) (bath bathe)

/ s z /   / ʃ ʒ /
(bus buzz) (rush rouge)

/ h / (he)

These nine sounds, four cognate pairs and voiceless 'h', maintain their position while breath is directed through an opening formed by the speech articulators narrow enough to cause emission of a friction-like sound. See pages 255-284 for more detail.

Affricates

/ t͡ʃ   d͡ʒ /
(ri<u>ch</u>   ri<u>dge</u>)

There are two affricates, one cognate pair, which consist of the short stop element from the stop-plosives /t, d/, and the longer fricative continuants /ʃ, ʒ/, blended together to sound as one. These sounds are represented in the words and corresponding IPA symbols, above. See pages 285-288 for more detail.

Glides

/ w /   / j /   / r /
(<u>w</u>e)   (<u>y</u>ou)   (red)

Glides begin in one position then quickly and seamlessly flow into the vowel sound that always follows. They do not quite fit the definition of consonants, sounds that are formed when the air is stopped or impeded during the course of its release through the mouth or nose. Glides are sometimes referred to as 'semi-vowels'.

The three gliding sounds occur only before vowels and never as the last sound of a word. In addition, if the shape and position for the glide is maintained too long, a vowel sound can be formed instead of the consonant.

The slight friction sound formed when producing the consonant /r/ allows its classification as both a fricative continuant and glide. A case can be made for either. It is included here to help remember that, like the other two glides, consonant /r/ is always followed by a vowel sound, and is never the last sound of a word. See pages 289-302 for more detail on the three glides.

Note. An 'r' in the spelling can also represent a vowel sound. This is introduced on pages 20-21 of the Vowel Overview.

The following chart categorizes the way or manner in which air is modified during formation of the consonant sound, in CAPITAL LETTERS. The next line notes the IPA symbol and includes a sample word containing the voiced sound, followed by a word with the voiceless partner sound, if one exists. A short description summarizes the place where the sound is modified when spoken, followed by a short summary word in the right column. Unless noted otherwise, the tongue tip rests down behind the lower front teeth when producing the sound.

The reader now has enough information to transcribe the words listed on page 29 using IPA symbols. All contain the vowel sound / i / (we).

Consonant Chart for Neutral American

voiced		voiceless			
			STOP-PLOSIVES		
d	feed	t	feet	tongue tip contacts the upper gum ridge	Alveolar
b	cab	p	cap	both lips articulate against each other	Bilabial
g	pig	k	pick	back of tongue contacts the soft palate	Velar
			CONTINUANTS		
			Nasal		
m	mom	*none*		both lips articulate against each other	Bilabial
n	nine	*none*		tongue tip contacts the upper gum ridge	Alveolar
ŋ	sing	*none*		back of tongue contacts the soft palate	Velar
			Lateral		
l	well	*none*		tongue tip contacts the upper gum ridge	Alveolar
			Fricative		
v	leave	f	leaf	lower lip contacts edge of upper front teeth	Labio-dental
ð	bathe	θ	bath	tongue tip contacts edge of upper front teeth	Dental
z	buzz	s	bus	tongue tip points toward upper gum ridge	Alveolar
ʒ	beige	ʃ	bash	tongue blade points toward upper gum ridge	Alveolar
		h	he	space between the vocal folds	Glottal
			AFFRICATES		
dʒ	ridge	tʃ	rich	tongue tip contacts the upper gum ridge	Alveolar
			GLIDES		
w	went	hw	why[1]	both lips round	Bilabial
j	you	*none*		tongue front arches toward the hard palate	Lingua-palatal
r	red	*none*		tongue tip points toward upper gum ridge	Alveolar

---

[1] The voiceless partner is spoken in Classical American and, occasionally, in Standard British.

VOWEL OVERVIEW

Vowels are formed when an uninterrupted stream of air is released through the mouth. The releasing air involves vibration of the vocal folds, which is referred to as voicing. Vibration, or voicing, can be felt externally by placing your fingertips on your throat while saying: *ahhhhh*.

Vowels are designated as **front**, **mid**, or **back**, depending on the area of the tongue that is actively arched during sound formation. This, in combination with the shape formed as a result of the position of the lower jaw and the lips, determines which vowel sound is actually spoken.

Parts of the Tongue

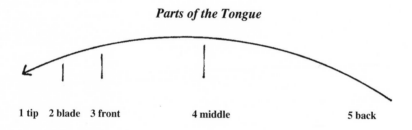

| 1 tip | 2 blade | 3 front | 4 middle | 5 back |

Overall Position of the Tongue Arch

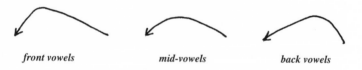

front vowels   *mid-vowels*   *back vowels*

The very tip of the tongue touches the back of the lower front teeth during vowel production and the soft palate is raised. This helps insure a complete lack of nasality on all vowel sounds as they release through the mouth, not the nose. An exception to the tip of the tongue placement occurs in the formation of Neutral American vowels and diphthongs of 'r', which are introduced on page 20-21 and 23-24.

Front Vowels

The first, most closed front vowel is: /i/ (we). To form the specific shape necessary for speaking this sound, the jaw is mostly closed, the tip of the tongue rests down behind the lower teeth, the front of the tongue arches high toward the front of the hard palate, and the lips are slightly spread.

If the jaw is allowed to relax progressively more open as the tongue tip rests behind the lower teeth, the arch of the tongue begins to flatten, the spreading of the cheeks decreases, and the shapes necessary for forming the remaining three Neutral American front vowels: /ɪ/ (will), /e/ (get), /æ/ (that) are formed.

If the jaw drops and the tongue arch flattens slightly more than for the /æ/ (that) sound, the front vowel represented by the symbol /a/ is formed. Though /a/ is not spoken as a vowel in NAS, it *is* spoken as the first sound of the diphthong in the words: my and now, represented by the corresponding IPA symbols: /aɪ̆/ and /aʊ̆/.

This is the sound that can be heard in some Bostonian's pronunciation of '*pahk the cahr in Hahvahd yahd*' or in certain southerner's pronunciation of pi*e* and by*e* where the second part of the sound is dropped. It is also spoken as a vowel in several accents and dialects, including Spanish and Irish. Since this sound is not used on its own as a vowel in Neutral American, there is no truly appropriate sample word. See page 422 for further discussion of this sound.

Key words to help remember Neutral American front vowels:

i   ɪ   e   æ   **(a)**
We will get that (*laugh—in some dialects*).

Additional sample words:

i	he, see, treat, achieve, receive, people, debris, fleas
ɪ	it, isn't, building, image, busy, window, wing, women
e	bet, many, quest, said, deaf, again, temper, shepherd
æ	hat, cash, plaid, sack, pal, man, lamb, mangle, rank
(a)	*none*

Phonetic symbols are usually placed between slashes / / in order to avoid confusing them with alphabetical letters, though slashes are sometimes eliminated when their absence will not cause confusion.

Mid-Vowels

It is necessary to understand stressed syllables before discussing the mid-vowels. A stressed syllable is that part of a word which receives the strongest emphasis. This is marked in IPA by / ' / before the stressed[1] syllable. It is used here, in combination with bolding, for emphasis and clarity.

The vowel sound in the stressed syllable of a word is generally *louder, longer,* and *higher* in pitch than those in the unstressed syllable(s), which offers a rhythmic contrast within the syllables of a word. A one-syllable word is considered stressed, even though there is no other syllable in the word to offer contrast, and it is not usually notated with a phonetic marker.

Mid-vowels, also known as central vowels, are formed with the jaw partially open, the middle of the tongue arching in the middle of the mouth, the soft palate raised, and the lips in a neutral position. Though in reality there are four mid-vowel sounds in Neutral American, they can be thought of as two sounds that both have a longer and shorter duration, and corresponding IPA symbols to reflect this duration or stress.

Vowel of 'r'. The first two mid-vowels that are differentiated by their duration or stress contain the letter 'r' in the spelling[2]. These sounds are illustrated by the spellings 'ER' and 'er', indicating a longer and shorter duration of the sound. This is reflected in IPA by the use of two different phonetic symbols, which can be thought of as rhythm markers.

When the 'ER' sound occurs in the stressed syllable and is longer in duration, as in: '**bur**ning, '**wor**thy, '**Ear**nest, and con'**cur**, it is represented phonetically by /ɝ/.

When the 'er' sound occurs in the unstressed syllable and is shorter in duration, as in '**fa**th*er*, '**su**g*ar*, '**ac**t*or*, and p*er*'**suade**, it is represented by /ɚ/.

---

[1] Stressed syllable markings used throughout this book are based on speaking sounds, rather than observing technical rules or dividing syllables according to spelling. See pages 57-61.

[2] Exception: 'colonel' is pronounced with /ɝ/ even though there is no 'r' in the spelling.

The tip of the tongue curls back from the lower teeth when forming Neutral American /ɝ/ and /ɚ/. This curling back, or retroflexion, results in 'r' coloring of the vowel, notated by the small 'curl' or 'tail' on the IPA symbol. Though mid-vowels do not require lip rounding, some people do round slightly when speaking these two sounds.

The word 'murmur' contains these vowels in the stressed and unstressed syllables and is transcribed: /ˈmɝmɚ/. Speak the word 'murmur' out loud. The lower jaw will drop to a slightly more open position for stressed /ɝ/ than it does for unstressed /ɚ/.

The two remaining mid-vowels are illustrated by the spellings 'UH' and 'uh', which indicate a longer and shorter duration of the sound. This is reflected in IPA by the use of two different symbols, which can be thought of as rhythm markers. When the 'UH' sound occurs in the stressed syllable and is longer in duration, as in ˈm<u>o</u>ney, ˈp<u>u</u>blic, t<u>**ough**</u>, it is represented in IPA by /ʌ/.

When the 'uh' sound occurs in an unstressed syllable and is shorter in duration, as in: ˈsof<u>a</u>, ˈNin<u>a</u>, p<u>u</u>ˈblicity, <u>a</u>ˈmazed, it is represented in IPA by /ə/. Unstressed /ə/ (<u>uh</u>) is also often used in weak forms of words (see pages 65-72).

The word 'above' contains this sound in both stressed and unstressed[1] syllables, and is transcribed: /əˈbʌv/. Speak the word 'above' out loud. The lower jaw will drop to a slightly more open position for stressed /ʌ/ than for unstressed /ə/.

Key words to help remember the mid-vowels

ɝ　ɚ　ə　ʌ
ˈ**mur**mur　aˈ**bove**

The tongue tip points up toward the alveolar ridge on /ɝ/ and /ɚ/. The tongue tip rests down behind the lower teeth for /ʌ/ and /ə/. This is represented in the diagram, above.

---

[1]　Unstressed syllables of words with 'un' prefixes (as in unhappy and unpleasant) and compound words (as in understood and teacup) are often transcribed with /ʌ/ rather than /ə/.

Back Vowels

Back vowels are made with the back of the tongue arching in relation to the raised soft palate, the tip of the tongue down behind the lower teeth, and the lips in a rounded position. The back of the tongue arch is very low and the lips are <u>un</u>rounded for /ɑ/ (f<u>a</u>ther), the most open back vowel sound.

The jaw is most closed, with the tongue arch most high, and the lips most rounded for /u/ (wh<u>o</u>) and, as the lower jaw opens more and the tongue arch drops, the shapes necessary for the /ʊ/ (w<u>ou</u>ld), /o/ (<u>o</u>'mit), /ɔ/ (<u>a</u>ll), and /ɑ/ (f<u>a</u>ther) sounds are formed[1].

Key words to help remember the back vowels:

u   ʊ   o   ɔ   (ɒ)[2]   ɑ

Wh<u>o</u> w<u>ou</u>ld <u>o</u>'mit <u>a</u>ll (*h<u>o</u>nest*) f<u>a</u>thers?

Additional sample words:

u	**who**	t<u>wo</u>, w<u>oo</u>, bl<u>ue</u>, gr<u>ew</u>, j<u>u</u>do, gl<u>oo</u>my, s<u>ui</u>t
ʊ	**would**	p<u>u</u>t, sh<u>ou</u>ld, t<u>oo</u>k, w<u>o</u>lf, b<u>oo</u>gie-w<u>oo</u>gie
o	**<u>o</u>'mit,**	<u>o</u>'asis, <u>o</u>'bese, <u>o</u>'dometer, <u>O</u>'hio, <u>o</u>'pacity
ɔ	**<u>a</u>ll**	cl<u>aw</u>, s<u>au</u>ce, w<u>a</u>ll, st<u>a</u>lk, l<u>o</u>ng, d<u>o</u>g, <u>o</u>ff[3]
(ɒ)	*none*	(*see footnote #2*)
ɑ	**f<u>a</u>thers**	t<u>o</u>p, <u>o</u>dd, cl<u>o</u>bber, w<u>a</u>tch, b<u>o</u>tch, R<u>o</u>ger

---

[1] There is much discrepancy on how to represent the **'oh'** sound in phonetics. Some dictionaries use /o/ in all positions in a word, some use /oŭ/, which represents two blended vowel sounds, and some make a distinction in the sound in stressed and unstressed syllables. Short /o/ is used in the Neutral American section of *Classically Speaking* to represent this sound in the unstressed first syllable, which occurs infrequently. This use facilitates the introduction of this sound along with the other vowels, and highlights the importance of rhythm in well-pronounced speech. The symbol /oŭ/ is used to represent this sound in all other positions in a word.

[2] The symbol /ɒ/ represents another back vowel sometimes referred to as the 'honest' sound. There is variation in opinion, among dictionaries and speech teachers alike, on the use of this sound and symbol in Neutral American. (I feel most Neutral American speakers do not use this sound, and teaching it as part of Neutral American Speech can be counter productive—especially for ESL actors studying NAS—since short, slightly lip-rounded /ɒ/ is often indicative of an accent or dialect. That said, there is difference in opinion....so listen to your teacher.) The /ɒ/ sound is included in the sentence above and in the vowel chart, so that the reader has an idea where this sound fits in with the other back vowels for future Classical American and Standard British study.

[3] Spellings to help differentiate /ɔ/ (<u>a</u>ll) and /ɑ/ (f<u>a</u>ther) words can be found on pages 148-149.

Diphthongs

Sounds composed of two of the previously covered vowels, seamlessly blended together to sound as one, are referred to as diphthongs.

Stress is on the first element of all diphthongs, the second element is rhythmically shorter as notated by / ˘ / over the second element in the IPA symbol. Altogether, there are ten diphthongs, which are generally divided into two groups:

(a) potentially long diphthongs: /eĭ/ (h<u>ey</u>), /aĭ/ (m<u>y</u>), /ɔĭ/ (b<u>oy</u>), /oŭ/ (g<u>o</u>), /aŭ/ (n<u>ow</u>)

(b) diphthongs of 'r' which have the short /ɚ / (<u>er</u>) sound as their second element: /ɪɚ̆ / (h<u>ere</u>'s), /eɚ̆ / (th<u>eir</u>), /ʊɚ̆ / (p<u>oor</u>), /ɔɚ̆ / (sp<u>or</u>ts), /ɑɚ̆ / (c<u>ar</u>)

Key words to help remember the potentially long diphthongs:

eĭ aĭ ɔĭ oŭ aŭ
H<u>ey</u> m<u>y</u> b<u>oy</u> g<u>o</u> n<u>ow</u>.

Key words to help remember the diphthongs of 'r':

ɪɚ̆ eɚ̆ ʊɚ̆ ɔɚ̆ ɑɚ̆
H<u>ere</u>'s th<u>eir</u> p<u>oor</u> sp<u>or</u>ts c<u>ar</u>.

Additional sample words containing **diphthongs**:

eĭ   <u>ai</u>d, <u>eigh</u>t, sl<u>ay</u>   ɪɚ̆   <u>ear</u>, st<u>eer</u>, t<u>ier</u>

aĭ   <u>I</u>, sk<u>y</u>, g<u>ui</u>de, m<u>igh</u>t   eɚ̆   <u>air</u>, wh<u>ere</u>, h<u>eirs</u>

ɔĭ   pl<u>oy</u>, g<u>oi</u>ter, <u>oy</u>ster   ʊɚ̆   s<u>ure</u>, y<u>our</u>, mat<u>ure</u>

oŭ   fl<u>ow</u>, c<u>o</u>de, d<u>ough</u>   ɔɚ̆   sh<u>ore</u>, w<u>ar</u>t, fl<u>oor</u>

aŭ   c<u>ow</u>, h<u>ou</u>se, l<u>ou</u>nge   ɑɚ̆   <u>are</u>, sc<u>ar</u>f, g<u>uar</u>d

Triphthongs

A triphthong is three vowel sounds blended to sound as one. There are two triphthongs that both have short /ɚ / (er) as the third element: /aɪɚ / (fire), /aʊɚ / (power). Depending on the rhythmic demands of the text, they can also be spoken as diphthongs followed by a vowel: /aɪ ɚ/ (fire) or /aʊ ɚ/ (power).

Diphthongs and triphthongs share the same attributes as pure vowel sounds: all are voiced, and are formed by an uninterrupted flow of air vibrating the vocal folds and releasing through the mouth.

The pure vowels that combine and blend are reflected in the phonetic symbols that represent each diphthong. For example, the /ɪɚ / (here) diphthong begins in the position and shape for /ɪ/ and then blends seamlessly into /ɚ/. A smooth movement from the shape of the first element through the shape of the second element results in each particular diphthong.

The first element is longer, louder, and usually more open, than the second and third elements. The shorter second and third elements are notated phonetically by a little unstressed symbol / ˘ / as a reminder of the rhythmic difference within the sound.

Key words to help remember the two possible triphthongs:

aɪɚ   aʊɚ

f<u>ire</u>   p<u>ower</u>

Additional sample words containing triphthongs:

aɪɚ   <u>ire</u>, exp<u>ire</u>, M<u>yer</u>, enqu<u>ire</u>, ch<u>oirs</u>, fr<u>iar</u>

aʊɚ   h<u>our</u>, <u>our</u>, dev<u>our</u>, sh<u>ower</u>, emp<u>ower</u>ing

The Vowel Chart

The following chart diagrams the shape and position of the articulators when forming Front, Mid and Back vowel sounds: lips (spread, neutral or rounded), lower jaw (most closed to most opened—from top to bottom on the chart), tongue arch (high, mid, low—from top to bottom on the chart). The left side of the chart reflects the front of the mouth, the right side, the back.

Vowel Chart

Front	Mid or Central	Back
Lips slightly spread **Lower jaw most closed**	**Lips neutral** **Lower jaw most closed**	**Lips most rounded** **Lower jaw most closed**
High i w<u>e</u> ↓ ɪ w<u>i</u>ll		u wh<u>o</u> **High** ʊ w<u>ou</u>ld ↓
Mid e g<u>e</u>t ↓	ɝ <u>ER</u> ɚ <u>er</u> ə <u>uh</u>	o <u>o</u>'mit **Mid** ↓
↓ æ th<u>a</u>t **Low** a* l<u>au</u>gh*	ʌ <u>UH</u>	ɔ˙ <u>a</u>ll ↓ ɒ* h<u>o</u>nest* ɑ f<u>a</u>thers **Low**
Lips neutral **Lower jaw most open**	**Lips neutral** **Lower jaw most open**	**Lips unrounded on /ɑ/** **Lower jaw most open**

Vowel, Diphthong and Triphthong Sound Relationships

All words begin with 'p' to focus on vowel, diphthong and triphthong sounds.

Front	Mid or Central	Back
i p<u>ea</u>		u p<u>ooh</u>
ɪ ɪɚ p<u>i</u>t, p<u>ier</u>		ʊ ʊɚ p<u>u</u>t, p<u>oor</u>
e eɪ eɚ p<u>e</u>t, p<u>ay</u>, p<u>air</u>	ɝ 'p<u>er</u>son	o oʊ p<u>o</u>'etic, 'p<u>oe</u>m
æ p<u>a</u>t	ɚ p<u>er</u>'suade	ɔ ɔɪ ɔɚ p<u>aw</u>, p<u>oi</u>se, p<u>ore</u>
a* aɪ aɪɚ aʊ aʊɚ	ə p<u>u</u>'blicity	ɒ* p<u>o</u>sh*
p<u>a</u>ss*, p<u>ie</u>, p<u>yre</u>, p<u>ow</u>, p<u>ower</u>	ʌ 'p<u>u</u>blic	ɑ ɑɚ p<u>a</u>, p<u>ar</u>

* Symbols and sample words followed by an asterisk represent sounds spoken in Classical American and/or Standard British, not Neutral American Speech.

IPA SYMBOLS
AND SAMPLE WORDS

VOWELS

All Voiced

Front

/i/	we, see
/ɪ/	will, is
/e/	get, end
/æ/	that, apple
/a/*	laugh*

Mid

/ɝ/	ER, 'person
/ɚ/	er, per'suade
/ə/	uh, pu'blicity
/ʌ/	UH, 'public

Back

/u/	who, blue
/ʊ/	would, hook
/o/	o'mit, o'asis
/ɔ/	all, claw
/ɒ/*	honest*
/ɑ/	fathers, drama

DIPHTHONGS

/eɪ/	hey, age
/aɪ/	my, eye
/ɔɪ/	boy, oil
/oʊ/	go, only
/aʊ/	now, out
/ɑʊ/*	now*

CONSONANTS

Voiced

/d/	did, feed
/b/	bib, cab
/g/	gap, pig
/m/	mom, him
/n/	nine, on
/ŋ/	sing, ringer
/l/	lily, well
/v/	vest, leave
/ð/	them, bathe
/z/	zoo, buzz
/ʒ/	azure, beige
/dʒ/	judge, ridge
/w/	went, we
/j/	you, yellow
/r/	red, pretty

Voiceless

/t/	tot, feet
/p/	pop, cap
/k/	cap, pick
/f/	fee, leaf
/θ/	thing, bath
/s/	sue, bus
/ʃ/	shush, bash
/h/**	he, hate
/tʃ/	church, rich
/hw/*	why*

DIPHTHONGS AND TRIPHTHONGS OF 'R'

/ɪɚ/	here's, ear
/eɚ/	their, air
/ʊɚ/	poor, tour
/ɔɚ/	sports, oar
/ɑɚ/	car, are
/aɪɚ/	fire, pyre
/aʊɚ/	power, hour
/ɑʊɚ/*	power*

---

* Sounds represented by these symbols and words are *not* covered in Neutral American, but are included for sound changes introduced in Classical American and Standard British.

** Technically, there is a voiced /ɦ/ that occurs between two vowel sounds. Voiced /ɦ/ and voiceless /h/ are nearly indistinguishable, and only /h/ is used throughout this book.

INTERNATIONAL
PHONETIC ALPHABET

Study & Practice

1. Make flashcards of the phonetic symbols.

2. Write words, phrases, or sentences in IPA. See if others can read out loud what has been written.

3. Make up and speak 'nonsense' sounds, words, or phrases out loud. See if others can transcribe what is being said in IPA. The speaker must be very clear and careful to repeat the 'nonsense' sound, word or phrase exactly the same each time it is spoken.

4. Divide the class into teams, one player from each team at the blackboard. A word, author's name, play title, etc. is spoken out loud and must be transcribed correctly for the team to get a point. The transcription can be timed as a race, or not, and can also be done with or without partners. The transcription can be done for Neutral American, Classical American, or Standard British.

5. Make up BINGO cards with the IPA symbols instead of letters of the alphabet. Call out the sounds represented by the symbols. Otherwise, the game is played just like BINGO.

6. HANGMAN can be played with phonetic symbols instead of the letters of the alphabet.

7. Crossword Puzzles. Create crossword puzzles with the answers in IPA transcription.

8. Phonetic Pillows. The brain child of Louis Colaianni, these wonderful pillows are made in the shape of the IPA symbols. They can be tossed, caressed, and used in ways which encourage a kinesthetic exploration of sound.

SAMPLE WORDS TRANSCRIBED IN IPA

Remember: one-syllable words are considered stressed.

1.	read / rid /	21.	loved / lʌvd /
2.	sting / sthɪŋ /	22.	wished / wɪʃtʰ /
3.	thug / θʌg /	23.	banks / bæŋkˌs /
4.	then / ðen /	24.	fluffed / flʌftʰ /
5.	calf / kʰæf /	25.	paused / pʰɔzd /
6.	whisk / wɪskʰ /	26.	clutches / ˈkˌlʌtˌʃɪz /
7.	fudge / fʌdʒ /	27.	snoozed / snuzd /
8.	worth / wɝθ /	28.	lumped / lʌmpˌtʰ /
9.	book / bʊkʰ /	29.	bearded / ˈbɪɚ̆dɪd /
10.	soothe / suð /	30.	faced / feɪstʰ /
11.	thunder / ˈθʌndɚ /	31.	annoyed / əˈnɔɪd /
12.	wealthy / ˈwelθi /	32.	pounded / ˈpʰaʊ̆ndɪd /
13.	hanger / ˈhæŋɚ /	33.	blindly / ˈblaɪ̆ndli /
14.	longer / ˈlɔŋgɚ /	34.	partners / ˈpʰɑɚ̆tˌnɚz /
15.	turning / ˈtʰɝ̆nɪŋ /	35.	orthodox / ˈɔɚ̆θədɑkˌs /
16.	girder / ˈgɝ̆dɚ /	36.	sharing / ˈʃeɚ̆rɪŋ /[1]
17.	attend / əˈtʰend /	37.	approached / əˈpˌroʊ̆tˌʃtʰ /
18.	pleasure / ˈpˌleʒɚ /	38.	admiring / ədˈmaɪ̆ɚ̆rɪŋ /
19.	reaches / ˈritˌʃɪz /	39.	orchards / ˈɔɚ̆tˌʃɚdz /
20.	things / θɪŋz /	40.	kimonos / kʰɪˈmoʊ̆noʊ̆z /

---

[1] When a vowel or diphthong of 'r' is followed immediately by another vowel or diphthong, a linking consonant /r/ is usually inserted in between, smoothly blending them together. Speakers are often unaware they are using a linking /r/. See page 294 for consonant /r/ and page 300 for additional information on linking with consonant /r/.

IPA TRANSCRIPTION

Consonants and Back Vowel Concentration

key words: wh<u>o</u> w<u>ou</u>ld <u>o</u>'mit[1] <u>a</u>ll f<u>a</u>thers

Numbers 1-13 and 19-31: Transcribe using the IPA symbols for consonants, back vowels, and the front vowel in 'w<u>i</u>ll'. Numbers 14-18 and 32-36: What is the word transcribed in IPA?

1. fall	_____	19. dogs	_____
2. loft	_____	20. blahs	_____
3. pull	_____	21. goods	_____
4. rude	_____	22. tossed	_____
5. chop	_____	23. Rob's	_____
6. talk	_____	24. squalls	_____
7. tock	_____	25. clauses	_____
8. lose	_____	26. Brook's	_____
9. obese	_____	27. cruises	_____
10. song	_____	28. fawned	_____
11. could	_____	29. viewed	_____
12. moth	_____	30. longed	_____
13. rouge	_____	31. cooked	_____
14. /stʰʊd/	_____	32. /spˌjud/	_____
15. /watˌʃ/	_____	33. /bʊkˌtʰ/	_____
16. /kˌrʊkʰ/	_____	34. /stʰupˌtʰ/	_____
17. /swɑv/	_____	35. /batˌʃtʰ/	_____
18. /sam, salm/	_____	36. /lɔntˌʃtʰ /	_____

---

[1] Remember, /o/ is used in the unstressed first syllable, only. See pages 148-149 for spelling guidelines for /ɔ/ (<u>a</u>ll) sounds. A complete list of phonetic symbols appears on page 26.

Answer key page 38

IPA TRANSCRIPTION

Consonants and Diphthongs

key words: hey my boy go now

Numbers 1-15 and 21-35: Transcribe using the IPA consonant, vowel, and diphthong symbols. Numbers 16-18 and 36-38: What is the word that is transcribed in IPA?

1. bay _____
2. joy _____
3. line _____
4. cope _____
5. out _____
6. bribe _____
7. poise _____
8. grade _____
9. town _____
10. boil _____
11. wild _____
12. stove _____
13. price _____
14. groin _____
15. south _____
16. /greĭv/ _____
17. /roŭg/ _____
18. /əd'vaĭs/ _____

19. Roy's _____
20. goats _____
21. Dave's _____
22. moist _____
23. doubts _____
24. crimes _____
25. raged _____
26. Mike's _____
27. bolsters _____
28. stages _____
29. toasted _____
30. striped _____
31. avoided _____
32. croaked _____
33. sliding _____
34. /ɪn'geĭdʒd/ _____
35. /'graŭndɪd/ _____
36. /pʰɚ'lɔĭnd/ _____

Answer key page 38

IPA TRANSCRIPTION

Consonants, Diphthongs and Triphthongs of 'r'

key words: h<u>ere</u>'s th<u>eir</u> p<u>oor</u> sp<u>or</u>ts c<u>ar</u> / f<u>ire</u> p<u>ower</u>

Transcribe using the IPA consonants and vowels, and the diphthongs and triphthongs of 'r'.

1. bear	_____	19. spear	_____
2. short	_____	20. hearts	_____
3. chart	_____	21. mature	_____
4. we're	_____	22. square	_____
5. tour	_____	23. restore	_____
6. clear	_____	24. perspire	_____
7. fair	_____	25. shower	_____
8. snort	_____	26. parsley	_____
9. harsh	_____	27. sworn	_____
10. pour	_____	28. cowers	_____
11. snarls	_____	29. wearable	_____
12. retorts	_____	30. remarked	_____
13. assure	_____	31. deplores	_____
14. abhors	_____	32. charming	_____
15. glares	_____	33. transpire	_____
16. career	_____	34. prayers	_____
17. orders	_____	35. starched	_____
18. argues	_____	36. conspire	_____

Answer key page 38

IPA TRANSCRIPTION

All Sounds[1] in the key words:

we will get that
'murmur a'bove
who would o'mit all fathers
hey my boy go now
here's their poor sports car
fire power

1. chairs _____
2. echos _____
3. sneers _____
4. market _____
5. portly _____
6. sincere _____
7. shining _____
8. employed _____
9. Queen _____
10. implied _____
11. hollow _____
12. clowns _____
13. patches _____
14. winked _____
15. modified _____

16. foil _____
17. cubes _____
18. spies _____
19. surely _____
20. overt _____
21. baked _____
22. trousers _____
23. strokes _____
24. witches _____
25. authors _____
26. smudged _____
27. neighbors _____
28. half hour _____
29. movie star _____
30. performance _____

---

[1] A complete list of phonetic symbols appears on page 26. Remember, /o/ is used in the unstressed first syllable only. Spelling guidelines for /ɔ/ (all) can be found on pages 148-149.

Answer key page 38

Diphthong Length

Diphthongs are two vowel sounds blended to sound as one. The first element is stressed and is therefore longer, louder, and more open than the rest of the sound. This is especially important to remember when lengthening or stressing a diphthong in an operative or key word in order to make a point.

Five Diphthongs Classified Long[1]

These five diphthongs can be remembered by the line:

eˑɪˑ   aˑɪˑ   ɔˑɪˑ   oˑʊˑ   aˑʊˑ

Hey my boy go now.

One dot follows each element of a long diphthong in IPA.

In the stressed syllable:

(a)   as the last sound of the word: day, why, ahoy, no, now

(b)   before one or more voiced consonants within the word: gave, size, soil, home, impound.

Short Diphthongs

These **same** five diphthongs are classified short in all other instances. In addition, **diphthongs and triphthongs of 'r'**, which are represented by the phrases *'here's their poor sports car'* and *'fire power'*, are always categorized as short and never transcribed with dots.

Note.   The practice transcription words on pages 29-36 can be transcribed with or without length markers. If you choose to transcribe with dots for length, use the answer key on pages 44-45.

---

[1] It is my experience that insisting a diphthong must be in the stressed *first* syllable of a word in order to be considered long overcomplicates, and serves as an ineffective learning tool for most actors, whether English is their first or second language. Therefore, for actors, I advocate the simplified version of the guideline listed above.

SOUND COMPARISONS

(transcribed in IPA with initial 'b' and with dots for length)

Remember: one-syllable words are considered stressed.

Front Vowels

/iː/ (we) as in: bean /biːn/
/ɪ/ (will) as in: bin /bɪn/
/e/ (get) as in: Ben /ben/
/æ/ (that) as in: ban /bæn/

Mid-Vowels

/ɜː/ (ER) as in: burn /bɜːn/
/ɚ/ (er) as in: burner /ˈbɜːnɚ/
/ə/ (uh) as in: Buddha /ˈbuːdə/
/ʌ/ (UH) as in: bun /bʌn/

Back Vowels

/uː/ (who) as in: boon /buːn/
/ʊ/ (would) as in: book /bʊk/
/o/ (oˈmit) as in: bodega /boˈdeˑɪˑgə/
/ɔː/ (all) as in: ball /bɔːl/
/ɑː/ (fathers) as in: bomb /bɑːm/

Diphthongs

/eˑɪˑ/ (hey) as in: bay /beˑɪˑ/
/aˑɪˑ/ (my) as in: bye /baˑɪˑ/
/ɔˑɪˑ/ (boy) as in: boy /bɔˑɪˑ/
/oˑʊˑ/ (go) as in: bone /boˑʊˑn/
/aˑʊˑ/ (now) as in: bow /baˑʊˑ/

/ɪɚ/ (here) as in: beer /bɪɚ/
/eɚ/ (their) as in: bear /beɚ/
/ʊɚ/ (poor) as in: boor /bʊɚ/
/ɔɚ/ (sports) as in: bore /bɔɚ/
/ɑɚ/ (car) as in: bar /bɑɚ/

Triphthongs

/aɪɚ/ (fire) as in: buyer /baɪɚ/
/aʊɚ/ (power) as in: bower /baʊɚ/

SAMPLE WORDS TRANSCRIBED IN IPA

(transcribed with dots for length[1], aspiration, and linking 'r')

1.	freed / **fri:d** /	21.	gloved / **glʌvd** /
2.	sling / **slɪŋ** /	22.	pushed / **pʰʊʃtʰ** /
3.	young / **jʌŋ** /	23.	thanks / **θæŋkˌs** /
4.	them / **ðem** /	24.	coughs / **kʰɔˑfs** /
5.	half / **hæf** /	25.	pauses / **ˈpʰɔ:zɪz** /
6.	whim / **wɪm** /	26.	touched / **tʰʌtˌʃtʰ** /
7.	ridge / **rɪdʒ** /	27.	bruised / **bru:zd** /
8.	mirth / **mɝˑθ** /	28.	zeros / **ˈzɪɚroʊz** /
9.	sugar / **ˈʃʊgɚ** /	29.	appeared / **əˈpʰɪɚd** /
10.	smooth / **smu:ð** /	30.	thumped / **θʌmpˌtʰ** /
11.	under / **ˈʌndɚ** /	31.	poised / **pʰɔˑɪˑzd** /
12.	deathly / **ˈdeθli** /	32.	Martha's / **ˈmɑðəθəz** /
13.	singer / **ˈsɪŋɚ** /	33.	quietly / **ˈkˌwaˑɪˑətˌli** /
14.	finger / **ˈfɪŋgɚ** /	34.	disgraced / **dɪsˈgreɪstʰ** /
15.	falling / **ˈfɔ:lɪŋ** /	35.	tornados / **tʰɔɚˈneˑɪˑdoʊz** /
16.	server / **ˈsɝ:vɚ** /	36.	compared / **kʰəmˈpʰeɚd** /
17.	drama / **ˈdrɑ:mə** /	37.	grounded / **ˈgraˑʊˑndɪd** /
18.	measured / **ˈmeʒɚd** /	38.	questions / **ˈkˌwestˌʃənz** /
19.	patches / **ˈpʰætˌʃɪz** /	39.	telephones / **ˈtʰeləfoʊnz** /
20.	strings / **stˌrɪŋz** /	40.	perspiring / **pʰəˈspʰaɪɚrɪŋ** /

---

[1] Remember: one-syllable words are considered stressed.

ANSWER KEY: transcribed with dots for length

Page 29—one vowel

1. /siː/
2. /tʰiː/
3. /liː/
4. /ʃiː/
5. /fiː/
6. /biː/
7. /biːd/
8. /iːz/
9. /iˑtˌʃ/
10. /kˌriˑkʰ/
11. /ðiː/
12. /sliˑpʰ/
13. /dʒiˑpʰ/
14. /jiˑstʰ/
15. /wiːv/

Page 30—three vowels

1. to (too, two)
2. wash
3. brews (bruise)
4. meets (meats)
5. docks
6. floozy
7. peeved
8. June
9. blues
10. blotch
11. bleach
12. creepy
13. shocks
14. queasy
15. pooch
16. /miː/
17. /aː/
18. /juː/
19. /tʰaˑpʰ/
20. /biˑtʰ/
21. /spʰaː/
22. /kʰiːz/
23. /gluː/
24. /ðiːz/
25. /θiˑf/
26. /ruːlz/
27. /dʒaːnz/
28. /ʃiˑtˌs/
29. /ˈwiːzi/
30. /ˈtˌʃuːzi/

Page 31—front vowels

1. /hiː/
2. /jes/
3. /bæd/
4. /fɪʃ/
5. /dʒɪm/
6. /pʰæθ/
7. /dʒækˌs/
8. /wen/
9. /rɪstʰ/
10. /siːdz/
11. /kˌwestʰ/
12. /θɪŋkˌs/
13. /ˈmætˌʃɪz/
14. /bliˑtˌʃtʰ/
15. /ˈtʰiːðɪŋ/
16. fans
17. hens
18. rings
19. Tim's
20. meals
21. banks
22. grief
23. sheets
24. drilled
25. wished
26. packed
27. penned
28. thanked
29. seethed
30. screeches

Page 32—mid-vowels

1. /tʰʌn/
2. /ðʌs/
3. /ˈpʰiˑtˌsə/
4. /θrʌstʰ/
5. /əˈtʰækʰ/
6. /ˈsʌni/
7. /dʒʌŋkˌtʰ/
8. /əˈmʌn/
9. /əˈniːmɪkʰ/
10. /ʌnˈdʌn/
11. achieve
12. thumbs
13. justice
14. busses
15. against
16. /ˈækˌtʰɚz/
17. /wɝˑstʰ/
18. /ˈhɝːmɪtʰ/
19. /ˈfiːvɚz/
20. /kʰɝˑstʰ/
21. /blɝːbz/
22. /əbˈzɝːvd/
23. /ˈtˌʃɝːlɪʃ/
24. /ˈpʰɝːmɪtˌs/
25. /pʰɚˈmɪtˌs/
26. treasures
27. covered
28. thunder
29. furthered
30. jumpers

THE DRAMA BOOK SHOP

250 West 40th St
New York, NY 10018
PHONE: (212) 944-0595
FAX: (212) 730-8739
TOLL FREE: 1-800-322-0595

524873 Reg 1 ID   7 10:33 am 05/31/16
DUPLICATE RECEIPT

S SPEAK WITH DISTIN	1 @ 39.99	39.99
S CLASSICALLY SPEAK	1 @ 32.95	32.95
SUBTOTAL		72.94
SALES TAX - 8.875%		6.47
TOTAL		79.41
AMERICAN EXPRESS PAYMENT		79.41

Account# XXXXXXXXXX2008 Exp Date 0320
Authorization# 286782   Clerk 7

I agree to pay the above total amount
according to the card issuer agreement.

No exchanges or refunds, incl. scripts.
www.dramabookshop.com

ANSWER KEY: transcribed with dots for length

Page 33—back vowels

1. /fɔːl/
2. /lɔˑftʰ/
3. /pʰʊl/
4. /ruːd/
5. /tˌʃɑˑpʰ/
6. /tʰɔˑkʰ/
7. /tʰɑˑkʰ/
8. /luːz/
9. /oˈbiˑs/
10. /sɔːŋ/
11. /kʰʊd/
12. /mɔˑθ/
13. /ruːʒ/
14. stood
15. watch
16. crook
17. suave
18. psalm

19. /dɔːgz/
20. /blɑːz/
21. /gʊdz/
22. /tʰɔˑstʰ/
23. /rɑːbz/
24. /skˌwɔːlz/
25. /ˈkˌlɔːzɪz/
26. /brʊkˌs/
27. /ˈkˌruːzɪz/
28. /fɔːnd/
29. /vjuːd/
30. /lɔːŋd/
31. /kʰʊkˌtʰ/
32. spewed
33. booked
34. stooped
35. botched
36. launched

Page 34—diphthongs

1. /beˈɪˑ/
2. /dʒɔˈɪˑ/
3. /laˈɪˑn/
4. /kʰoŭpʰ/
5. /aŭtʰ/
6. /braˈɪˑb/
7. /pʰɔˈɪˑz/
8. /greˈɪˑd/
9. /tʰaˈŭˑn/
10. /bɔˈɪˑl/
11. /waˈɪˑld/
12. /stʰoˈŭˑv/
13. /pˌraĭs/
14. /grɔˈɪˑn/
15. /saŭθ/
16. grave
17. rogue
18. advice

19. /rɔˈɪˑz/
20. /goŭtˌs/
21. /deˈɪˑvz/
22. /mɔĭstʰ/
23. /daŭtˌs/
24. /kˌraˈɪˑmz/
25. /reˈɪˑdʒd/
26. /maĭkˌs/
27. /ˈboˑŭˑlstʰə˞z/
28. /ˈstʰeˈɪˑdʒɪz/
29. /ˈtʰoŭstʰɪd/
30. /stˌraĭpˌtʰ/
31. /əˈvɔˈɪˑdɪd/
32. /kˌroŭkˌtʰ/
33. /ˈslaˈɪˑdɪŋ/
34. engaged
35. grounded
36. purloined

Page 35—diphth/triphthongs of 'r'

1. /beə˞/
2. /ʃɔə̆tʰ/
3. /tˌʃaə̆tʰ/
4. /wɪə̆/
5. /tʰʊə̆/
6. /kˌlɪə̆/
7. /feə̆/
8. /snɔə̆tʰ/
9. /haə̆ʃ/
10. /pʰɔə̆/
11. /snaə̆lz/
12. /rɪˈtʰɔə̆tˌs/
13. /əˈʃʊə̆/
14. /əbˈhɔə̆z/
15. /gleə̆z/
16. /kʰəˈrɪə̆/
17. /ˈɔə̆də˞z/
18. /ˈaə̆gjuz/

19. /spʰɪə̆/
20. /haə̆tˌs/
21. /mə tˌʃʊə̆/
22. /skˌweə̆/
23. /rɪˈstʰɔə̆/
24. /pʰəˈspʰaĭə̆/
25. /ʃaʊə̆/
26. /ˈpʰaə̆sli/
27. /swɔə̆n/
28. /kʰaʊə̆z/
29. /ˈweə̆rəbl/
30. /rɪˈmaə̆kˌtʰ/
31. /dɪˈpˌlɔə̆z/
32. /ˈtˌʃaə̆mɪŋ/
33. /tˌrænˈspʰaĭə̆/
34. /pˌreə̆z/
35. /stʰaə̆tˌʃtʰ/
36. /kʰənˈspʰaĭə̆/

Page 36—all sounds

1. /tˌʃeə̆z/
2. /ˈekʰoŭz/
3. /snɪə̆z/
4. /ˈmaə̆kʰɪtʰ/
5. /ˈpʰɔə̆tˌli/
6. /sɪnˈsɪə̆/
7. /ˈʃaˈɪˑnɪŋ/
8. /ɪmˈpˌlɔˈɪˑd/
9. /kˌwiːn/
10. /ɪmˈpˌlaˈɪˑd/
11. /ˈhaːloŭ/
12. /kˌlaˈŭˑnz/
13. /ˈpʰætˌʃɪz/
14. /wɪŋkˌtʰ/
15. /ˈmaːdəfaĭd/

16. /fɔˈɪˑl/
17. /kˌjuːbz/
18. /spʰaˈɪˑz/
19. /ˈʃʊə̆li/
20. /oˈvɜˑˑtʰ/
21. /beĭkˌtʰ/
22. /ˈtˌraˈŭˑzə˞z/
23. /stˌroŭkˌs/
24. /ˈwɪtˌʃɪz/
25. /ˈɔˑθə˞z/
26. /smʌdʒd/
27. /ˈneˈɪˑbə˞z/
28. /hæf aŭə̆/
29. /ˈmuːvi stʰaə̆/
30. /pʰəˈfɔə̆məns/

NEUTRAL AMERICAN DIALECT

AUDIO SELECTIONS▶
Carman Lacivita and Patricia Fletcher

RHYTHM HIGHLIGHTERS

"Contenting myself with the certainty that Music, in its various modes of metre, rhythm, and rhyme, is of so vast a moment in Poetry as never to be wisely rejected—is so vitally important an adjunct, that he is simply silly who declines its assistance..."

(Edgar Allan Poe: The Poetic Principle)

The following items accentuate or highlight the rhythmic qualities inherent in spoken English, and are crucial for effectively playing well-pronounced characters or adjusting contemporary speech to the demands of classical texts.

Rhythm Highlighters Section

Rhythm Highlighters pertaining to specific vowels and consonants are covered in specific sound sections, including:

Linking

To Avoid Glottal Attack and Glottal Fry

Many speakers, especially younger contemporary actors, have a habit of interrupting the formation of initial vowel sounds with a **glottal** stop, or sudden closing of the space between the vocal folds in the throat. Tensing the vocal folds in this manner explodes the breath and initiates vowel sounds with a slight popping noise, giving them a harsh, choppy quality.

Note: You may be familiar with the glottal pronunciation of 'be<u>tt</u>er', 'bu<u>tt</u>er' and 'bo<u>tt</u>le' in the *Cockney* dialect, when the medial consonant /t/ is replaced by a glottal stop.

This approach to initiating sound is especially common in actors speaking with emphasis or expressing themselves while in a highly emotional state. But vowels exploded from the glottis in the throat are much less open, clear, informative, or expressive than those uninterrupted in their release through an open throat. Also, undue stress placed on the vocal mechanism from continued use of glottal attacks can contribute to serious vocal problems.

To break the habit of beginning vowel production with a glottal stop, try **linking** the vowel that begins a word to the last sound of the previous word. This will help avoid the initial 'pop' and promote an uninterrupted, forward release of breath and sound through the mouth.

AUDIO 1▶ **linking words to avoid glottal attacks**

> To show‿an‿unfelt sorrow‿is‿an‿office
> Which the false man does‿easy.
>
> (Macbeth: II, iii, 136)
>
> There‿are such‿a lot‿of vulgar‿and‿ unpleasant‿and‿offensive
> people‿among the‿other civilians.
>
> (Chekhov: Three Sisters)
>
> Come, come‿away!
> The sun‿is high, and we‿outwear the day.
>
> (Henry V: IV, ii, 62)

The symbol for linking to the previous word: **/ ‿ /** is used in the remaining practice phrases in this section, though linking is ultimately at an actor's discretion. I suggest marking your own script until the habit of linking sounds is firmly established. Do not link with an 'r' sound if there is no 'r' in the spelling, see **intrusive 'r'** on pages 129-130 and pages 153-154.

PHRASES linking words to avoid glottal attacks

1. saying yes‿or no
2. paying for‿Adam
3. wherever you‿are
4. going with‿Annie
5. thinking‿of‿Evelyn

6. today‿it‿isn't
7. someone‿else‿is
8. closing‿all doors
9. knowing‿about‿it
10. filling‿in‿all blanks

SENTENCES linking words to avoid glottal attacks

1. Take action!

2. What's in your eye?

3. Who is after you in line?

4. The animals are in cages.

5. Hiking isn't for everyone.

6. The IRS did what I asked.

7. Those apples are unwashed.

8. Benjamin left after auditioning.

9. They all lived happily ever after!

10. Has everyone already eaten dinner?

11. He asked to play a part in *Everyman*.

12. The opening night party is at Sardi's.

13. This sofa isn't comfortable anymore.

14. Japan and China are on our itinerary.

15. Do vocal warm-ups before all auditions.

16. They rehearsed every evening last week.

17. That idiomatic expression is everywhere.

18.   She's not exaggerating: they had eleven callbacks.

19.   Dad dreams of vacationing in the sun every February.

20.   They're both excellent actors and they're in my acting class.

When a vowel sound begins a sentence or new phrase, and there is no previous sound to link with, extra care and practice is required to avoid initiating sound with a glottal attack.

Gently place your hand on your throat and begin the <u>first</u> word in the pair below by elongating the initial 'h'. Notice the smooth flow of breath as it moves from the middle of the torso, up through the relaxed throat, carrying the vowel that follows 'h' through the mouth. Breathe. Speak the <u>second</u> word of the pair. Focus on repeating the sensation of a smooth, open-throated release of breath that carries sound through the mouth without any stoppage in the throat.

WORDS avoiding glottal attack on initial words

hi – eye	hit – it	hail – ale	heart – art
heat – eat	haul –all	ham – am	hand – and
hate – ate	hair – air	head – Ed	halter – alter
heel – eel	hive – I've	Henry – any	heave – even
hash – ash	hem – Emma	hamper – amp	heavy – Evan

Another approach is to form the *shape*[1] necessary to speak the initial vowel on an open-throated intake of breath. Then, smoothly release the vowel through that shape on a tension-free exhalation with no closing, catching, stopping, or interruption in the throat. This technique should be used for brief practice, not in everyday life or in performance.

The IPA symbol /ʔ/ below represents a glottal sound. It is used here as a reminder to avoid beginning with a glottal attack.

PHRASES linking and avoiding glottal attack on initial words

1.	ʔ as‿is	6.	ʔ always‿acting
2.	ʔ interesting‿image	7.	ʔ isn't‿alienated
3.	ʔ evening‿activities	8.	ʔ about‿an‿hour
4.	ʔ anything‿Edith‿asks	9.	ʔ outside‿at‿Evan's
5.	ʔ unaccountable‿action	10.	ʔ eventually‿interred

---

[1] Specific shapes necessary for forming all sounds are covered in the individual sound chapters.

SENTENCES linking and avoiding initial glottal attack on initial words

1. Avoid oysters.

2. Oliver exhausts.

3. Avery is an angel.

4. Embroider everything.

5. Insist on oil free ointment.

6. *As You Like It* ended early.

7. Ida idolizes opulent operas.

8. Evelyn's earrings are opaque.

9. Unsolicited advice is annoying.

10. Insight is extremely underrated.

11. Alvin Anderson's always invited.

12. Awesome adventures are often admired.

13. At eighty-eight, aging Abe is inexhaustible.

14. 'An eye for an eye' isn't an admirable outlook.

15. Arthur's amazing agent arranged the appointment.

16. Evening attire is expressly indicated on the invitation.

17. Intoxication inevitably evolves into obnoxious behavior.

18. After an hour, irate Irene still waited for an announcement.

Preventing glottal fry: many contemporary speakers have a habit of tensing the muscles of the throat and stopping the release of breath, especially during vowel sounds at the ends of phrases or sentences—rather than continuing the forward release of breath and sound through an open throat through the end of the word and thought. The resulting raspy, throaty sound is sometimes referred to as a **glottal fry**.

Muscles of the throat, larynx, and outer abdominal area should remain relaxed during inhalation, and breath release should initiate from the middle of the torso, not from the throat and larynx. This forward release must continue, through the last sound of the last word, without any experience of forcing or squeezing on the final sounds.

Key Words
& Stressed Syllables

English is a wonderfully rhythmic language, composed of varying combinations of stressed and unstressed syllables within words, and stressed and unstressed words within phrases and sentences. Recognizing stress patterns and understanding the contribution stress makes to rhythm, inflected speech and clarity of expression, can increase the likelihood an actor will be sensitive to a character's rhythmic delivery when interpreting any text, from Shakespeare to Beckett to Mamet.

I would define, in brief, the Poetry of words as

'The Rhythmical Creation of Beauty'.
(Edgar Allan Poe: The Poetic Principle)

Syllables. A one-syllable word contains only one vowel sound, as in 'tea', one diphthong sound, as in 'tie', or one triphthong sound, as in 'tire'. Though a word like 'f<u>ame</u>' has two letters that are associated with vowel sounds, the final 'e' is silent. Remember to consider sound, not spelling.

If a one-syllable word is **operative** or **key** to the meaning being expressed, the entire word will be emphasized or stressed. Any contrast in stress will be between this one-syllable word and other less important words in the sentence. One possible choice, demonstrated on Audio 2 and marked below, follows.

AUDIO 2▶ **stressing key words**

To think upon my **pomp** shall be my **hell.**

(2 Henry VI: II, iv, 27)

Do all men **kill** the things they do not **love**?
(The Merchant of Venice: IV, i, 66)

'Tis **he. Slink** by, and **note** him.

(As You Like It: III, ii, 252)

Read through the following sentences and notice how meaning and implication change, depending on the word receiving stress.

> **Chris**, I don't want pizza now.
> Chris, **I** don't want pizza now.
> Chris, I **don't** want pizza now.
> Chris, I don't **want** pizza now.
> Chris, I don't want **pizza** now.
> Chris, I don't want pizza **now**.

As you see, actors need to choose carefully, placing stress on words that clearly communicate their point. This usually involves: nouns, action verbs, adjectives and adverbs, though it is not usually necessary to stress more than one word per phrase, or unit of thought. Stressing too many words can cause as much confusion and lack of clarity as stressing too few.

When an operative or key word contains more than one syllable, as in: 'crying', 'prefer', or 'peaceful', the vowel sound in the stressed syllable is usually contrasted (or highlighted) by making it louder, longer, and higher in pitch than the rest of the word. This is influenced by many variables, including the thought being communicated, and the emotional life and intention of the speaker.

Paying attention to stressed syllables, especially in key words and phrases, is a useful way to add variety, musicality, and increased intelligibility to one's speech and to avoid a monotone delivery.

A stressed syllable in a word can be notated in IPA by placing a / ' / mark in front of it; **bolding** will also used for additional clarity. Selections in Audio 3, below, are marked with both to reflect the speakers' choices. When working with a microphone, stress is subtler than when speaking for the stage.

AUDIO 3► **stressed syllables of key words**

Just sitting here 'pra**tt** ling with Miss 'Ju**lie**.

(Strindberg: Miss Julie)

Think you I am no 'stronger than my **sex**,
Being so 'father'd and so 'husbanded?

(Julius Caesar: II, i, 296)

The **tongues** of 'dying **men**
En'force a'ttention like **deep** 'harmony.

(Richard II: II, i, 5)

As previously stated, stressed syllable markings used throughout this book are based on pronunciation, rather than observing technical rules or dividing syllables according to spelling combinations.

a'**wake**   '**fla**vor   de'**mure**ly

ri'**dic**ulous   unin'**ten**tional   respecta'**bil**ity

The contrast in rhythm and pitch between the stressed and unstressed syllables in the words 'awake' and 'flavor' could be represented:

a'**wake**   short **LONG**   tuh **TUM**

'**fla**vor   **LONG** short   **TUM** tuh

Energetically speak the following words. Notice if the vowel of the *stressed* syllable is louder, longer, and higher in pitch than the vowel(s) in the unstressed syllable(s).

WORDS with stressed syllables marked

re'**ply**	'**trai**tor	a'**pplaud**	de'**ny**
'**fa**ding	'**poi**son	a'**lar**ming	'**chim**ing
'**sat**isfied	'**mor**ning	de'**tained**	'**in**tercom
com'**plain**	'**poun**ding	com'**pressed**	un'**nat**ural
re'**spon**sive	de'**stroyed**	'**ban**ishment	'**pros**perous

Hint: If you are having difficulty discerning the stressed syllable, place your hand on the underside of your chin. The jaw is usually most open on the vowel sound of the stressed syllable. If you are still having difficulty, try over-stressing various syllables. The 'correct' choice will probably become more apparent.

WORDS with stressed syllables unmarked

robber	avenue	serial	sailor
soberly	contain	about	patent
account	allowed	media	dignity
lionized	limerick	absurd	display
deceived	legislate	limestone	libretto
belonging	bachelor	turpentine	particle
chaperone	probably	inscrutable	equality

NEUTRAL AMERICAN TEXT key words, stressed syllables. *Underline your choice key words and speak aloud, with attention to stressed syllables. Find a balance: stressing too many words is as unclear as stressing too few.*

I've been <u>thinking</u> of setting up a new line of <u>business</u>.

(Ibsen: Ghosts)

Fie, my lord, fie! A soldier, and afeard?

(Macbeth: V, i, 36)

Nina, how strange it is that I should be seeing you. Why would you not let me see you?

(Chekhov: The Seagull)

Alas! Yes, family life is certainly not always so pure as it ought to be.

(Ibsen: Ghosts)

We turn up our noses at one another, but life is passing all the while.

(Chekhov: The Cherry Orchard)

DOCTOR PINCH. Give me your hand and let me feel your pulse.
ANTIPHOLUS. There is my hand, and let it feel your ear.

(The Comedy of Errors: IV, iv, 52)

I may neither choose who I would, not refuse who I dislike; so is the will of a living daughter curb'd by the will of a dead father.

(The Merchant of Venice: I, ii, 23)

GREMIO. O this learning, what a thing it is!
GRUMIO. O this woodcock, what an ass it is!

(The Taming of the Shrew: I, ii, 159)

From THE CASK OF AMONTILLADO

Edgar Allan Poe

The thousand injuries of Fortunato I had borne as best I could; but when he ventured upon insult, I vowed revenge. You, who so well know the nature of my soul, will not suppose, however, that I gave utterance to a threat. *At length* I would be avenged; this was a point definitively settled—but the very definitiveness with which it was resolved, precluded the idea of risk. I must not only punish, but punish with impunity. A wrong is unredressed when retribution overtakes its redresser. It is equally unredressed when the avenger fails to make himself felt as such to him who has done the wrong.

From **THE TAMING OF THE SHREW**

William Shakespeare

Choose your key words carefully, in order to make the following conversation clear.

LUCENTIO.	Pray you sit down,
	For now we sit to chat as well as eat.
PETRUCHIO.	Nothing but sit and sit, and eat and eat!
BAPTISTA.	Padua affords this kindness, son Petruchio.
PETRUCHIO.	Padua affords nothing but what is kind.
HORTENSIO.	For both our sakes, I would that word were true.
PETRUCHIO.	Now, for my life, Hortensio fears his widow.
WIDOW.	Then never trust me if I be afeard.
PETRUCHIO.	You are very sensible, and yet you miss my sense:
	I mean Hortensio is afeard of you.
WIDOW.	He that is giddy thinks the world turns round.
PETRUCHIO.	Roundly replied.
KATHERINE.	Mistress, how mean you that?
WIDOW.	Thus I conceive by him.
PETRUCHIO.	Conceives by me! how likes Hortensio that?
HORTENSIO.	My widow says, thus she conceives her tale.
PETRUCHIO.	Very well mended. Kiss him for that, good widow.
KATHERINE.	"He that is giddy thinks the world turns round":
	I pray you tell me what you meant by that.
WIDOW.	Your husband, being troubled with a shrew,
	Measures my husband's sorrow by his woe:
	And now you know my meaning.
KATHERINE.	A very mean meaning.
WIDOW.	Right, I mean you.
KATHERINE.	And I am mean indeed, respecting you.
PETRUCHIO.	To her, Kate!
HORTENSIO.	To her, widow!
PETRUCHIO.	A hundred marks, my Kate does put her down.
HORTENSIO.	That's my office.
PETRUCHIO.	Spoke like an officer. Ha' to thee, lad!

Drinks to Hortensio.

(V, ii, 10-37)

Noun / Verb Variations

There are words whose stress and meaning can vary depending on their use as nouns, verbs, or adjectives. Some words commonly used as both nouns and verbs follow.

Nouns	**Verbs**
1ˢᵗ syllable stressed)	(2ⁿᵈ syllable stressed)
LONG short **TUM** tuh	short **LONG** **TUM** tuh
ˈcompound	comˈpound
ˈcontent	conˈtent
ˈcontest	conˈtest
ˈcontract	conˈtract
ˈcontrast	conˈtrast
ˈconvert	conˈvert
ˈdefect	deˈfect
ˈdiscourse	disˈcourse
ˈextract	exˈtract
ˈfrequent	freˈquent
ˈimport	imˈport
ˈinsult	inˈsult
ˈobject	obˈject
ˈperfect	perˈfect
ˈpermit	perˈmit
ˈpervert	perˈvert
ˈpresent	preˈsent
ˈproduce	proˈduce
ˈprogress	proˈgress
ˈproject	proˈject
ˈrebel	reˈbel
ˈrecord	reˈcord
ˈsubject	subˈject
ˈsurvey	surˈvey
ˈsuspect	suˈspect
ˈtorment	torˈment

AUDIO 4▶ noun / verb variations

And tor'**ment** each other to death?

(Strindberg: Miss Julie)

ı

Fancy—to be able to write on such a '**subject** as that!

(Ibsen: Hedda Gabler)

Come, come, dis'**patch**, the Duke would be at dinner.

(Richard III: III, iv, 94)

SENTENCES noun / verb variations

1. Don't subject me to studying that subject.

2. Let me present you with this lovely present.

3. She's a rebel who rebels against everything!

4. I feel I must contest the results of the contest.

5. You insult by reading from that book of insults.

6. Vanilla extract is extracted from the vanilla bean.

7. For the record, I recorded my first record in 1970.

8. I suspect that the suspect is still living in Manhattan.

9. I am content after hearing the contents of the review.

10. I will defect to the other side unless you correct this defect.

NEUTRAL AMERICAN TEXT noun / verb variations. *Mark the stressed syllable of words that vary between noun and verb, and speak aloud.*

The object and the pleasure of mine eye.

(A Midsummer Night's Dream: IV, i, 170)

I cannot project mine own cause so well.

(Antony and Cleopatra: V, ii, 121)

Content yourself. God knows I lov'd my niece.

(Much Ado About Nothing: V, i, 87)

O, that record is lively in my soul!

(Richard II: I, i, 30)

And to the nightingale's complaining notes
Tune my distresses and record my woes.

(The Two Gentlemen of Verona: V, iv, 5)

A woman sometimes scorns what best contents her.

(The Two Gentlemen of Verona: III, i, 93)

Thus was I, sleeping, by a brother's hand
Of life, of crown, of queen, at once dispatch'd.

(Hamlet: I, v, 74)

Let's follow him, and pervert the present wrath
He hath against himself.

(Cymbeline: II, iv, 151)

And mark what object did present itself
Under an old oak, whose boughs were moss'd with age
And high top bald with dry antiquity.

(As You Like It: IV, iii, 103)

First, heaven be the record to my speech,
In the devotion of a subject's love.
Tend'ring the precious safety of my prince,
And free from other misbegotten hate,
Come I appellant to this princely presence.

(Richard II: I, i, 30)

I know a wench of excellent discourse,
Pretty and witty; wild, and yet, too, gentle;
There will we dine. This woman that I mean,
My wife (but, I protest, without desert)
Hath often times upbraided me withal.

(The Comedy of Errors: III, I, 109)

It is a melancholy of mine own, compounded of many simples
extracted from many objects.

(As You Like It: IV, i, 15)

Weak Forms

Weak forms, sometimes referred to as vowel reductions, are specific words that have two pronunciations: a strong form (sf), which uses a longer, more prominent vowel sound, and a weak form (wf), which uses a shorter vowel sound. In most cases, the vowel in the weak form of a word is the short /ə/ (uh) sound, also known as the 'schwa' sound.

Articles, auxiliary verbs, pronouns (including personal, possessive and demonstrative), prepositions and connectives all have weak forms. Using weak forms helps rhythmically focus attention onto more important or informative key words, while maintaining a relaxed, conversational rhythm.

The following is marked as spoken in the audio selection.

AUDIO 5▶ **weak forms**

   tə   ə   əz   əz   ə

To **wake** a **wolf** is as **bad** as **smell** a **fox**.

(2 Henry IV: I, ii, 155)

        ə   əv   ðəts   ðə

There 's not a **note** of **mine** that' s **worth** the **'not**ing.

(Much Ado About Nothing: II, iii, 55)

      ðə   əv ðə

'Memory, the **'ward**er of the **brain**.

(Macbeth: I, vii, 65)

ARTICLES: The choice of weak form in this case depends on the first sound of the word that follows the article.

Strong form			Weak form
a	**eĭ**	followed by a consonant sound use	**ə**
an	**æn**	followed by a vowel sound use	**ən**

The weak form of the word 'a', /ə/, prevails unless 'a' is being stressed to make a point. In that uncommon instance /eĭ/ is spoken. Compare:

Weak form   I'd like a <u>ticket</u>.

Strong form   I'd like <u>a</u> ticket.

$$ə \qquad\qquad\qquad\qquad ə$$
Sometime a horse I'll be, sometime a hound,
$$ə \quad ə \qquad\qquad\qquad\qquad ə$$
A hog, a headless bear, sometime a fire.

(A Midsummer Night's Dream: III, I, 108)

Remember: The article **'a'** is not used (in writing or speaking) before words that begin with a vowel; **'an'** is used, in either its strong or weak form.

PHRASES *'a'* followed by consonants / *'an'* followed by vowels

/ə/	/ə/	/ən/	/ən/
1. a key	a jolt	an ant	an altar
2. a box	a fact	an exam	an oboe
3. a talk	a date	an event	an action
4. a play	a song	an addict	an actress
5. a script	a thing	an animal	an umpire
6. a snack	a bottle	an excuse	an opinion
7. a check	a printer	an emotion	an illusion
8. a knock	a chorus	an audition	an incident
9. a couch	a change	an umbrella	an evening
10. a movie	a promotion	an intention	an argument

SENTENCES *'a'* followed by consonants / *'an'* followed by vowels

1. Give me a break.

2. That was an exciting event.

3. It's an exact duplicate of a very old antique.

4. What an inspired thought; that's a great idea!

5. An ounce of prevention is worth a pound of cure.

6. I'll have a piece of cake with a scoop of ice cream.

7. I have a feeling an announcement will be made soon.

8. Creating an artistic environment is a challenging job.

9. As a matter of fact, I'd like to buy a ticket for a hit show.

10. They had a great time on an ocean liner in the Caribbean.

Strong form		Weak form
the ðɪ	when followed by a consonant sound use	ðə
	when followed by a vowel sound use	ðɪ (or) ðɪ

ðə

SHYLOCK. *Is that the law?*

ðɪ

PORTIA. *Thyself shalt see the‿act.*

(The Merchant of Venice: IV, i, 314)

PHRASES *'the'* followed by consonants and vowels

	/ðə/	/ðə/	/ðɪ/ or /ðɪ/	/ðɪ/ or /ðɪ/
1.	the way	the job	the‿item	the‿ad
2.	the cast	the day	the‿ache	the‿act
3.	the sink	the fish	the‿extra	the‿end
4.	the play	the one	the‿apple	the‿eyes
5.	the time	the best	the‿author	the‿actor
6.	the craft	the wait	the‿energy	the‿oven
7.	the news	the truth	the‿opening	the‿action
8.	the notes	the stage	the‿audition	the‿interest
9.	the place	the worst	the‿intention	the‿address
10.	the boxer	the traffic	the‿academic	the‿argument

SENTENCES *'the'* followed by consonants and vowels

1. The agency closed its door at the end of the day.

2. The sign-in sheet at the audition was full by 6 a.m.

3. The attorney couldn't defend the criminal's actions.

4. Delaying the shooting was the last thing he wanted.

5. The last time we visited the theatre, the lights went out.

6.   The waitress brought the coffee first, then the dessert.

7.   The knives and forks were all purchased just for the event.

8.   The singers scheduled a vocal warm-up before the concert.

9.   All the entertainers were applauded at the end of the show.

10.   The reading was a huge success; the actors were wonderful.

AUXILIARY VERBS. The verbs in the following list are commonly used either alone in a sentence as the main verb, or in combination with another verb as auxiliary verb.

am	are	can	could	do	does
had	has	have	must	was	should

When used alone as the main verb, as in the second column, the strong form is spoken and the word is stressed. When used as the auxiliary verb, as in the third column, the weak form is used to focus attention onto the more descriptive main verb that comes after, which is stressed. Phonetic transcription of strong and weak forms is included above the word, below. *Read across.*

<u>VERB</u>	<u>Strong Form</u>	<u>Weak Form</u>
	æm	əm
am	Yes I **am**!	I am **here**.
	ɑə̆	ə̆
are	You **are**?	Bob and Tim are **gone**.
	kæn	kən
can	They **can**.	They can **leave**.
	kʊd	kəd
could	We **could**.	We could **see** that.
	du	də (or dʊ)
do	You **do**?	What do you **want**?
	dʌz	dəz
does	He **does**.	Does it **work**?
	hæd	həd (or əd)
had	I wish I **had**.	I wish I had **known**.
	hæz	həz (or əz)
has	Yes, he **has**.	He has been **hurt**.

3. **(from)**   Where are you <u>from</u>? I'm fr~~o~~m New York.

4. **(some)**   I've had <u>some</u> day! Now, I need s~~o~~me rest.

5. **(that)**   They told me th~~a~~t I won; do you believe <u>that</u>?

6. **(of)**   I'm thinking ~~o~~f you; that's what I'm thinking <u>of</u>.

7. **(must)**   We m~~u~~st go to a show sometime; we really <u>must</u>!

8. **(was)**   I w~~a~~s going to confirm it. Really, I <u>was</u>.

9. **(had)**   I wish I h~~a~~d known. I really wish I <u>had</u>.

10. **(for)**   Who's that <u>for</u>; is it fo~~r~~ you?

NEUTRAL AMERICAN TEXT weak forms. *Draw a line through words with weak forms or write the appropriate IPA symbol above the weak form word. Speak out loud, highlighting key words.*

~~A~~ new <u>bonnet</u> ~~and~~ ~~a~~ new <u>parasol</u>!

(Ibsen: Hedda Gabler)

Brilliant! You should have been an actor!

(Strindberg: Miss Julie)

It is the part of men to fear and tremble.

(Julius Caesar: I, iii, 54)

Soft you; a word or two before you go.

(Othello: V, ii, 338)

From time to time I have acquainted you…

(The Merry Wives of Windsor: IV, vi, 8)

Condemning some to death and some to exile.

(Coriolanus: I, vi, 34)

In peace there's nothing so becomes a man
As modest stillness and humility.

(Henry V: III, i, 3)

What a delight it is to have you again, as large as life, before
my very eyes!

(Ibsen: Hedda Gabler)

From **THE PURLOINED LETTER**

Edgar Allan Poe

Why, the fact is, we took our time, and we searched *everywhere*. I have had long experience in these affairs. I took the entire building, room by room; devoting the nights of a whole week to each. We examined, first, the furniture of each apartment. We opened every possible drawer; and I presume you know that, to a properly trained police-agent, such a thing as a '*secret*' drawer is impossible. Any man is a dolt who permits a 'secret' drawer to escape him in a search of this kind.

THE RAINY DAY

Henry Wadsworth Longfellow

The day is cold, and dark, and dreary;
It rains, and the wind is never weary;
The vine still clings to the mouldering wall,
But at every gust the dead leaves fall,
And the day is dark and dreary.

My life is cold, and dark, and dreary,
It rains, and the wind is never weary,
My thoughts still cling to the mouldering Past,
But the hopes of youth fall thick in the blast,
And the days are dark and dreary.

Be still, sad heart! and cease repining;
Behind the clouds is the sun still shining;
Thy fate is the common fate of all,
Into each life some rain must fall,
Some days must be dark and dreary.

From **SHADOW—A PARABLE**

Edgar Allan Poe

The year had been a year of terror, and of feelings more intense than terror for which there is no name upon the earth. For many prodigies and signs had taken place, and far and wide, over the sea and land, the black wings of the Pestilence were spread abroad. To those, nevertheless, cunning in the stars, it was not unknown that the heavens wore an aspect of ill; and to me, the Greek Oinos, among others, it was evident that now had arrived the alternation of that seven hundred and ninety-fourth year when, at the entrance of Aires, the planet Jupiter is conjoined with the red ring of the terrible Saturnus. The peculiar spirit of the skies, if I mistake not greatly, made itself manifest, not only in the physical orb of the earth, but in the souls, imaginations, and meditations of mankind.

From **ALICE IN WONDERLAND**

Lewis Carroll

Tied around the neck of the bottle was a paper label, with the words "DRINK ME" beautifully printed on it in large letters.

It was all very well to say "Drink me," but the wise little Alice was not going to do *that* in a hurry. "No, I'll look first," she said, "and see whether it's marked '*poison*' or not"; for she had read several nice little stories about children who had got burnt, and eaten up by wild beasts, and other unpleasant things, all because they *would* not remember the simple rules their friends had taught them: such as, that a red-hot poker will burn you if you hold it too long; and that, if you cut your finger *very* deeply with a knife, it usually bleeds; and she had never forgotten that, if you drink much from a bottle marked "poison," it is almost certain to disagree with you, sooner or later.

However, this bottle was *not* marked "poison," so Alice ventured to taste it, and finding it very nice (it had, in fact, a sort of mixed flavour of cherry-tart, custard, pine-apple, roast turkey, toffy, and hot buttered toast), she very soon finished it off.

78

Pause

Perhaps the most rhythmically useful tool available when speaking is silence. A pause is cessation of speech (silence) in the middle or end of verbalization for any number of reasons, the most popular – breathing!

Speak the following sentence, which is written without punctuation. Make sure any pause taken for breath does not interfere with the 'unit of thought' or idea being expressed.

I have of late but wherefore I know not lost all my mirth forgone all custom of exercises and indeed it goes so heavily with my disposition that this goodly frame the earth seems to me a sterile promontory this most excellent canopy the air look you this brave o'erhanging firmament this majestical roof fretted with golden fire why it appeareth nothing to me but a foul and pestilent congregation of vapors.

(Hamlet: II, ii, 295)

Some playwrights are extremely precise in their use of punctuation; for example, Harold Pinter, Edward Albee, and David Mamet. When ignored, it is to the actor's detriment.

The punctuation is very useful in the following:

TESMAN. *What... are you staring at?*
PAUSE.
Hedda... ?
HEDDA. *The leaves. They're so yellow... withered.*
TESMAN. *Well, it is September.*
PAUSE.
HEDDA. *Think of it! September... already.*
SILENCE.

(Ibsen: Hedda Gabler)

Sometimes pauses are needed in order to avoid confusion and are thus used for **clarity**. Parentheses are used in the following example to delineate pauses:

I do affect the very ground (which is base) where her shoe (which is
baser) guided by her foot (which is basest) doth tread.

(Love's Labor's Lost, I, ii, 167)

There is often a slight pause within a line of verse called a **caesura**, indicated by **/** in the sample below. The line may or may not be marked with punctuation, but a caesura can serve to clarify the thought or offer a pause for dramatic effect:

He talks to me **/** *that never had a son.*

(King John: III, iv, 91)

AUDIO 7▶ **dramatic pause**

Some rise by sin, and some by virtue **/** fall.

(Measure for Measure: II, i, 38)

Just think: Midsummer Day, in a stifling train, packed in with
that mob of families all gaping at me; train stalled in the station,
when you want **/** to fly!

(Strindberg: Miss Julie)

The inaudible and noiseless foot **/** of time.

(Twelfth Night: V, iii, 4)

Changes in the pace, speed, or tempo of the delivery, coupled with pauses, can be a very effective tool for breaking up established patterns and adding dramatic effect.

Some actors, gifted with an internal sense of rhythm, have perfect 'timing' and possess an innate feeling for precisely when to begin or end a line, phrase, laugh, or pause. But there are also some purely technical considerations that can be helpful.

A longer 'dramatic' pause can be used as a set-up before an important idea, or for underscoring a point after an idea has been introduced. But such dramatic pauses must be earned. There is a direct relationship between one's pace and energy when speaking and the amount of time 'earned' that can be 'spent' on a pause. In other words, actors should establish an enlivened delivery first, so they have something with which to balance the length of the pause.

The slower the pace, the shorter the pause; the quicker the pace and higher the energy level, the more time earned for an engaging pause.

It is important to remember that pausing is not emptiness in time and space. The thought must continue. The character stops for a reason—to decide what to say next, to allow something to settle in, to recover his/her composure, etc. The pause is related to the moments before and after and must reflect that by being filled.

When a pause occurs in the middle of a thought, an upward, double or even level inflection immediately preceding the pause can subtly communicate that the speaker is not yet finished, and can increase the time 'earned' for the pause.

It is often effective to 'break' the pause by returning to speech on a lower pitch, especially if upward inflection was used immediately before pausing, while being sensitive to the need to re-establish or 'pick up' the pace.

In summary, 'pace', 'pitch', then 'pause' are the technical underpinnings, but any pause should be driven and substantiated by the character's wants and needs as expressed through the text.

NEUTRAL AMERICAN TEXT pause and dramatic pause. *Decide where a dramatic pause might be possible, mark the text, and then speak the text aloud.*

It's your duty / to go on the stage.
(Chekhov: The Seagull)

Thou art, as you are all, a sorceress.
(The Comedy of Errors: IV, iii, 66)

You surely do not suppose that I have nothing better to do than to study such publications as these?
(Ibsen: Ghosts)

You argue like a man who has had enough. You are satisfied and so you are indifferent to life, nothing matters to you. But even you will be afraid to die.
(Chekhov: The Seagull)

Uncle, what could be more hopeless and stupid than my position?
(Chekhov: The Seagull)

From **THE MASQUE OF THE RED DEATH**

Edgar Allan Poe

The "Red Death" had long devastated the country. No pestilence had ever been so fatal, or so hideous. Blood was its Avatar and its seal—the redness and the horror of blood. There were sharp pains, and sudden dizziness, and then profuse bleeding at the pores, with dissolution. The scarlet stains upon the body and especially upon the face of the victim, were the pest ban which shut him out from the aid and from the sympathy of his fellow-men. And the whole seizure, progress and termination of the disease, were the incidents of half an hour.

From **THREE SUNDAYS IN A WEEK**

Edgar Allan Poe

A very "fine old English gentleman," was my grand-uncle Rumgudgeon, but unlike him of the song, he had his weak points. He was a little, pursy, pompous, passionate semicircular somebody, with a red nose, a thick skull, a long purse, and a strong sense of his own consequence. With the best heart in the world, he contrived, through a predominant whim of contradiction, to earn for himself, among those who only knew him superficially, the character of a curmudgeon. Like many excellent people, he seemed possessed with a spirit of tantalization, which might easily, at a casual glance, have been mistaken for malevolence. To every request, a positive "No!" was his immediate answer; but, in the end—in the long, long end—there were exceedingly few requests which he refused. Against all attacks upon his purse he made the most sturdy defense; but the amount extorted from him, at last, was generally in direct ratio with the length of the siege and the stubbornness of the resistance. In charity no one gave more liberally or with a worse grace.

LITERARY DEVICES

An immortal instinct, deep within the spirit of man, is thus, plainly, a sense of the Beautiful. This it is which administers to his delight in the manifold forms, and sounds, and odors, and sentiments amid which he exists.

(Edgar Allan Poe: The Poetic Principle)

Increased sensitivity to the palate of sounds and rhythms that make up spoken words and phrases can be promoted through an awareness of the following commonly used literary devices.

Rhyme

Rhyme is the reoccurrence of the same last sound, or last few sounds, in two or more words.

AUDIO 8 A▶ **rhyme**

The time is out of joint – O cursed sp<u>ite</u>,
That ever I was born to set it <u>right!</u>

(Hamlet: I, v, 188)

Your hands than mine are quicker for a fr<u>ay</u>;
My legs are longer though, to run aw<u>ay</u>.

(A Midsummer Night's Dream: III, ii, 342)

Mount, mount, my soul! thy seat is up on h<u>igh</u>,
Whilst my gross flesh sinks downward, here to d<u>ie</u>.

(Richard II: V, v, 112)

Assonance

Reoccurrence of vowel or diphthong sounds within two or more words or syllables is called assonance.

AUDIO 8 B▶ **assonance**

A h<u>o</u>rse! a h<u>o</u>rse! my kingdom f<u>or</u> a h<u>o</u>rse!

(Richard III: V, iv, 7)

To w<u>ee</u>p is to make l<u>e</u>ss the d<u>e</u>pth of gr<u>ie</u>f.

(3 Henry IV: II, i, 85)

L<u>i</u>ght, seeking l<u>i</u>ght, doth l<u>i</u>ght of l<u>i</u>ght begu<u>i</u>le.

(Love's Labor's Lost: I, i, 77)

Alliteration

Alliteration is the reoccurrence of the initial consonant sounds in two or more words.

AUDIO 8 C▶ **alliteration**

<u>B</u>less thee, <u>B</u>ottom! <u>b</u>less thee!

(A Midsummer Night's Dream: III, i, 118)

I will not <u>st</u>ruggle, I will <u>st</u>and <u>st</u>one-<u>st</u>ill.

(King John: IV, i, 76)

This <u>m</u>usic <u>m</u>ads <u>m</u>e; let it sound no <u>m</u>ore.

(Richard II: V, v, 61)

Consonance

Consonance is the reoccurrence of medial or ending consonant sounds, not necessarily preceded by the same vowel sounds, in two or more words.

AUDIO 8 D▶ **consonance**

Gra<u>ce</u> me no gra<u>ce</u>, nor un<u>cle</u> me no un<u>cle</u>.

(Richard II: II, iii, 87)

That which ha<u>th</u> made them drunk ha<u>th</u> made me bold;
What ha<u>th</u> quench'd them ha<u>th</u> given me fire.

(Macbeth: II, ii, 1)

O fle<u>sh</u>, fle<u>sh</u>, how art thou fi<u>sh</u>ified!

(Romeo and Juliet: II, iv, 37)

Anaphora

Anaphora refers to the repetition of words at the beginning of two or more clauses. Repetition of words should be noted anywhere in the sentence.

AUDIO 8 E▶ **anaphora**

<u>Past</u> hope, <u>past</u> cure, <u>past</u> help!

(Romeo and Juliet: IV, i, 45)

<u>O</u> sleep! <u>O</u> gentle sleep!

(2 Henry IV: III, i, 5)

You care not who sees your <u>back</u>. Call you that <u>back</u>ing of your friends? A plague upon such <u>back</u>ing!

(1 Henry IV: II, iv, 149)

Onomatopoeia

Words in which the sounds suggest the meaning are onomatopoeic.

AUDIO 8 F▶ **onomatopoeia**

<u>Fight</u> till the <u>last</u> <u>gasp</u>.

(1 Henry VI: I, ii,127)

<u>Gallop</u> <u>apace</u>, you <u>fiery</u>-<u>footed</u> steeds.

(Romeo and Juliet: III, ii, 1)

<u>Blow</u>, winds, and <u>crack</u> your cheeks! <u>rage</u>! <u>blow</u>!

(King Lear: III, ii, 1)

Imagery

Imagery refers to the use of words that create vivid pictures or images in the mind of the listener. See all previous entries, along with the following.

AUDIO 8 G▶ **imagery**

At first the infant,
Mewling and puking in the nurse's arms.

(As You Like It: II, vii 143)

RHYTHM TRACK This vowel is one of five[1] that can be categorized as long, half-long, or short depending on its position in the word and the sounds that follow. Notice the variation in the length[2] of this sound, *reading across*:

long /i:/	long /i:/	half-long /iˑ/	short /i/
me	meal	meek	slimy
pea	peal	peach	lippy
see	seed	seat	sassy
bee	bean	beast	baby
agree	green	Greek	angry

This sound is **long /i:/** in a stressed syllable:

(a)   when it's the last sound of the word

(b)   when it's followed by a voiced consonant

PHRASES long /i:/

1.	cedar tree	6.	freed eagles
2.	yes, please	7.	green leaves
3.	mean thieves	8.	illegal to ski
4.	agrees to clean	9.	breathing easily
5.	seems reasonable	10.	team's achievement

This sound is **half-long /iˑ/** in a stressed syllable when followed by a voiceless consonant.

PHRASES half-long /iˑ/

1.	no sheets	6.	tired feet
2.	seeks Keith	7.	takes a peek
3.	peace on earth	8.	day at the beach
4.	dog on a leash	9.	washes with bleach
5.	fond of peaches	10.	filled with disbelief

This sound is **short /i/** when in an unstressed syllable or when used in the weak form of: he, me, she, we, be. Short /i/ is often represented by the spelling 'y' in an unstressed syllable at the end of a word.

---

[1] The five vowels that can be categorized long, half-long or short can be remembered from the line: 'All drama uses these words'. The eight other vowels, which are always categorized as short, can be remembered from the phrase: 'Mother took a poetics class'.

[2] Length indicators, or dots, used in IPA notation are optional (see pages 39-40). This section is marked to promote increased awareness and to aid those studying lengths.

PHRASES short /i/

1.	no vacancy	6.	my balcony
2.	awfully good	7.	joined Equity
3.	given priority	8.	filled a cavity
4.	what a rivalry	9.	very gracefully
5.	not particularly	10.	lots of activity

Note: /i/ (we) is not marked for length from this point on.

SENTENCES /i/ (we) various lengths

1. Steve, you're bleeding.

2. Truthfully, there's no vacancy.

3. He's leaving this evening it seems.

4. The carpet needs to be steam cleaned.

5. I believe you're my team leader, Deena.

6. Police caught the thieves fleeing the scene.

7. Overeating is not the only cause of obesity.

8. That was the creepiest movie I've ever seen!

9. I need to have this completed by this evening.

10. Teaching Edith how to water-ski was tedious.

11. There's no fee. Every human being gets in free.

12. Let's eat! I'd like an omelet with cheese, please.

13. Remembering to breathe helps me speak more clearly.

14. Lisa grieved over her beagle's death from heart disease.

15. She needs anesthesia for that medical procedure, I believe.

SOUND CHECK #1: /i/ **before the consonant /l/.** The back of the tongue should remain relaxed and uninvolved while moving the tongue tip from behind the lower teeth to touch the upper gum ridge on /il/ combinations, so that /j/ is not inserted between the two sounds. In other words, speak 'eel', not 'ee**juh**l'.

WORDS /i/ before /l/

feel	veal	keel	seal
real	deal	zeal	he'll
peel	we'll	steal	spiel
appeal	unreal	squeal	meal
feeling	Camille	genteel	ideal

PHRASES /i/ before /l/

1. real appeal
2. break the seal
3. squeals at eels
4. wheels and deals
5. kneeling on steel
6. reeling it in
7. feels the ordeal
8. peals of laughter
9. the meal of meals
10. shouldn't steal seals

SENTENCES /i/ before /l/

1. I feel Neil is ideal for the part.
2. They're optimistic and audition with zeal.
3. We'll meet after the show, if you feel like it.
4. Did you ever see *Let's Make a Deal* on TV?
5. That teal cashmere sweater feels great in the cold.
6. That's by one of my favorite authors: Eugene O'Neill.
7. The actor slipped on the banana peel, to peals of laughter.
8. Her head was reeling and she almost keeled over on stage.
9. What an ordeal, I broke my heel in the middle of the scene.
10. Leigh was cast as MISS BEALE in the Broadway production.

NEUTRAL AMERICAN TEXT /i/ (we). *Mark the following and then speak out loud.*

/i/ before /l/:

The day will steal upon thee suddenly.

(Middleton & Rowley: The Changeling)

O now doth Death line his dead chaps with steel.

(King John: II, i, 352)

We must be brief when traitors brave the field.

(Richard III: IV, iii, 57)

Oh—ideals, ideals! If only I were not such a coward!

(Ibsen: Ghosts)

He'll learn before he quickly turns his heel,
That he's been booted face to face—with steel!

(Rostand: Cyrano de Bergerac)

Bow, stubborn knees, and heart, with strings of steel,
Be soft as sinews of the new-born babe!

(Hamlet: III, iii, 70)

/i/ various positions:

As in this world there are degrees of evils,
So in this world there are degrees of devils.

(Webster: The White Devil)

All that we see or seem
Is but a dream within a dream.

(Poe: A Dream Within a Dream)

Oh sin foul and deep!
Great faults are winked at when the Duke's asleep.

(Tourneur: The Revenger's Tragedy)

QUEEN.   Why seems it so particular with thee?
HAMLET.   Seems, madam? Nay, it is, I know not "seems".

(Hamlet: I, ii, 75)

Methought I heard a voice cry, "Sleep no more!
Macbeth does murder sleep"—the innocent sleep,
Sleep that knits up the ravell'd sleeve of care.

(Macbeth: II, ii, 32)

/ ɪ / (wɪll)

The shape necessary for speaking the second front vowel /ɪ/ is nearly identical to that of the previous front vowel /i/. The jaw is mostly closed with the tongue tip resting down behind the lower teeth. The front of the tongue is arched high toward the front of the hard palate, and the lips and cheeks are slightly spread. When speaking /ɪ/, the articulators are slightly more open and relaxed with the tongue arched slightly lower.

AUDIO 11 A ▶ /ɪ/ (wɪll)

    ɪ ɪ   ɪ   ɪ
I'll kɪll hɪm; by thɪs sword, I wɪll.

(Henry V: II, i, 100)

        ɪ
Soft stɪllnɪss and the night
 ɪ   ɪ
Bɪcome the touchɪs of sweet harmony.

(The Merchant of Venice: V, i, 56)

     ɪ   ɪ   ɪ   ɪ
The wɪll, the wɪll! we wɪll hear Caesar's wɪll!

(Julius Caesar: III, ii, 139)

WORDS /ɪ/ (wɪll)

Initial	Medial	Final
ʔ if	fist	*
ʔ itch	sing	*
ʔ isn't	dish	*
ʔ India	bring	*
ʔ interest	million	*

Note: * this sound does not occur in the final position in NAS.

RHYTHM TRACK Sounds can be of various lengths and the time spent on the expression of any spoken sound is, hopefully, linked to an actor's intention or point of view. That said, /ɪ/ (wɪll) is short, crisp, and bright, especially in comparison to /i/ (wē).

PHRASES /ɪ/ (wi̱ll)

1.	invi̱si̱ble i̱nsides	6.	li̱ttle bi̱t of gi̱n
2.	bri̱sk si̱ster Li̱nda	7.	i̱nclined to wi̱n
3.	chi̱ps and mi̱nt di̱p	8.	mi̱ssi̱ng i̱nsects
4.	Mi̱ss Bri̱tt's i̱nsti̱nct	9.	shi̱pped on a whi̱m
5.	i̱mmensely i̱mproved	10.	si̱ppi̱ng pi̱nk dri̱nks

SOUND CHECK #1 Rhythm Highlighter: use unstressed /ɪ/ prefixes. A prefix is a small group of letters added to the *beginning* of a base word, or root, that affects the meaning. Several prefixes have more than one pronunciation in contemporary American speech. The advantage of using /ɪ/ (wi̱ll) instead of /i/ (we̱), /ə/ (uh) or /e/ (ge̱t), is that it highlights the contrast in rhythm and musicality between the unstressed and stressed syllables, while keeping the prefix short, forward in the mouth, and clear.

AUDIO 11 B▶ /ɪ/ prefix

ɪ
And now re'**mains**

ɪ
That we find out the cause of this e'**ffect,**

i
Or rather say, the cause of this '**defect,**

ɪ   ɪ
For this e'**ffect** de'**fec**tive comes by cause.

(Hamlet: II, ii, 100)

ɪ   ɪ
There, at the moated grange, re'**sides** this de'**jec**ted Mariana.

(Measure for Measure: III, i, 264)

ɪ   ɪ   ɪ
I will not ex'**cuse** you, you shall not be ex'**cus'd**, ex'**cu**ses shall

ɪ
not be admitted, there is no ex'**cuse** shall serve, you shall not

ɪ
be ex'**cus'd**.

(2 Henry IV: V, i, 4)

This variation in rhythm and pitch within the word can be represented:

LONG
short   (*or*)   tuh **TUM**

WORDS /ɪ/ (wi̱ll) prefix (common spellings left column)

be   be'come, be'fore, be'friend, be'hoove, be'jewel, be'reft

de   de'cline, de'crease, de'part, de'rive, de'stroy, de'tain

e   e'ffect, e'llipse, e'longate, e'lude, e'quate, e'quip, e'rase

i   i'llicit, i'lliterate, i'magine, i'mmune, i'rrational, i'talics

ne   ne'gate, ne'glect, ne'gotiate, ne'farious, ne'matic

pre   pre'caution, pre'cede, pre'clude, pre'dict, pre'fer, pre'vent

re   re'bel, re'cede, re'cite, re'cline, re'flect, re'form, re'lated

se   se'clude, se'cure, se'date, se'duce, se'lect, se'rene

PHRASES /ɪ/ (wi̱ll) prefix

1. re'peat after me
2. be'hind the door
3. pre'fers pre'vention
4. re'strain from e'rupting
5. i'maginative negoti'ation
6. no de'ception
7. re'hearsing now
8. i'llegal de'tention
9. be'fore or be'tween
10. precipi'tation tonight

Use the short **/ɪ/** (wi̱ll) sound instead of the **/e/** (ge̱t) sound in the following prefixes:

         ɪ
em   em'balm, em'barrassed, em'bark, em'brace

         ɪ
en   en'courage, en'joy, en'liven, en'trenched

When 'ex' in the prefix is followed by a *voiceless* consonant, the prefix is pronounced **/ɪks/** as in ex'pense. When 'ex' in the prefix is followed by a *voiced* sound, the prefix is pronounced **/ɪgz/** as in ex'act.

ex   ex'**pense**, ex'**cel**, ex'**pend**, ex'**plore**, ex'**tent**

ex   ex'**act**, ex'**alt**, ex'**amine**, ex'**ample**, ex'**haust**

ɪks

ɪgz

ADDITIONAL PHRASES /ɪ/ (wi̱ll) prefix

1.	ex'**amines** it	6.	always ex'**act**
2.	em'**braces** her	7.	ex'**plained** later
3.	too ex'**haus**ting	8.	not an ex'**cep**tion
4.	en'**joy**ing living	9.	overly ex'**pen**sive
5.	ex'**pelled** at once	10.	carefully em'**balmed**

SENTENCES /ɪ/ (wi̱ll) prefix

1. If he recovers, he'll present the award.

2. The fire was immediately extinguished.

3. The reclusive farmer began to feel lonely.

4. Be exact when you examine the evidence.

5. She was determined to attend the premiere.

6. Can you explain why you refused to reply?

7. I thought that demented species was extinct.

8. I prefer you refrain from referring to your notes.

9. The expressive performance was strangely seductive.

10. Bill isn't prepared to take a salary reduction in December.

SOUND CHECK #2 Rhythm Highlighter: use /ɪ/ in unstressed suffixes and word endings. A suffix is a small group of letters added to the *end* of a base word, or root, that affects the meaning. Using the short /ɪ/ (wi̱ll) sound highlights the contrast in rhythm and musicality between the stressed and unstressed syllables. Common spellings include: 'i' (ing, ish, ity, ive), 'a' (age, ate) and 'e' (ed, et, es, ess, est, less, ness).

AUDIO 11 C▶ /ɪ/ suffix

ɪ
Thou 'basest thing, avoid hence, from my sight!

(Cymbeline: I, i, 125)

ʊə̆
To be furious
ɪ
Is to be 'frighted out of fear.

(Antony and Cleopatra: III, xiii, 194)

How sharper than a serpent's tooth it is
ɪ
To have a 'thankless child!

(King Lear: I, iv, 288)

This variation in rhythm and pitch can by represented:

LONG short   (*or*)   **TUM** tuh

WORDS /ɪ/ (w<u>i</u>ll) **suffix** (common spellings left column)

ing	'doing, 'going, 'saying 'seeing, 'talking, 'writing
ish	'bookish, 'childish, 'greenish 'selfish, 'squeamish
ity	ca'pacity, lumin'osity, ra'pacity, ve'racity
ive	cre'ative, ex'pressive, 'missive, 'passive, pro'gressive
age	'baggage, 'marriage, 'passage, 'savage, 'scrimmage
ate[1]	'aggregate, 'fortunate, i'mmediate, 'passionate
ed	in'fected, 'heeded, 'planted, 'pleaded, pro'tected
et	'basket, 'carpet, 'closet, 'market, 'picket, 'pocket
es	'breezes, 'crushes, 'misses, 'pauses, 'prices, 'wishes

---

[1] When the 'ate' ending occurs in words used as *verbs*, it is often pronounced /eɪ̆t/ (<u>ate</u>) as in: estim<u>ate</u>, intim<u>ate</u>, advoc<u>ate</u>. For example: "Estim<u>ate</u> the price".

ess   ˈhostess, ˈshepherdess, ˈsorceress, ˈwaitress

est   ˈbiggest, ˈboldest, ˈhappiest, ˈluckiest, ˈsmartest

less   ˈcareless, ˈhelpless, ˈsleepless, ˈthoughtless, ˈuseless

ness   ˈfondness, ˈfriendliness, ˈgoodness, ˈhappiness

PHRASES /ɪ/ (wi̱ll) suffix

1.	my ˈgoodness	6.	quite ˈhopeless
2.	what auˈdacity	7.	an ˈaverage day
3.	very ˈpassionate	8.	ˈfalling to ˈpieces
4.	not the ˈcheapest	9.	transˈmitted diˈseases
5.	ˈnothing ˈgranted	10.	placed on the ˈcabinet

SENTENCES /ɪ/ (wi̱ll) suffix

1. Rummage through the closet.

2. After marriage, they took a pilgrimage.

3. The actress received massive media coverage.

4. Goodness, we're hopelessly and helplessly lost.

5. She loved that snippet of lighthearted dialogue.

6. That is the rarest of jewels: in fact, it's priceless.

7. He's decisive and perceptive, though a bit peevish.

8. The corporate executive was immediately promoted.

9. The ineffective faucet was made of the weakest materials.

10. Damage from the storm that ravaged the area was minimal.

SPECIAL ATTENTION Remember to speak /ɪ/ (wi̱ll) *not* /i/ (we̱):

(a)   when 'ing' occurs in the root of a word

(b)   in 'ing' suffixes

There should be no 'off-glide' or addition of an 'uh' sound, on the final voiced /ŋ/ 'ng'. See additional practice on page 246.

NEUTRAL AMERICAN TEXT /ɪ/ (wi̱ll). *Mark the following and then speak out loud.*

/ɪ/ before /l/:

I   I   I   I
Error i' th' bill, sir, error i' th' bill!

(The Taming of the Shrew: IV, iii, 145)

I'll gild the faces of the grooms withal,
For it must seem their guilt.

(Macbeth: II, ii, 53)

At morn—at noon—at twilight dim—
Maria! thou hast heard my hymn!
In joy and woe—in good and ill—
Mother of God, be with me still!

(Edgar Allan Poe: Hymn)

Achilles will not to the field to-morrow.

(Troilus and Cressida: II, iii, 162)

/ɪ/ prefixes and suffixes:

But let us give him burial as becomes.

(Titus Andronicus: I, i, 347)

You shall offend him and extend his passion.

(Macbeth: III, iv, 56)

Falling in, after falling out, may make them three.

(Troilus and Cressida: III, i, 103)

Thou grumblest and railest every hour on Achilles.

(Troilus and Cressida: II, i, 32)

Why, what a gorgeous bonnet you've been investing in!

(Ibsen: Hedda Gabler)

Oh, his relations have entirely washed their hands of him.

(Ibsen: Hedda Gabler)

He made confession of you,
And gave you such a masterly report
For art and exercise in your defense,
And for your rapier most especial.

(Hamlet IV, vii, 95)

104

There is no tarrying here.

(Troilus and Cressida: II, iii, 258)

The least allusion to the...cartilage...
Alas, may prove a fatal sacrilege!

(Rostand: Cyrano de Bergerac)

The lowest and most dejected thing of fortune.

(King Lear: IV, i, 3)

Shall the Orphanage buildings be insured or not?

(Ibsen: Ghosts)

I'll assume you were merely exaggerating, or engaging in
what's commonly known as flattery.

(Strindberg: Miss Julie)

Singing, or howling, braying, barking, all
As their wild fancies prompt 'em.

(Middleton & Rowley: The Changeling)

You men of Cyprus, let her have your knees.
Hail to thee, lady! and the grace of heaven,
Before, behind thee, and on every hand,
Enwheel thee round!

(Othello: II, i, 84)

Truly, shepherd, in respect of itself, it is a good life; but in respect that
it is a shepherd's life, it is naught. In respect that it is solitary, I like it
very well; but in respect that it is private, it is a very vile life. Now in
respect it is in the fields, it pleaseth me well; but in respect it is not in
the court, it is tedious.

(As You Like It: III, ii, 13)

Shall I tell you a lie? I do despise a liar as I do despise one that is
false, or as I despise one that is not true.

(The Merry Wives of Windsor: I, i, 68)

O villain, villain! His very opinion in the letter. Abhorred villain!
unnatural, detested, brutish villain! worse than brutish! Go, sirrah,
seek him; I'll apprehend him. Abominable villain! Where is he?

(King Lear: I, ii, 75)

SOUND CHECK #2: /e/ before /l/. Arch the tongue forward in the mouth in order to avoid a dull, lax vowel sound when speaking **/el/** combinations.

---

bell	cell	fell	gel
hell	Nell	tell	yell
smell	shell	expel	quell
propel	Ravel	dwell	retell
compel	dispel	personnel	unwell

PHRASES /e/ before /l/

1.	self-help	6.	a cappella
2.	sells jelly	7.	Elmer Fudd
3.	felt svelte	8.	Helen's fella
4.	dinner bell	9.	farewell to elves
5.	health and wealth	10.	blond bombshell

SENTENCES /e/ before /l/

1. Do tell, Mel, who rang the bell?

2. Twelve elk became unwell eating elm trees.

3. Anyone remember *The Lawrence Welk Show*?

4. Cornell tightened his belt, then felt like belching.

5. Ed was compelled to delve into the books on the shelf.

6. Well, when overwhelmed with jealousy, elephants yell.

7. It's a delicate situation, so Ellen's walking on egg shells.

8. Tell Mr. Roosevelt mademoiselle has had a fainting spell.

9. In a nutshell, our motel is the worst in the commonwealth.

10. Nell's clientele prefer *Velvet* hair gel; it penetrates the cells.

NEUTRAL AMERICAN TEXT /e/ (get). *Mark the following and then speak out loud.*

/e/ before 'm' or 'n':

               e

I will be mild and gentle in my words.

(Richard III: IV, iv, 161)

If we shadows have offended,
Think but this, and all is mended.

(A Midsummer Night's Dream: V, i, 423)

O, it is excellent
To have a giant's strength; but it is tyrannous
To use it like a giant.

(Measure for Measure: II, ii, 107)

L. MACBETH.
Did not you speak?
MACBETH.　　　　　When?
L. MACBETH.　　　　　　　　Now.
MACBETH.　　　　　　　　　　As I descended?

(Macbeth: II, ii, 16)

QUEEN.　Hamlet, thou hast thy father much offended.
HAMLET.　Mother, you have my father much offended.

(Hamlet: III, iv, 9)

That ever-living man of memory,
Henry the Fifth.

(1 Henry VI: IV, iii, 51)

Ah, let me live in prison all my days,
And when I give occasion of offense,
Then let me die, for now thou hast no cause.

(3 Henry VI: I, iii, 43)

What, sir, not yet at rest? The King's a-bed.
He hath been in unusual pleasure, and
Sent forth great largess to your offices.

(Macbeth: II, i, 12)

And turning to his men,
Quoth our brave Henry then,
'Though they be one to ten,
Be not amazéd.
Yet have we well begun,
Battles so bravely won
Have ever to the sun
By fame been raiséd.

(Michael Drayton: Ballad of Agincourt)

No longer session hold upon my shame,
But let my trial be mine own confession.
Immediate sentence then, and sequent death,
Is all the grace I beg.

(Measure for Measure: V, i, 371)

/e/ before /l/:

Who lives and dares but say thou didst not well
When I was got, I'll send his soul to hell.

(King John: I, i, 271)

The bell invites me.
Hear it not, Duncan, for it is a knell,
That summons thee to heaven or to hell.

(Macbeth: II, i, 62)

SCROOP.   Both young and old rebel,
              And all goes worse than I have power to tell.
K. RICHARD. Too well, too well thou tell'st a tale so ill.

(Richard II: III, ii, 119)

If you did wed my sister for her wealth,
Then for her wealth's sake use her with more kindness:
Or if you like elsewhere, do it by stealth.

(The Comedy of Errors: III, ii, 5)

Hear the sledges with the bells –
Silver bells!
What a world of merriment their melody foretells!
How they tinkle, tinkle, tinkle,
In the icy air of night!
While the stars that oversprinkle
All the heavens seem to twinkle
With a crystalline delight;
Keeping time, time, time,
In a sort of Runic rhyme,
To the tintinnabulation that so musically wells
From the bells, bells, bells, bells,
Bells, bells, bells –
From the jingling and the tinkling of the bells.

(Edgar Allan Poe: The Bells)

/ æ / (th<u>a</u>t)

Form the shape for the fourth front vowel /æ/ (th<u>a</u>t) by resting the tip of the tongue down behind the lower teeth and dropping the lower jaw substantially more open than for the previous /e/ (g<u>e</u>t) sound. This will lessen the front tongue arch noticeably to a low, almost flat position in relationship to the hard palate. The cheeks and lips remain neutral but energized as sound releases forward through the mouth.

AUDIO 13► /æ/ (th<u>a</u>t)

(weak form or æ)   æ   æ
The princess shall have her castle.

(Ibsen: The Master Builder)

æ (or weak form)   æ
I <u>am</u> not bound to please thee with my <u>a</u>nswers.

(The Merchant of Venice: IV, i, 65)

æ   æ
Things p<u>a</u>st redress are now with me p<u>a</u>st care.

(Richard II: II, iii, 171)

WORDS /æ/ (th<u>a</u>t)

Initial	Medial	Final
? after	slap	*
? actor	habit	*
? assets	traffic	*
? agitate	attack	*
? aspirin	casting	*

RHYTHM TRACK Although /æ/ (th<u>a</u>t) is classified as short, it is generally longer than either /ɪ/ (w<u>i</u>ll) or /e/ (g<u>e</u>t) when spoken.

Note: If Spanish is your first language, position the front tongue arch slightly higher and more forward than for the Spanish pronunciation represented by the letter 'a'. The jaw may also need to close slightly more.

PHRASES /æ/ (th<u>a</u>t)

1.	scr<u>a</u>tchy p<u>a</u>tch	6.	f<u>a</u>shionable <u>a</u>ds
2.	<u>a</u>ctually <u>a</u>cting	7.	st<u>a</u>cks of sn<u>a</u>cks
3.	h<u>a</u>ppy <u>a</u>crob<u>a</u>ts	8.	dis<u>a</u>strous j<u>a</u>cket
4.	<u>a</u>thletic <u>a</u>ctivity	9.	enthusi<u>a</u>stic cl<u>a</u>pping
5.	p<u>a</u>ckage to <u>A</u>frica	10.	h<u>a</u>bit of st<u>a</u>shing c<u>a</u>sh

---

SOUND CHECK #1: Speak the vowel /æ/ rather than /ē̃æ/ diphthong by keeping the throat, tongue, cheeks, and jaw relaxed as the tongue arches low in the mouth. Some speakers from the Great Lakes area, NYC, Boston, etc. 'slide' from /e/ to /æ/ while over-tensing the articulators. This results in a bright, nasal diphthong represented by /ē̃æ/. The wavy line over /ē/ represents nasality.

Breathe in, then speak the following words on the releasing breath. The throat, tongue, cheeks, and jaw should remain relaxed, with the tongue arched low. You can also pinch your nose during the vowel to check that sound is releasing through the mouth, not the nose. Sound *should* release through the nose on /m n ŋ/, so do not pinch your nose on those sounds.

WORDS speak the pure vowel /æ/ rather than /ē̃æ/ diphthong

Jack	crash	batch	task
sassy	nasty	faster	gasp
apple	savage	tablet	sadly
match	Athens	lavish	black
casting	laughter	passive	master

PHRASES speak the pure vowel /æ/ rather than /ē̃æ/ diphthong

1.	<u>a</u>fter th<u>a</u>t	6.	h<u>a</u>ppy d<u>a</u>ds
2.	b<u>a</u>d tr<u>a</u>ffic	7.	l<u>a</u>st S<u>a</u>turday
3.	M<u>a</u>tt's st<u>a</u>sh	8.	h<u>a</u>ppen to <u>a</u>sk
4.	b<u>a</u>ck tr<u>a</u>cking	9.	l<u>a</u>cks the f<u>a</u>cts
5.	tr<u>a</u>ctor coll<u>a</u>psed	10.	sm<u>a</u>shed gl<u>a</u>sses

SENTENCES speak the pure vowel /æ/ rather than /ē̃æ/ diphthong

1. Perhaps Jack is an insomniac.

2. Cathy, let's practice chatting in Latin.

3.   Jack's black cat sat basking in the sun.

4.   Wear something practical (but not tacky).

5.   After the accident, they took drastic action.

6.   We were hired to enact the historical battle.

7.   What's that scratching sound, Mr. Thatcher?

8.   Brad, your socks are attractive, but don't match.

9.   Actually, overacting can detract from the scene.

10.   They ran out of gas on the way to the track meet.

11.   Collect the facts before preparing your income tax.

12.   Congratulations; your advertisement is fascinating.

13.   The fragile sound of distant bagpipes was a bit magical.

14.   As an actor, Maxwell is a craftsman; he's great at accents.

15.   I'm baffled how they photographed workers on the scaffold.

SOUND CHECK #2 special case: /æ/ before 'm', 'n', 'g', 'ng', 'nk' need not be a pure vowel sound in NAS[1], but it should not be overly tense or nasalized.

/æn/	/æm/	/æg/	/æŋ/	/æŋk/	/æŋg/
man	slam	tag	rang	rank	angle
frantic	lamb	rags	hang	stank	dangle
fanned	clams	ragged	slang	blank	bangle
bandage	champ	snagged	clang	Hank	mangle
standard	damage	haggard	banged	thanks	strangle

PHRASES /æ/ relaxed (th<u>a</u>t) before / n, m, g, ŋ, ŋk, ŋg /

1. <u>a</u>ngry D<u>a</u>nny
2. c<u>a</u>mpus pr<u>a</u>nk
3. cl<u>a</u>nging t<u>a</u>nks
4. p<u>a</u>mpered <u>A</u>nnie
5. unm<u>a</u>nageable b<u>ag</u>s

6. dr<u>a</u>nk br<u>a</u>ndy
7. b<u>a</u>nkrupt H<u>a</u>nk
8. f<u>a</u>ncy pl<u>a</u>nning
9. <u>a</u>nxious to th<u>a</u>nk
10. Th<u>a</u>nksgiving h<u>a</u>m

---

[1] Classical American dialect does require pure /æ/. See pages 349-352 for instructional material.

SENTENCES /æ/ relaxed (th<u>a</u>t) before / n, m, g, ŋ, ŋk, ŋg /

1. Nancy stared blankly.

2. What's the plan, Chan?

3. Brand saw the damage firsthand.

4. Did Blanche escape the avalanche?

5. Thankfully, I have a fantastic landlady.

6. Who won the break dancing championship?

7. That anchorman's office is overly cramped.

8. Can we wrangle Yankee tickets for Sammy?

9. The telegram advised Ann: see France firsthand.

10. The band cancelled; they all have swollen glands.

11. The champion's remarks are considered sacrosanct.

12. Hank's Mustang vanished while he was in the bank.

13. Our clan formed a caravan and drove to the Grand Slam.

14. The man in command of expanding Disneyland is grand.

15. Are you sure camcorders are banned in the theatre? I am.

æ

For stony limits ′c<u>a</u>nnot hold love out.

(Romeo and Juliet: II, ii, 67)

Stress is usually placed on the second syllable of the word 'cannot' in contemporary material and on the first syllable of the word in classic text, as in the selection from *Romeo and Juliet*, above.

SOUND CHECK #3: speak pure, open /æ/ before /l/. The tongue tip contacts the upper gum ridge and does not protrude between the teeth on /l/.

---

shall	alp	pal	scalp
value	aloe	talon	alpine
tallow	ballot	callow	gallop
scallop	gallon	gallows	valiant
morale	callous	salvage	shallow

116

PHRASES clear /æ/ before /l/

1.	valley girls	4.	valiant gal
2.	salad dressing	5.	falcon's talons
3.	Italian ballads	6.	California canal

SENTENCES clear /æ/ before /l/

1. Psychoanalysis demands confidentiality, Allen.

2. Sally is expected at the rally on Valentine's Day.

3. Valerie maintains her vitality by cutting calories.

NEUTRAL AMERICAN TEXT /æ/ (that). *Mark the following and speak out loud.*

/æ/ before 'm', 'n', 'g', 'ng', 'nk':

æ
How well I understand her, if only she knew!

(Chekhov: The Cherry Orchard)

Rage like an angry boar chafed with sweat?

(The Taming of the Shrew: I, ii, 202)

Why not face matters as they stand?
Perhaps m'sieur finds it a trifle...grand?

(Rostand: Cyrano de Bergerac)

Everyone can master a grief but he that has it.

(Much Ado About Nothing: III, ii, 28)

CASSIUS. Stand ho!
BRUTUS. Stand ho! Speak the word along.
1 SOLDIER. Stand!
2 SOLDIER. Stand!
3 SOLDIER. Stand!

(Julius Caesar: IV, ii, 32)

O, my offense is rank, it smells to heaven.

(Hamlet: III, iii, 36)

Post back with speed, and tell him what hath chanc'd.

(Julius Caesar: III, I, 287)

EMILIA. What will you give me now
For that same handkerchief?
IAGO. What handkerchief?
EMILIA. What handkerchief?
Why, that the Moor first gave to Desdemona.

(Othello: III, iii, 305)

/æ/ various positions:

Ay me, unhappy,
To be a queen, and crown'd with infamy!

(2 Henry VI: III, ii, 70)

Wast thou mad,
That thus so madly thou didst answer me?

(The Comedy of Errors: II, ii, 11)

We are glad the Dauphin is so pleasant with us,
His present and your pains we thank you for.
When we have match'd our rackets to these balls,
We will in France, by God's grace, play a set
Shall strike his father's crown into the hazard.
Tell him he hath made a match with such a wrangler
That all the courts of France will be disturb'd
With chaces. And we understand him well.

(Henry V: I, ii, 259)

And thereof came it that the man was mad.

(The Comedy of Errors: V, i, 68)

For that matter, he was away from home himself—he was traveling.

(Ibsen: Hedda Gabler)

Rats!
They fought the dogs and killed the cats,
And bit the babies in the cradles,
And ate the cheeses out of the vats,
And licked the soup from the cooks' own ladles,
Split open the kegs of salted sprats,
Made nests inside men's Sunday hats,
And even spoiled the women's chats
By drowning their speaking
With shrieking and squeaking
In fifty different sharps and flats.

(Robert Browning: Pied Piper of Hamelin)

MID-VOWELS

See Overview pages 18-26

/ ɝ / (ER)

Form the shape for the stressed mid-vowel /ɝ/ (ER) by relaxing the jaw half open, arching the middle of the tongue high near the hard palate, lifting the *tip* up behind the alveolar ridge and curling it slightly back, as sound releases through the mouth. Rounding the lips is not necessary, though many people do.

The tongue tip rests down behind the lower front teeth for all vowels, diphthongs, and triphthongs, *except* those that contain the strong or weak vowels of 'r': /ɝ/ (ER), /ɚ/ (er).

AUDIO 14▶ stressed /ɝ/ (ER)

I see thee compass'd with thy kingdom's **pe<u>ar</u>l**.
ɝ

(Macbeth: V, ix, 22)

Th'ob'**s<u>er</u>v'd** of all ob'**s<u>er</u>v**ers, quite, quite down!
ɝ   ɝ   ɚ

(Hamlet: III, i, 154)

My **w<u>or</u>ds** fly up, my thoughts remain below:
ɝ

W<u>or</u>ds without thoughts never to heaven go.
ɝ   ɚ

(Hamlet: III, iii, 97)

WORDS stressed /ɝ/ (ER)

Initial	Medial	Final
ʔ ˈerr	ˈlearn	ˈsir
ʔ ˈirk	ˈpurple	ˈfur
ʔ ˈurge	ˈthirsty	ˈstir
ʔ ˈearly	ˈperson	inˈfer
ʔ ˈearth	reˈhearsal	conˈcur

RHYTHM TRACK: This sound can be categorized as long, half-long, or, in rare instances, short.[1] This depends on its position in the word and the sounds that follow. Notice the variation in lengths while *reading across*:

long /ɝ:/	long /ɝ:/	half-long /ɝ·/	half-long /ɝ·/
infer	fern	firth	flirt
blur	blurb	blurt	burp
burr	burn	birth	burst
purr	perm	purse	perch
were	worm	worth	worst

This sound is **long /ɝ:/** in a stressed syllable:

(a)   when it is the last sound of the word

(b)   when it is followed by a voiced consonant

PHRASES long /ɝ:/

1.	girls in a hurry[2]	6.	swirl and twirl
2.	too early to worry	7.	girlish mermaid
3.	encouraged courage	8.	nourishing curry
4.	surge in subservience	9.	currant preserves
5.	thoroughly concerned	10.	conservative journal

This sound is **half-long /ɝ·/** in a stressed syllable when followed by a voiceless consonant.

PHRASES half-long /ɝ·/

1.	perky worker	6.	purple circle
2.	reimburse Percy	7.	birthday shirt
3.	lurching curtsey	8.	worship dessert
4.	perfect rehearsal	9.	cursing merchants
5.	immersed in work	10.	search for a purpose

---

[1] Length indicators (or dots) used in IPA notation are optional (see pages 39-40). This section is marked to promote increased awareness and to aid those studying lengths.

[2] Many words in these phrases are pronounced with the stressed vowel /ɝ:/ before the consonant /r/ in Neutral American Speech, as in hurry: / hɝːri/.

A slightly **shorter** /ɝ/ can be spoken in weak forms of 'her', 'were' and 'sir'. In almost all other cases, the short version of this sound represented by the symbol /ɚ/ is spoken in unstressed syllables. The following selection contains the weak form of /ɝ/, fully-long stressed /ɝ:/, and the unstressed vowel /ɚ/.

weak forms: ɝ (or) ɚ   ɝ: ɚ ɚ
They w<u>er</u>e villains, m<u>urder</u>ers. The will, read the will!

(Julius Caesar: III, ii, 156)

Note: /ɝ/ (<u>ER</u>) is not marked for length from this point on.

SENTENCES /ɝ/ (<u>ER</u>) various lengths

1.   Turn the toast before it burns.

2.   You certainly deserved first prize.

3.   Blackbirds chirped in the birch tree.

4.   Burt splurged on tickets to the circus.

5.   He asserts that nursing is worthy work.

6.   Do crossword puzzles use code words?

7.   Certainly, surgeons must be reimbursed.

8.   The most overworked interns are in research.

9.   I'm concerned. We need more rehearsal time.

10.   This superb herb dressing isn't sold commercially.

11.   Her blurred version of events concerned the attorney.

12.   It was confirmed. Someone hacked into the network.

13.   Detergent will wash that dessert off your favorite shirt.

14.   I heard the colonel cursing when his job was terminated.

15.   The anniversary circular was published Thursday the 30th.

SOUND CHECK #1: clear /ɝl/ combinations. Do not pull down or flatten the middle of the tongue as the <u>tip</u> moves to touch the upper gum ridge for /l/, or else /ə/ (<u>uh</u>) may be inserted between /ɝ/ and /l/. Speak 'girl' not 'gir**uhl**'.

WORDS /ɝ/ before /l/

girl	early	purl	curl
hurl	pearl	surly	skirl
twirl	whirl	early	burly
world	unfurl	churl	furlough
Shirley	underworld	Merlin	Sherlock

PHRASES /ɝ/ before /l/

1. early bird
2. other worldly
3. old chorus girl
4. lovely showgirl
5. surly underworld
6. burly Earl
7. hurled pearls
8. the third world
9. thirsty cowgirl
10. mother-of-pearl

SENTENCES /ɝ/ before /l/

1. Earl was cast in *Hurly Burly*.

2. Shirley Temple had the curliest hair.

3. Swirl and twirl, they told the showgirl.

4. Were the sails furled or unfurled, sailor?

5. Pearls wrapped in burlap? That's absurd.

6. The directions instruct: knit one, purl two.

7. The whole world watched *That Girl* on TV.

8. The skirl of bagpipes was heard early today.

9. Sherlock cursed the surly underworld character.

10. We heard the whirr as the whirligig beetle whirled about.

NEUTRAL AMERICAN TEXT stressed /ɝ/ (ER). *Mark the following and speak out loud.*

/ɝ/ before /l/:

          ɝ   ɝ

Hector was stirring early.

(Troilus and Cressida I, ii, 51)

CLASSICALLY SPEAKING   NEUTRAL AMERICAN /ɝ/

My master is of churlish disposition.

(As You Like It: II, iv, 80)

There is another comfort than this world.

(Measure for Measure: V, i, 49)

Be opposite with a kinsman, surly with servants.

(Twelfth Night: II, v, 149)

/ɜ/ various positions:

O, sir, content you;
I follow him to serve my turn upon him.

(Othello: I, i, 41)

Balm of hurt minds, great nature's second course,
Chief nourisher in life's feast.

(Macbeth: II, ii, 36)

Words spoke in tears
Are like the murmurs of the waters; the sound
Is loudly heard, but cannot be distinguished.

(Tourneur: The Revenger's Tragedy)

Put money in thy purse; follow thou the wars; defeat thy favor with an
usurp'd beard. I say put money in thy purse. It cannot be long that
Desdemona should continue her love to the Moor—put money in thy
purse—nor he his to her.

(Othello: I, iii, 339)

CASSIUS. When Caesar liv'd, he durst not thus have mov'd me.
BRUTUS. Peace, peace, you durst not so have tempted him.
CASSIUS. I durst not?
BRUTUS. No.
CASSIUS. What? durst not tempt him?
BRUTUS.   For your life you durst not.

(Julius Caesar: IV, iii, 58)

LEONTES. Once more, take her hence.
PAULINA. A most unworthy and unnatural lord
         Can do no more.
LEONTES.   I'll ha' thee burnt.
PAULINA.   I care not:
        It is a heretic that makes the fire,
        Not she which burns in't.

(The The Winter's Tale: II, iii, 112)

/ ɚ / (er)

Form the shape for speaking unstressed /ɚ/ (er) by relaxing the jaw half open, slightly more than for stressed /ɝ/, arching the middle of the tongue high near the hard palate, lifting the tip up behind the alveolar ridge and curling it slightly back, while releasing sound through the mouth. Lip rounding is not required.

AUDIO 15▶ **short, unstressed /ɚ/ (er)**

                ɚ   ɚ   ɚ
I said an '**eld**<u>er</u> '**sold**i<u>er</u>, not a '**bett**<u>er</u>.
                ɚ
Did I say "'**bett**<u>er</u>"?

(Julius Caesar: IV, iii, 56)

            ɚ
I have no '**fur**th<u>er</u> with you.

(Coriolanus: II, iii, 173)

            ɚ   ɚ
I re'**mem**b<u>er</u> him well, and I re'**mem**b<u>er</u> him '**wor**thy of thy praise.

(The Merchant of Venice: I, ii, 120)

WORDS short, unstressed /ɚ/ (er)

Initial[1]	Medial	Final
*	cur'tail	'sister
*	sur'mise	'actor
*	ger'mane	'sugar
*	per'suade	'favor
*	fer'mentable	'theatre

RHYTHM TRACK /ɚ/ (er) occurs in unstressed syllables and is, therefore, always short. It may help to think of /ɚ/ (er) as a shorter, more relaxed /ɝ/ (ER).

---

[1] The word 'urbane' *could* be placed here, though it's sometimes transcribed /ɝ/ (ER).

WORDS unstressed /ɚ/ (er)

water	over	diner	owner
never	cover	father	matter
savor	anger	traitor	mother
brother	either	singer	Virginia
remember	permission	perspective	neighbor

PHRASES unstressed /ɚ/ (er)

1.	older surfer	6.	teacher's sister
2.	calling the waiter	7.	blistered fingers
3.	wider paper cutter	8.	failure to censure
4.	picture of glamour	9.	sculptured leather
5.	wonderful structure	10.	bothersome computer

WORDS with stressed /ɝ/ (ER) and unstressed /ɚ/ (er)

'server	'turner	'girder	'stirrer
'cursor	'purser	'fervor	'Mercer
'bursar	'learner	'further	'burner
'furniture	'murder	dis'burser	'Herbert
'worshiper	'murmur	con'server	'pervert

SENTENCES unstressed /ɚ/ (er)

1. Expect better weather in November.

2. Do me a favor, please pass the sugar.

3. Hector registered for officer training.

4. Edgar is a tenured professor at Vassar.

5. The caterer sent dinner over via messenger.

6. That singer gave a spectacular performance.

7. Actors often think dinner tastes better after the show.

8. Do me a favor and audition Leonard for the tenor part.

9. I feel like seeing a lighter play, one filled with laughter.

10. Smother the mixture in vinegar, then cover and let simmer.

NEUTRAL AMERICAN TEXT unstressed **/ə/** (<u>er</u>). *Mark the following and speak out loud.*

ə
Farewell, sweet lord, and sist<u>er</u>.

(King Lear: III, vii, 21)

He hath a lady, wiser, fairer, truer,
Than ever Greek did couple in his arms.

(Troilus and Cressida: I, iii, 275)

Suffer? I'll suffer you to be gone, I'll suffer you
To come no more; what would you have me suffer?

(Tourneur: The Revenger's Tragedy)

Turned apostle now, our demon brother?
Smite one nostril, and he turns the other!

(Rostand: Cyrano de Bergerac)

Thou'lt come no more,
Never, never, never, never, never.

(King Lear: V, iii, 308)

Her father is no better than an earl,
Although in glorious titles he excel.

(1 Henry VI: V, v, 37)

Never to be able to work again! Never—never! A living
death! Mother, can you imagine anything so horrible!

(Ibsen: Ghosts)

Of course, I'm clever, cleverer than plenty of other people,
but happiness does not consist of merely being clever.

(Chekhov: Three Sisters)

K. RICHARD. Should dying men flatter with those that live?
GAUNT.   No, no, men living flatter those that die.
K. RICHARD. Thou, now a-dying, sayest thou flatterest me.
GAUNT.   O no, thou diest, though I the sicker be.

(Richard II: II, i, 88)

/ ə / (<u>uh</u>)

Form the shape for always short /ə/ (<u>uh</u>) by resting the tongue tip down behind the lower teeth, with the lips and cheeks relaxed in a neutral position, opening the jaw a little more than for /ɚ/ (<u>er</u>), and arching the middle of the tongue slightly toward the center of the mouth.

AUDIO 16 A▶ **short, unstressed**[1] **/ə/ (<u>uh</u>).**

ə   ə ə   ə   ə ə
I <u>am</u> 'Cinn<u>a</u> th<u>e</u> poet, I <u>am</u> 'Cinn<u>a</u> th<u>e</u> poet.

(Julius Caesar: III, iii, 29)

ə   ə   ə   ə
<u>A</u> proper man <u>as</u> one shall see in <u>a</u> summer's day; <u>a</u> most
             ə
lovely 'gentl<u>ema</u>n-like man.

(A Midsummer Night's Dream: I, ii, 86)

ə   ə
There's law <u>and</u> 'warr<u>ant</u>, lady, for my curse.

(King John: III, i, 184)

WORDS short, unstressed /ə/ (<u>uh</u>).

Initial	Medial	Final
a'far	'legacy	'sofa
a'bout	con'trol	'Lisa
a'ffirm	com'pare	'diva
a'ttempt	'adamant	'salsa
a'ccount	mathema'tician	'pizza

Avoid a glottal attack on the first sound of the word in the first column.

RHYTHM TRACK The sound /ə/ (<u>uh</u>), sometimes referred to as the **'schwa'**, occurs in unstressed syllables and is always short. It is a shorter, more relaxed version of stressed /ʌ/ (<u>UH</u>). It is also spoken in many weak forms of words. Weak forms are covered in the Rhythm Highlighter section, pages 65-72.

---

[1] Possible weak forms using /ə/ (<u>uh</u>) are also marked.

WORDS short, unstressed /ə/ (uh)

about	again	agree	sofa
arrest	aroma	affect	cola
annoy	facility	ahead	Martha
police	pedigree	legacy	cadaver
maternal	ashamed	tonight	sedative

PHRASES short, unstressed /ə/ (uh)

1. above contempt	6. pathetic award
2. affordable again	7. agreeable affect
3. atrocious formula	8. Atlanta, Georgia
4. confirm complaints	9. afraid or annoyed
5. supposedly comedic	10. American diploma

SOUND CHECK #1 Rhythm Highlighter: use /ə/ (uh) in unstressed suffixes and word endings. Highlight the contrast in rhythm and musicality between stressed and unstressed syllables by using short /ə/ on unstressed suffixes and word endings commonly spelled: 'ance', 'ence', 'ant', 'ent', 'ous', 'man', 'ment'.

AUDIO 16 B▶ /ə/ suffix and word endings

Here have we war for war and blood for blood,
      ə   ə
Con'trolment for con'trolment: so answer France.

(King John: I, i, 19)

You could easily nab a husband one fine day! A rich
     ə
'Englishman, why not?

(Strindberg: Miss Julie)

    ə   ɪ
Good 'sentences, and well pronounc'd.

(The Merchant of Venice: I, ii, 10)

Though contemporary speakers often use the short /ɪ/ (will) sound on the following suffixes, instead of the more traditional /ə/ (uh), it is useful to learn to distinguish /ɪ/ (will) from /ə/ (uh) for future dialect study.

WORDS /ə/ schwa suffix (common spellings left column)

ance   a'cquaintance, 'arrogance, 'countenance, 'entrance, 'radiance, 'resonance, 'utterance

ence   'abstinence, 'eminence, 'essence, 'impudence, 'insolence, 'truculence, 'violence, 'virulence

ant   a'ssistant, 'dissonant, 'dominant, ex'travagant, lieu'tenant, 'petulant, 'recreant, 'servant, 'tenant

ent   'eloquent, 'excellent, fla'vescent, 'imminent, o'bedient, re'silient, 'regent, superin'tendent

ous   am'biguous, am'bitious, 'bigamous, 'copious, 'dangerous, 'marvelous, 'nervous, odo'riferous

man   'ottoman, 'Scotsman, de'liveryman, 'fisherman, 'Frenchman, 'henchman, 'statesman, 'doorman

ment   a'ppeasement 'argument a'rraignment, 'instrument, 'ligament, 'regiment, re'quirement, re'sentment

PHRASES /ə/ schwa suffix and word endings

1. the best 'postman
2. especially 'tenuous
3. tipping the 'doorman
4. wonderfully 'fragrant
5. well-known 'statesman
6. not 'prevalent
7. very ob'noxious
8. unnoticed 'absence
9. unreleased 'statement
10. offers some re'sistance

SENTENCES /ə/ schwa suffix and word endings

1. What a surprising development.

2. They enjoyed the absence of violence.

3. A glorious event is planned in remembrance.

4. The actor was paid a pittance for his appearance.

5. The assessment confirmed their interdependence.

6. What statesman was convicted of embezzlement?

7. He engendered resentment from the management.

8. His doorman works undercover for the government.

9. Prepayment was demanded at the restaurant's entrance.

10. A highwayman has taken up residence in the basement.

SOUND CHECK #2: intrusive, unstressed vowel of 'r'. When words end in the 'schwa' sound /ə/ (uh) and there is no 'r' in the spelling, do not add /ɚ/ (er). Pronounce 'sofa' not 'sofer'. Also, do not not link to another vowel sound by inserting the consonant /r/. Speak: The sofa is dirty. Not: The sofer is dirty.

WORDS final /ə/ (uh) with no intrusive /ɚ/ (er)

'aura	'quota	'pizza	'Russia
i'dea	'Linda	'Africa	'comma
a'rena	'melba	an'tenna	ba'nana
A'merica	'Emma	Ye'shiva	The'resa
no'stalgia	'Martha	am'brosia	'Georgia

PHRASES final /ə/ with no intrusive /ɚ/ (er) or linking /r/

1. Cuba incident
2. no idea about it
3. Aretha asks him
4. seeing Lisa angry
5. media advertisements
6. Martha isn't
7. diarrhea ends
8. China involved
9. Australia advised
10. pasta isn't cooked

SENTENCES final /ə/ with no intrusive /ɚ/ (er) or linking /r/

1. Sophia is buying soda in the market.

2. Is the panda in the zoo pregnant yet?

3. Diana, are mimosas made with Coca Cola?

4. Zelda is a prima donna and loves her tiara.

5. Let's have pizza and watch the Oscars, Eva.

6. The saga of Attila in China is on TV tonight.

7.   Nina's idea of traveling to Cuba is appealing.

8.   Brenda and Emma are working on the agenda.

9.   PORTIA isn't listed on the casting notice after all.

10.   Cleopatra looks beautiful wearing magenta in the Sahara.

NEUTRAL AMERICAN TEXT   unstressed /ə/ (<u>uh</u>). *Mark the following and speak out loud.*

schwa suffixes, word endings, weak forms:

ə   ə   ə ə   ə
My judg<u>ment</u> is the judg<u>ment</u> <u>of</u> th<u>e</u> law.

(Strindberg: The Father)

So every bondman in his own hand bears
The power to cancel his captivity.

(Julius Caesar: I, iii, 101)

It was the owl that shriek'd, the fatal bellman,
Which gives the stern'st good-night.

(Macbeth: II, ii, 3)

To the contrary I have express commandment.

(The The Winter's Tale: II, ii, 8)

A document in madness, thoughts and remembrance fitted.

(Hamlet: IV, v, 178)

Yes, my thoughtlessness had consequences, my dear Judge.

(Ibsen: Hedda Gabler)

My lord, I know not what the matter is, but to my judgment your highness is not entertain'd with that ceremonious affection as you were wont. There's a great abatement of kindness appears as well in the general dependants as in the Duke himself also, and your daughter.

(King Lear: I, iv, 58)

AUTOLYCUS. I am robb'd sir...
CLOWN   . What, by a horseman, or a footman?
AUTOLYCUS. A footman, sweet sir, a footman.
CLOWN.   Indeed, he should be a footman by the garments he has
            left with thee. If this be a horseman's coat, it hath seen
            very hot service.

(The The Winter's Tale: IV, iii, 61)

/ ʌ / (UH)

Form the shape for stressed or strong /ʌ/ (UH) by resting the tongue tip down behind the lower teeth with the lips and cheeks relaxed and neutral, opening the jaw a little more than for /ə/ (uh), arching the middle of the tongue low in the mouth, and releasing sound through the mouth.

AUDIO 17► **stressed /ʌ/ (UH)**

ʌ
Avaunt, you 'cullions!

(Henry V: III, ii, 20)

ʌ　　　　　　　　ʌ
If it were done, when 'tis done, then 'twere well
ʌ
It were done quickly.

(Macbeth: I, vii, 1)

ʌ
A'dultery?

ʌ
Thou shalt not die. Die for a'dultery?

(King Lear: IV, vi, 110)

WORDS stressed /ʌ/ (UH)

Initial	Medial	Final
up	gum	*
'ugly	'trouble	*
'uncle	'wonder	*
'other	'chunky	*
'under	be'loved	*

Do not begin words in the initial column with a glottal attack.

RHYTHM TRACK Stressed /ʌ/ (UH) is classified as a short vowel, though it is longer than unstressed /ə/ (uh), which is also classified as short.

PHRASES /ʌ/ (UH)

1.	lucky in love	6.	uncle in London
2.	butter crunch	7.	double or nothing
3.	sunny summer	8.	comforting cuddle
4.	just dumb luck	9.	judged to be drunk
5.	brunch or lunch	10.	a month of Sundays

SENTENCES stressed /ʌ/ (UH)

1. I'm ready for my close-up.

2. Young Judd was stage-struck.

3. Speak up, Douglas, you're mumbling.

4. Gus signaled 'thumbs up' when he won.

5. Is your new puppy named Fluffy or Puffy?

6. The crumbling mummy was discovered in the sun.

7. Hundreds have wondered where thunder comes from.

8. They're casting for a handsome, honey-tongued lover.

9. I have a hunch it will take months to finish these puzzles.

10. Any discussion will involve dozens of cousins and brothers.

11. One impulsive summer crush is a must for any young adult.

12. Royal flush? Eyes fluttering, blood pumping—he's bluffing!

When 'un' is added as a prefix to the beginning of a word, it is spoken and transcribed in IPA with strong /ʌ/, even though the sound is technically in the unstressed syllable. Also, compound words are often transcribed with strong /ʌ/ in the unstressed syllable, for example: under'go, under'graduate, 'teacup.

PHRASES /ʌ/ (UH) prefix and compound words

1.	unlikely buyer	6.	unsound advice
2.	unearned income	7.	unvoiced ending
3.	unfriendly waiter	8.	handcuffed culprits
4.	undisciplined fun	9.	unhappy underneath
5.	unwatered buttercups	10.	unkempt and undone

SOUND CHECK #1: /ʌl/ (UHL) combinations. Relax the lower jaw open and speak strong, stressed /ʌ/ (UH) before bringing the tongue tip up to touch the gum ridge on /l/. Do not round the lips or /o/ may be spoken instead of /ʌ/.

---

dull	sulk	pulp	result
cull	hulk	ulcer	culture
skull	adult	pulse	ulcerous
culprit	consult	bulge	repulsive
vulture	impulse	dulcet	revulsion

PHRASES /ʌ/ before /l/

1. dull bulb
2. pop culture
3. sulking culprits
4. result of adultery
5. impulsive vulture
6. ultra dull
7. sullied hull
8. bulging seagulls
9. compulsive gulping
10. divulged his revulsion

SENTENCES /ʌ/ before /l/

1. Is mulch repulsive? Mull that over.

2. The culvert was flooded during the storm.

3. Skulking and sulking can give you ulcers.

4. Lullabies have such soothing dulcet tones.

5. Convulsions resulted in injury, they divulged.

6. All applicants to culinary school were insulted.

7. They found the cult culpable of occult practices.

8. Multinational cultural institutions were consulted.

9. The bulkhead rested on the fulcrum during repairs.

10. Mr. Tull won't divulge where the bulbs are planted.

11. I'd like to indulge my impulse to vacation on the gulf.

12. She felt sullen and vulnerable in the sultry evening air.

13. Adultery: the marriage nullified, the culprit pulverized.

NEUTRAL AMERICAN TEXT   stressed /ʌ/ (UH). *Mark the following and speak aloud.*

/ʌ/ before /l/:

         ʌl
Away you sc<u>ull</u>ion!

(2 Henry IV, II, i, 59)

Sing in our sweet lullaby,
Lulla, lulla, lullaby, lulla, lulla, lullaby.

(A Midsummer Night's Dream: II, ii, 14)

Your pulsidge beats as extraordinarily as heart would desire.

(2 Henry IV: II, iv, 23)

No doubt the murd'rous knife was dull and blunt.

(Richard III, IV, iv, 227)

/ʌ/ various positions:

I am undone!

(The Merry Wives of Windsor: IV, ii, 41)

O coz, coz, coz, my pretty little coz, that thou didst know how many fathom deep I am in love!

(As You Like It: IV, i, 205)

O blood, blood, blood!

(Othello: III, iii, 451)

Finds brotherhood in thee no sharper spur?
Hath love in thy old blood no living fire?
Edward's seven sons, whereof thyself art one,
Were as seven vials of his sacred blood.

(Richard II: I, ii, 9)

Oh, nonsense! Your love touches me, but I can't reciprocate it—
that's all.

(Chekhov: The Seagull)

1 WITCH. Here I have a pilot's thumb,
        Wrack'd as homeward he did come.
3 WITCH. A drum, a drum!
        Macbeth doth come.

(Macbeth: I, iii, 28)

BACK VOWELS

See Overview pages 18-26

/ u / (wh<u>o</u>)

Form the shape necessary for speaking the first back vowel sound /u/ (wh<u>o</u>) by closing the jaw almost completely, resting the tip of the tongue down behind the lower teeth, arching the back of the tongue high toward the front of the soft palate, sinking the cheeks, rounding the lips, and releasing sound through the mouth.

AUDIO 18▶ /u/ (wh<u>o</u>)

                                                u
Why, he is the Prince's jester, a very dull f<u>oo</u>l.
                                (Much Ado About Nothing: II, i, 138)

                                        u
We cannot fight for love, as men may d<u>o</u>.
                   u   u
We should be w<u>oo</u>'d, and were not made to w<u>oo</u>.
                                (A Midsummer Night's Dream: II, i, 241)

            u   u   u
Draw thy t<u>oo</u>l, here comes tw<u>o</u> of the house of Montag<u>ue</u>s.
                                (Romeo and Juliet: I, i, 31)

WORDS /u/ (wh<u>o</u>)

Initial	Medial	Final
ʔ Uzi	truth	two
ʔ oops	tomb	woo
ʔ ooze	move	blue
ʔ oodles	boom	stew
ʔ oomph	assume	canoe

RHYTHM TRACK This sound can be categorized as long, half-long or short depending on its position in the word and the sounds that follow.[1] Notice the variation in lengths. *Read across.*

long /u:/	long /u:/	half-long /u·/	short /u/
flu	floozy	flute	curfew
Jew	June	juice	statue
rue	room	Ruth	routine
shoe	shooed	shoot	cashew
taboo	booed	booth	boutique

This sound is **long /u:/** in a stressed syllable:

(a)　　when it's the last sound of the word

(b)　　when it's followed by a voiced consonant

PHRASES long /u:/

1.	true blue	6.	gloomy tomb
2.	brew booze	7.	choose cartoons
3.	wounded poodle	8.	imprudent shoes
4.	afternoon snooze	9.	drooling kangaroos
5.	zounds to you too	10.	concluded the review

This sound is **half-long /u·/** (who) in a stressed syllable when followed by a voiceless consonant.

PHRASES half-long /u·/

1.	loose suit	6.	brutes in boots
2.	oops, a blooper	7.	gruesome truth
3.	introducing Zeus	8.	exclusive troops
4.	shoots the jukebox	9.	juice, not vermouth
5.	plays hoops on the roof	10.	smooching pooches

Short /u/ (who) is spoken when in the unstressed syllable, or when used in the weak forms of the words 'do' and 'you'.

---

[1] Length indicators (or dots) used in IPA notation are optional (see pages 39-40). This section is marked to promote increased awareness and to aid those studying lengths.

PHRASES /ʊ/ (w<u>ou</u>ld)

1.	sugar c<u>oo</u>kies	6.	t<u>oo</u>k a b<u>u</u>llet
2.	st<u>oo</u>d in dark s<u>oo</u>t	7.	l<u>oo</u>ks cr<u>oo</u>ked
3.	w<u>ou</u>ld like Br<u>oo</u>ke	8.	c<u>ou</u>ld be a b<u>oo</u>king
4.	mist<u>oo</u>k the w<u>o</u>man	9.	g<u>oo</u>d s<u>u</u>gar p<u>u</u>dding
5.	l<u>oo</u>ks for g<u>oo</u>d b<u>oo</u>ks	10.	w<u>oo</u>den h<u>oo</u>ks sh<u>oo</u>k

SENTENCES /ʊ/ (w<u>ou</u>ld)

1. They're bullish on America.

2. The woman lost her footing.

3. Your hood's on crooked, Butch.

4. Could you, should you, would you?

5. He tripped on the cushion underfoot.

6. Tell us about your boyhood in Brooklyn.

7. My favorite store, Woolworth's, is kaput.

8. No one likes being called a goody-goody.

9. The woman misunderstood and pushed Brooke.

10. Should you bully the butcher when he's cooking?

11. He was in charge of finding firewood on the kibbutz.

12. Who is the good-looking man playing BOLINGBROKE?

13. The anchorwoman interviewed the barefooted onlookers.

SOUND CHECK #1: Compare the short, more open /ʊ/ (w<u>ou</u>ld) sound with the longer, more closed and energetically lip-rounded **/u/** (wh<u>o</u>). *Read across.*

/ʊ/	/u/	/ʊ/	/u/
put	pool	cookie	kook
good	goose	hook	who
stood	stewed	book	booth
foot	food	shook	shoed
would	woo	look	Luke

PHRASES   short /ʊ/ (w<u>ou</u>ld) and longer /u/ (wh<u>o</u>)

1.	h<u>oo</u>ded statue	6.	sh<u>ou</u>ldn't shoot
2.	baref<u>oo</u>t Hugo	7.	c<u>oo</u>ked couscous
3.	w<u>o</u>manly wooer	8.	r<u>u</u>ral route ruined
4.	p<u>u</u>lling the pooch	9.	b<u>u</u>lletproof booth
5.	brutal Miss Br<u>oo</u>ks	10.	g<u>oo</u>d-l<u>oo</u>king Lucy

SENTENCES   /ʊ/ (w<u>ou</u>ld) and /u/ (wh<u>o</u>)

1. Brooding isn't good for you.

2. They overtook the crooks in Utah.

3. Wooden spoons are best for cooking.

4. Rookie cops should use bulletproof vests.

5. Take a good look; then tell me if this is crooked.

SOUND CHECK #2: /ʊ/ (w<u>ou</u>ld) before /l/. Be sure to speak short /ʊ/ before the consonant /l/ in the following words, rather than the longer /u/ (wh<u>o</u>) sound.

---

bull	wool	pull	full
wolf	bullet	Fuller	fulfill
pulley	pulpit	fulsome	wolves

PHRASES   /ʊ/ before /l/

1.	f<u>u</u>lly f<u>u</u>ll	6.	w<u>oo</u>ly b<u>u</u>lly
2.	cries w<u>o</u>lf	7.	B<u>u</u>lgarian b<u>u</u>lls
3.	woman in w<u>oo</u>l	8.	pushed the p<u>u</u>lpit
4.	p<u>u</u>lling the p<u>u</u>lley	9.	would see w<u>o</u>lves
5.	books about b<u>u</u>llets	10.	w<u>oo</u>lens from Wooster

SENTENCES   /ʊ/ before /l/

1. Butch named his team the 'Brooklyn Bullets'.

2. Mr. Woolsey drinks nothing but hot bullion.

3. Was Sandra Bullock in *Dancing with Wolves*?

4. Fuller should fulfill his dream of selling cookies.

5. Wouldn't you prefer wearing wool in the woods in winter?

> **SOUND CHECK #3:** Compare /ʊ/ (w**ou**ld) and /ʌ/ (**UH**). Speak /ʊ/ with the jaw mostly closed, the lips slightly rounded and the back of the tongue arched. Speak /ʌ/ with the jaw more open, the lips unrounded and the middle of the tongue slightly arched. *Read across.*

/ʊ/	/ʌ/	/ʊ/	/ʌ/
put	putt	could	cud
would	what	look	luck
bull	bulb	soot	such
stood	stud	book	buck
hook	Huck	shook	shucks

PHRASES /ʊ/ and /ʌ/

1. rushing br**oo**ks
2. l**oo**king for lunch
3. p**u**shed the punks
4. b**oo**ked a bus tour
5. the w**o**man wasn't

6. baref**oo**t ushers
7. puffing and p**u**lling
8. combustible b**u**llets
9. sh**ou**ldn't have sunk
10. c**oo**ked for customers

SENTENCES /ʊ/ and /ʌ/

1. You look lovely, Brooke.

2. I wonder if that's deadwood.

3. Crooks will be fully punished.

4. She held the bundle to her bosom.

5. We took the Chunnel into London.

NEUTRAL AMERICAN TEXT /ʊ/ (w**ou**ld). *Mark the following and speak out loud.*

/ʊ/ before /l/:

        ʊl   ʊl

Your w**ol**f no longer seems to be a w**ol**f
Than when she's hungry.

                                      (Webster: The White Devil)

Some to the common pulpits, and cry out.

                                      (Julius Caesar: III, i, 80)

144

/ʊ/ various positions:

Bless'd pudding!

(Othello: II, i, 253)

I grant I am a woman; but withal
A woman that Lord Brutus took to wife.
I grant I am a woman; but withal
A woman well reputed, Cato's daughter.

(Julius Caesar: II, i, 292)

Wake Duncan with thy knocking! I would thou couldst!

(Macbeth: II, ii, 71)

Upon my lips—in ambush, there, he stood—
My foe, a lackey; his sword, a log of wood!

(Rostand: Cyrano de Bergerac)

O Rosalind, these trees shall be my books,
And in their barks my thoughts I'll character,
That every eye which in this forest looks
Shall see thy virtue witness'd every where.

(As You Like It: III, ii, 5)

ELEANOR.   There's a good mother, boy, that blots thy father.
CONSTANCE. There's a good grandame, boy, that would blot thee.
AUSTRIA.   Peace!

(King John: II, i, 132)

I would the college of the Cardinals
Would choose him Pope and carry him to Rome

(2 Henry VI: I, iii, 61)

PAULINA. I say, I come
            From your good queen.
LEONTES. Good queen?
PAULINA. Good queen, my lord, good queen, I say good queen,
            And would by combat make her good, so were I
            A man...

(The The Winter's Tale: II, iii, 57)

/ o / (o̱'mit)

Form the shape for speaking the third back vowel sound, <u>unstressed</u> /o/ (o̱'mit), by opening the jaw and relaxing the articulators slightly more than for the previous /ʊ/ sound. The jaw will be half open, the tip of the tongue resting behind the lower teeth, the back of the tongue arched half-high toward the soft palate and the lips gently rounded in the shape of an 'o'.

AUDIO 20► /o/ (o̱'mit) **in the first, unstressed syllable**

       o
Beauty pro̱'voketh thieves sooner than gold.

(As You Like It: I, iii, 110)

       o
I would the gods had made thee po̱'etical.

(As You Like It: III, iii, 16)

    o
Farewell! O̱'thello's occupation's gone!

(Othello: III, iii, 357)

WORDS /o/ (o̱'mit) **in the first, unstressed syllable**

Initial	Medial	Final
o'mit	mo'saic	*
o'vert	do'main	*
o'mega	no'bility	*
o'vation	co'quette	*
o'mission	bro'chure	*

RHYTHM TRACK /o/ (o̱'mit) is short, and occurs in the unstressed first syllable—as the first sound of the word or as the vowel in the first syllable.[1] The diphthong /oʊ̆/ is spoken in all other instances. (Pure /o/ is common in many accents, including: Spanish, Irish, Italian and Scottish.)

---

[1] This sound is represented many ways in dictionaries: as a diphthong in all positions in a word, as a vowel in all positions, and as a vowel or diphthong depending on its stress in a word. It is presented here as a vowel sound in the first, unstressed syllable of a word for its rhythmic implications, and to introduce this sound in context with the vowels.

Short **/ə/** (<u>uh</u>) is very often spoken instead of **/o/** in Neutral American, especially in words that begin with 'o', 'co', 'do', 'po', 'pro', 'so' in the spelling:

object, oblige, oblivion, obscene, obscure, observe, occasion, occult, occur, offend, offense, official, Olympics, opinion, oppress, Othello, command, convert, domestic, dominion, polemic, police, polite, possess, potential, proceed, proclaim, produce, profess, profound, promote, pronounce, protrude, provoke, society, solemnity, solution

PHRASES initial unstressed /o/ (<u>o</u>'mit)

1.	beautiful <u>o</u>asis	6.	on pr<u>o</u>bation
2.	this N<u>o</u>vember	7.	finds great h<u>o</u>tels
3.	gorgeous l<u>o</u>cale	8.	check the n<u>o</u>tation
4.	seems gr<u>o</u>tesque	9.	h<u>o</u>listic viewpoints
5.	finding a v<u>o</u>cation	10.	cute k<u>o</u>ala sighting

SENTENCES initial unstressed /o/ (<u>o</u>'mit)

1.   It's a very romantic locale.

2.   They decided to cooperate.

3.   Sophia always obeys the law.

4.   She received a standing ovation.

5.   Young O'Neill is Olympic material.

6.   Opaque glass was omitted from the model.

7.   The loquacious young man courted Odetta.

8.   A donation was requested at Yosemite National Park.

9.   The Oasis, a holistic hotel, is featured in the brochure.

10.   Is there a relationship between ovarian cancer and obesity?

NEUTRAL AMERICAN TEXT initial unstressed /o/ (<u>o</u>'mit). *Mark the following and speak out loud.*

o

Most pleasing it is, and <u>o</u>doriferous.

(Middleton & Rowley: The Changeling)

What if we do omit
This reprobate till he were well inclin'd?

(Measure for Measure: IV, iii, 73)

If he bid you set it down, obey him.

(The Merry Wives of Windsor: IV, ii, 109)

Therefore omit him not, blunt not his love,
Nor lose the good advantage of his grace.

(2 Henry IV: IV, iv, 27)

But that's all one; omittance is no quittance.

(As You Like It: III, v, 133)

Then true noblesse would
Learn him forbearance from so foul a wrong.

(Richard II: IV, I, 119)

I induced you to resume the yoke of duty and obedience!

(Ibsen: Ghosts)

The following selections could be spoken with pure /o/ or /ə/.

I will proclaim thee, Angelo, look for't!

(Measure for Measure: II, iv, 151)

How all occasions do inform against me.

(Hamlet: IV, iv, 32)

And if we thrive, promise them such rewards
As victors wear at the Olympian games.

(3 Henry VI: II, iii, 52)

Yea, brother Richard, are you offended too?

(3 Henry VI: IV, i, 19)

When water-drops have worn the stones of Troy,
And blind oblivion swallow'd cities up.

(Troilus and Cressida: III, ii, 186)

Suppose they take offense without a cause?

(3 Henry VI: IV, i, 14)

/ ɔ / (a̲ll)

Form the shape for the fourth back vowel /ɔ/ (a̲ll) by resting the tip of the tongue down behind the lower teeth, opening the jaw substantially more than for the previous /o/ sound, dropping the back of the tongue arch to a half-low position, and very slightly sinking the cheeks, which will slightly round the lips. This sound is sometimes referred to as the 'claw' sound, as the articulators tend to take the shape of the written IPA symbol: /ɔ/.

AUDIO 21▶ /ɔ/ (a̲ll)

     ɔ   ɔ

I a̲lways dream I'm under a ta̲ll tree in a dark wood.

                     (Strindberg: Miss Julie)

     ɔ

Kill Cla̲udio.

         (Much Ado About Nothing: IV, i, 289)

     ɔ   ɔ

And o̲ftentimes excusing of a fa̲ult

  ʌ   ɔ

Doth make the fa̲ult the worse by th' excuse.

                   (King John: IV, ii, 30)

WORDS /ɔ/ (a̲ll)

Initial	Medial	Final
ʔ awe	chalk	jaw
ʔ ought	flaunt	saw
ʔ awful	coffee	paw
ʔ always	sought	draw
ʔ August	daughter	thaw

The sound /ɔ/ is commonly represented by the spellings:

all	wall	tall	small	squall
alk	walk	balk	chalk	stalk
aw	law	saw	bawd	dawn
au	auction	sauce	daughter	audition

The sound /ɔ/ is also suggested[1] by the spellings:

og	log	smog	frog	dog
of(f)	often	soft	coffee	loft
os(s)	cross	toss	across	gloss
oth	cloth	moth	broth	froth
ong	song	belong	wrong	strong
ought	ought	bought	sought	fought

The word 'water' is pronounced with /ɔ/ (all), not /ɑ/ (father) in NAS.

RHYTHM TRACK This sound can be categorized as long, half-long or short, depending both on its position in the word and on the sounds that follow it.[2] Notice the variation in length of this sound in the following. *Read across.*

long /ɔ:/	**half-long /ɔ·/**	**short /ɔ/**
ball	balk	albeit
awe	aught	Australia
awed	ought	autumnal
pawn	paucity	Paulina
cause	caught	Caucasian

This sound is **long /ɔ:/** in a stressed syllable:

(a)   when it's the last sound of the word

(b)   when it's followed by a voiced consonant

PHRASES long /ɔ:/

1.	gnawed paws	6.	flawed straws
2.	finds the cause	7.	implausible law
3.	bawdy Mr. Shaw	8.	clawed Claudius
4.	appalled by *Jaws*	9.	draws an audience
5.	applause, applause	10.	marauding alderman

---

[1] There is discrepancy and difference of opinion, among dictionaries and teachers alike, whether words are pronounced with /ɔ/ (all) or /ɑ/ (father). Some also suggest /ɒ/ as an option. Though there are a few exceptions to the guidelines presented above, they are included in an attempt to offer a manageable, recognizable organization of words by sound and spelling, for both well-pronounced characters and/or for classical text. These guidelines are then referred to, and systematically altered when moving on to the Classical American and Standard British dialects.

[2] Length indicators (or dots) used in IPA notation are optional. This section is marked to promote increased awareness and to aid those studying lengths.

This sound is **half-long /ɔ·/** in a stressed syllable when followed by a voiceless consonant.

PHRASES half-long /ɔ·/

1.	awful faucet	6.	cautions Austin
2.	saucy sausage	7.	exhausting walk
3.	caught talking	8.	awkwardly taught
4.	brought hawks	9.	fraught with chalk
5.	unlawfully sought	10.	awesome thoughts

Short /ɔ/ is spoken when in the unstressed syllable.

WORDS short /ɔ/

already	augment	albeit	alright
austere	authentic	Almighty	Warsaw
Augustus	audacious	Australian	audition

Note: /ɔ/ (all) is not marked for length from this point on.

PHRASES /ɔ/ various lengths

1.	draws on cloth	6.	authentic talk
2.	haunted walkway	7.	gawky authors
3.	awkward songster	8.	enthralling waterfall
4.	all the daughter saw	9.	wall covered in chalk
5.	bought fresh prawns	10.	ought to be thoughtful

SENTENCES /ɔ/ (all) various lengths

1. What an exhausting talk!

2. Claude, the offer is a fraud.

3. How often do you go walking?

4. Dawn, are you working offline?

5. Store the softest cloth in mothballs.

6. His brother-in-law is from Arkansas.

7. The entire audience coughed at once.

8. Does your dog travel abroad with you?

9. There's no alternative but to be cautious.

10. They launched the boat off the boardwalk.

11. You're stalling; please fix the faulty faucet.

12. Without chalk, Dawn could no longer draw.

13. Saul becomes lost in thought when drawing.

14. They talked and talked for hours over coffee.

15. Paula always serves sweet sausage in autumn.

16. The applause from the auditorium was audible.

17. That small saucepan is filled with scalding water.

18. That's an awful song coming from that automobile.

19. They were appalled when she wallpapered the office.

20. The cost is automatically deducted from your account.

SOUND CHECK #1: Distinguish between /ɔ/ (all) and /ɑ/ (father) sounds in the following. Refer to the spelling guidelines on the previous pages 148-149.

WORDS comparing /ɑ/ (father) and /ɔ/ (all) *Read across.*

/ɑ/	/ɔ/	/ɑ/	/ɔ/
wok	walk	Tom	talk
stop	stall	pot	pall
drop	draw	John	jaw
dock	dawn	lot	lawn
shop	Shaw	hock	hawk
bob	bauble	crop	crawl
sot	sought	tot	taught

PHRASES /ɑ/ (father) and /ɔ/ (all)

1. flawed clocks
2. moms talking
3. saw the drama
4. a small omelet
5. not applauding

6. calling John
7. fond of Paula
8. caught Donna
9. lots of drawings
10. awfully odd drama

SENTENCES /ɑ/ (f<u>a</u>ther) and /ɔ/ (<u>a</u>ll)

1. Lots of small tots walk and talk.

2 Gosh, Falstaff's voice is too soft.

3. Audrey set the wok on the sidewalk.

4. They called 'bravo' after father's song.

5. Not feeling well? Sip some hot broth.

6. What's causing the cost of tacos to rise?

7. Am I wrong? I thought Tom lost his job.

8. They often call Tom for a small donation.

9. Hot chocolate is always good for business.

10. The disc jockey played that long, long song.

11. Thousands of actors responded to the cattle call.

12. Robert was too nauseous to enjoy the panorama.

13. Dawn and Don always look suave in silk pajamas.

14. Who's that on the opposite sidewalk, John or Paul?

15. The sonata wafted through the office building, calming all.

Hush-a-bye, baby, on the tree top,
When the wind blows, the cradle will rock;
When the bough breaks, the cradle will fall;
Down will come baby, cradle and all.
(Mother Goose: Hush-a-Bye)

SOUND CHECK #2: /ɔ/ (<u>a</u>ll) before consonant /l/. Drop the jaw open to the shape and position for /ɔ/ rather than beginning this sound combination with the more closed /ʊ/ (w<u>ou</u>ld) shape. Also, maintain the sunken cheeks and tongue arch as the tongue tip touches the upper gum ridge for /l/ to avoid inserting short /ə/ (<u>uh</u>) or /wə/ (w<u>uh</u>) before /l/. Speak 'all' not '**oo**all' or '**awuh**ll'.

Don't talk, that's all.

(Chekhov: The Cherry Orchard)

She was as false as water.

(Othello: V, ii, 134)

Why, what a caterwauling dost thou keep!

(Titus Andronicus: IV, ii, 57)

I have decked the sea with drops full salt.

(The Tempest: I, ii, 155)

Yet all goes well, yet all our joints are whole.

(1 Henry IV: IV, i, 83)

All—all expired save thee—save less than thou:
Save only the divine light in thine eyes—
Save but the soul in thine uplifted eyes.
I saw but them—they were the world to me.
I saw but them—saw only them for hours—
Saw only them until the moon went down.

(Poe: To Helen)

And thou, O wall, O sweet, O lovely wall,
That stand'st between her father's ground and mine!
Thou wall, O wall, O sweet and lovely wall,
Show me thy chink, to blink through with mine eyne!

(A Midsummer Night's Dream: V, I, 174)

CROWD.   Boo! boo!
JODELET.   Yes, yes! And the same unto you all!
BELLEROSE. Time we all went home now—!
JODELET.   Clear the hall!

(Rostand: Cyrano de Bergerac)

ANGELO.   Condemn the fault and not the actor of it?
            Why, every fault's condemn'd ere it be done.
            Mine were the very cipher of a function,
            To fine the faults whose fine stands in record,
            And let go by the actor.
ISABEL.   O just but severe law!

(Measure for Measure: II, ii, 37)

/ɔ/ various positions:

I'll make them pay; I'll sauce them.

(The Merry Wives of Windsor: IV, iii, 8)

Thou dost usurp that title now by fraud,
For in that shell of mother breeds a bawd.

(Tourneur: The Revenger's Tragedy)

While you two talk this out, I'll go shave!

(Strindberg: Miss Julie)

He says, my lord, your daughter is not well.

(King Lear: I, iv, 50)

Conscience is but a word that cowards use,
Devis'd at first to keep the strong in awe.

(Richard III: V, iii, 309)

He calls us rebels, traitors, and will scourge
With haughty arms this hateful name in us.

(1 Henry IV: V, ii, 39)

Thou call'dst me dog before thou hadst a cause,
But since I am a dog, beware my fangs.

(The Merchant of Venice: III, iii, 6)

A small writer, particularly when he is not successful, seems to
himself clumsy, awkward, unnecessary...

(Chekhov: The Seagull)

KING.   To this point hast thou heard him
         At any time speak aught?
SURVEYOR.   He was brought to this
         By a vain prophecy of Nicholas Henton.

(Henry VIII: I, ii, 145)

When law can do no right,
Let it be lawful that law bar no wrong;
Law cannot give my child his kingdom here,
For he that holds his kingdom holds the law;
Therefore since law itself is perfect wrong,
How can the law forbid my tongue to curse?

(King John: III, i, 185)

/ ɑ / (f<u>a</u>ther)

Form the shape for the fifth back vowel **/ɑ/** (f<u>a</u>ther) by resting the tip of the tongue down behind the lower front teeth, opening the lower jaw slightly more than for the previous back vowel sound **/ɔ/** (<u>a</u>ll), relaxing the back of the tongue low in the mouth and releasing sound through the mouth with the lips <u>un</u>rounded. The muscles of the throat and cheeks remain relaxed throughout.

AUDIO 22▶ */ɑ/* (f<u>a</u>ther)

              ɑ

And through his cloak, his sword thrust out to m<u>o</u>ck

           ɑ

The ruffled feathers of a strutting c<u>o</u>ck!

(Rostand: Cyrano de Bergerac)

         ɑ

All this is nothing; you shall see an<u>o</u>n

        ɑ

A place you little dream <u>o</u>n.

(Middleton & Rowley: The Changeling)

  ɑ   ɑ   ɑ

Oh, "f<u>a</u>ther,"—"f<u>a</u>ther"! I never knew anything of f<u>a</u>ther.

(Ibsen: Ghosts)

WORDS /ɑ/ (f<u>a</u>ther)

Initial	Medial	Final
? ox	sobs	*
? on	palm	*
? opt	drama	*
? omelet	topping	*
? obvious	common	*

RHYTHM TRACK This sound can be categorized as long, half-long or short depending on its position in the word and the sounds that follow.[1] Notice the variation in lengths while reading the words that follow out loud. *Read across.*

---

[1] Length indicators (or dots) used in IPA notation are optional (see pages 39-40). This section is marked to promote increased awareness and to aid those studying lengths.

long /ɑ:/	half-long /ɑ·/	short /ɑ·/
nod	not	nuance
rod	rot	(*occurs very rarely*)
mob	mop	
lodge	lots	
blond	block	

This sound is **long /ɑ:/** in a stressed syllable:

(a)   when it's the last sound of the word

(b)   when it's followed by a voiced consonant

PHRASES long /ɑ:/

1.	spa massage	6.	John's collie
2.	holiday lodge	7.	monstrous job
3.	modern college	8.	scholarly mom
4.	blond bombshell	9.	snobby robbers
5.	five-dollar omelet	10.	twenty-third Psalm

This sound is **half long /ɑ·/** in a stressed syllable when followed by a voiceless consonant.

PHRASES half-long /ɑ·/

1.	stocky doctor	6.	posh watches
2.	shot of Scotch	7.	lots of peacocks
3.	boxes of pasta	8.	forgotten operas
4.	shops in Washington	9.	yachts in the tropics
5.	improper stock option	10.	popular cotton socks

Short /ɑ/ is spoken in unstressed syllables, which occurs very rarely.

Note: /ɑ/ (father) is not marked for length from this point on.

SENTENCES /ɑ/ various lengths

1.   Mom shopped for pasta.

2.   It's impossible to contact Robert.

3.   The dropped stop watch stopped running.

4.   Solid dark chocolate is not considered toxic.

5.   Robin had a calming massage at the health spa.

6.   My father's cell phone is probably not turned on.

7.   The rockers feasted on hot popcorn, pasta, and nachos.

8.   They all raced nonstop around the block, then dropped.

9.   Manhattan co-ops are uncommonly expensive property.

10.   Tom will be waiting in the lobby at the Renaissance drama.

NEUTRAL AMERICAN TEXT /ɑ/ (f<u>a</u>ther). *Mark the following and speak out loud.*

/ɑ/ various positions:

           ɔ
Discuss unto me, art thou officer,
        ɑ   ɑ
Or art thou base, c<u>o</u>mmon, and p<u>o</u>pular?

                       (Henry V: IV, i, 37)

It shall be call'd "Bottom's Dream," because it hath no bottom.
              (A Midsummer Night's Dream: IV, i, 215)

Abjure this magic, turn to God again.
Ay, and Faustus will turn to God again.
To God? He loves thee not.
The God thou servest is thine own appetite.
                    (Marlowe: Doctor Faustus)

CASSIO. Welcome, Iago; we must to the watch.
IAGO.   Not this hour, lieutenant; 'tis not yet ten o' th' clock.
                    (Othello: II, iii, 12)

GRUMIO.   Knock, sir? whom should I knock? Is there any man
          has rebus'd your worship?
PETRUCHIO. Villain, I say, knock me here soundly.
GRUMIO.   Knock you here, sir? Why, sir, what am I, sir, that I
          should knock you here, sir?
PETRUCHIO. Villain, I say, knock me at this gate.
              (The Taming of the Shrew: I, ii, 6)

LONG DIPHTHONGS

See Overview pages 18-26

/ eĭ / (h<u>ey</u>)

Form /eĭ/ (h<u>ey</u>) by beginning in the shape and position for the third front vowel /e/ (g<u>e</u>t), then seamlessly blending into the second front vowel /ɪ/ (w<u>i</u>ll). The jaw will close slightly and the front tongue arch will lift during the blend.

Stress is on the first element of all diphthongs. The second element is rhythmically shorter as notated by / ˘ / in the IPA symbol.

AUDIO 23▶ /eĭ/ (h<u>ey</u>)

>   eĭ   eĭ
> For the red blood r<u>ei</u>gns in the winter's p<u>a</u>le.
>
> (The The Winter's Tale: IV, iii, 4)
>
>   eĭ   eĭ   eĭ
> I pr<u>ay</u> thee, good Hor<u>a</u>tio, w<u>ai</u>t upon him.
>
> (Hamlet: V, i, 293)
>
>   eĭ   eĭ
> A wicked d<u>ay</u>, and not a holy d<u>ay</u>!
>
> (King John: III, i, 83)

WORDS /eĭ/ (h<u>ey</u>)

Initial	Medial	Final
ʔ age	raid	day
ʔ aid	lake	hay
ʔ ace	faint	stay
ʔ ape	brain	relay
ʔ aim	praise	matinee

RHYTHM TRACK This sound can be categorized as long or short depending on its position in the word and the sounds that follow.

When the duration of the sound is long, a 'dot' follows each element of the symbol. Keep in mind that diphthongs consist of two blended vowels, so they can be wonderfully expressive, even when categorized as short.

This sound is **long /e·ĭ·/** in a stressed syllable:

(a)   when it's the last sound of the word

(b)   when it's followed by a voiced consonant

This sound is **short** in all other instances.

PHRASES long /e·ĭ·/

1.	bathes today	6.	snail mail
2.	displays rage	7.	plays at Shea
3.	explains to Dave	8.	made the grade
4.	pays for lemonade	9.	persuaded Wayne
5.	dismayed by the delay	10.	chained to the stage

PHRASES short /eĭ/

1.	dates Kate	6.	apes fate
2.	great shape	7.	erased mistakes
3.	wastes paste	8.	face with makeup
4.	eight debates	9.	displaced glaciers
5.	hates pancakes	10.	disgraceful skates

Note: /eĭ/ (pay) is not marked for length from this point on.

SENTENCES /eĭ/ various lengths

1.   Jane is off to Norway on Monday.

2.   Did you say 'checkmate', Lorraine?

3.   The gray fire escape is strangely shaped.

4.   Subway stations are being painted today.

5. The play received raves in all the daily papers.

6. Laurence Olivier was great in *The Entertainer*.

7. Grace, I'm midway through your essay on Spain.

8. Who is playing KATE in *The Taming of the Shrew*?

9. They gave first aid in the freight train at the station.

10. They were not 'on the same page' and were enraged.

11. There's no debate; Adrian is a great conversationalist.

12. Failure to obey was a grave mistake and chaos reined.

13. Everyone is acquainted with heartache; it's no disgrace.

14. Dr. Abe's patients are grateful and sing his praises daily.

15. By the way, Craig's application to the Navy was misplaced.

SOUND CHECK #1: /eĭl/ combinations. The middle and back of the tongue should remain relaxed and uninvolved when moving the tongue tip from its position resting down behind the lower teeth on /eĭ/, up to touch the upper gum ridge on /l/. Otherwise, an /ə/ (uh) or /jə/ (yuh) sound will be inserted before the /l/. In other words, speak 'hail' rather than 'haiuhl' or 'haiyuhl'.

/eĭl/	/eĭl/	/eĭl/	/eĭl/
jail	rail	nail	fail
flail	kale	dale	mail
scale	whale	snail	assail
ale/ail	sale/sail	inhale	they'll
tail/tale	gale/Gail	hail/hale	pail/pale

PHRASES /eĭ/ before /l/

1. the Holy Grail
2. tells great tales
3. needs an inhaler
4. raising pay scales
5. gray whale sighting
6. daily mail
7. veils on sale
8. the third rail
9. pale assailants
10. frail from ailments

SENTENCES /eĭ/ before /l/

1. Grades are pass/fail in Airedale.

2. If the ginger ale is stale, have a cocktail.

3. Hail the mailmen, both male and female.

4. Ms. Hale, what does studying Braille entail?

5. They tried to pay on a sliding scale, to no avail.

6. The trailer for the movie failed to generate sales.

7. Gale, you can't buy wholesale at Bloomingdales.

8. Abigail played FLORENCE NIGHTINGALE in pigtails.

9. The blackmailer was nailed by police and put in jail.

10. Evil Dale is impaled in the fairy tale, so good prevails.

NEUTRAL AMERICAN TEXT /eĭ/ (h<u>ey</u>). *Mark the following and speak out loud.*

/eĭ/ before /l/:

      eĭ   eĭ   eĭ
"A s<u>ail</u>, a s<u>ail</u>, a s<u>ail</u>!"

(Othello: II, i, 51)

Let not search and inquisition quail.

(As You Like It: II, ii, 20)

PETRUCHIO. Whose tongue?
KATHERINE. Yours, if you talk of tales, and so farewell.
PETRUCHIO. What, with my tongue in your tail?

(The Taming of the Shrew: II, i, 216)

MACBETH.   If we should fail?
L. MACBETH.   We fail?
           But screw your courage to the sticking place,
           And we'll not fail.

(Macbeth: I, vii, 59)

All hail, Macbeth, hail to thee, Thane of Cawdor!

(Macbeth: I, iii, 49)

/eǐ/ various positions:

Or shall we give the signal to our rage.

(King John: II, i, 265)

Poor Cyrano! We must find a gentle way
To tell Roxanne. What does the doctor say?

(Rostand: Cyrano de Bergerac)

The grave doth gape, and doting death is near.

(Henry V: II, i, 61)

To solemnize this day the glorious sun
Stays in his course and plays the alchemist.

(King John: III, i, 78)

You lie, in faith, for you are call'd plain Kate,
And bonny Kate, and sometimes Kate the curst;
But Kate, the prettiest Kate in Christendom.

(The Taming of the Shrew: II, i, 185)

NYM.   You'll pay me the eight shillings I won of you at betting?
PISTOL.   Base is the slave that pays.

(Henry V: II i, 94)

Had he been ta'en, we should have heard the news;
Had he been slain, we should have heard the news.

(3 Henry VI: II, i, 4)

Reputation, reputation, reputation! O, I have lost my reputation!
I have lost the immortal part of myself, and what remains is bestial.
My reputation, Iago, my reputation!

(Othello: II, iii, 262)

Down, down I come, like glist'ring Phaëton,
Wanting the manage of unruly jades.
In the base court? Base court, where kings grow base,
To come at traitors' calls and do them grace.
In the base court, come down? Down court! Down king!

(Richard II: III, iii, 178)

8. Guy arrives disguised, so he's not recognized.

9. What a triumphant recital; you're highly admired.

10. I'm standing-by in *The Prime of Miss Jean Brodie*.

11. I advise you to stop whining; whiners are despised.

12. The bride is marrying the pilot Friday evening at five.

13. Shall we wine and dine in Wyoming or Thailand, Ryan?

14. My advice? Lengthen your spine for improved alignment.

15. The way the sun is shining on this mild day is just sublime.

SOUND CHECK #1: /aĭ/ before a *voiceless* consonant. The jaw should be mostly open with a slight front of the tongue arch for the first element /a/, so that /ə/ (uh) is not spoken instead (for very well-pronounced characters or when speaking classical/poetic text). 'Rhyming' /aĭ/ sounds in the word pairs that follow may be useful for spotting variations in pronunciation. Also note, the second element of this diphthong, though rhythmically shorter, should not be eliminated. This is important for individuals from the South and Mid-west.

WORD PAIRS /aĭ/ before a voiceless consonant *Read across.*

tie/type	hi/hype	lie/life	vie/vice
pie/pike	my/mike	eye/ice	my/might
rye/right	fry/fright	why/wife	nigh/night

WORDS /aĭ/ before a voiceless consonant

life	rife	wife	strife
hike	like	plight	strike
pipe	right	spices	thrice
tight	stripe	device	slight
mighty	insightful	dislike	birthright

PHRASES /aĭ/ before a voiceless consonant

1.	so nice	6.	too tight
2.	she's bright	7.	not tonight
3.	the good life	8.	feisty advice
4.	more than likely	9.	iced or spiced
5.	height and might	10.	just delightful

SENTENCES /aĭ/ before a voiceless consonant

1. Can I play the spiteful sprite?

2. Have you seen *White Nights*?

3. What an extremely bright playwright.

4. Is there a hyphen in the word 'housewife'?

5. Most everyone dislikes cellulite; am I right?

6. No one will be on-site after midnight tonight.

7. It fell off the Eiffel tower and had to be spliced.

8. I didn't see the sign at night because of its height.

9. Swipe the card and the price of the item is sighted.

10. When cast as the fighter, he began taking vitamins.

11. It's unlikely the vice president will make this flight.

12. Would you like that tight little item in red or white?

13. The fishwife had a large pike caught in her windpipe.

14. In hindsight, it might have been better to avoid sunlight.

15. She priced the toy rifle for Mike but bought a kite instead.

SOUND CHECK #2: When /aĭ/ is followed immediately by /l/ within a word a short schwa may be inserted, with the resulting pronunciations: /aĭl/ *or* /aĭ əl/, depending on the rhythm of the text. The back of the tongue must remain relaxed and uninvolved so a /j/ (you) sound is not inserted between /aĭ/ and /l/ or between /aĭ/ and /əl/. Speak the word: 'wild' or 'wiuhld', *not* 'wiyyuhld'.

I'll	file	bile	dial
rile	trial	Nile	vile
pile	mild	wild	trial
awhile	guile	style	Lyall
while/wile	child	revile	denial

PHRASES /aɪ̆/ and /aɪ̆ ə/ before /l/

1.	hair styling	6.	love child
2.	lot of smiles	7.	mile after mile
3.	fair and mild	8.	all Francophiles
4.	no crocodiles	9.	puerile behavior
5.	down the aisle	10.	wild on the Nile

SENTENCES /aɪ̆/ and /aɪ̆ ə/ before /l/

1. The juvenile has style.

2. Are there crocodiles in the Nile?

3. What vile behavior, defiling the files.

4. Have that wild child be quiet for awhile.

5. The mild smile on the Mona Lisa beguiles.

6. Compile all reviews of *Buried Child* in a pile.

7. Kyle disguised himself, then tried to rile Lyle.

8. The reviled pedophile couldn't receive a fair trial.

9. I'll while away the time for awhile on a desert isle.

10. They cancelled their trip down the aisle, then reconciled.

NEUTRAL AMERICAN TEXT /aɪ̆/ (my). *Mark the following and speak out loud.*

/aɪ̆/ and /aɪ̆ ə/ before /l/:

aɪ̆
Will you be patient? Will you stay awhi<u>le</u>?

(Julius Caesar: III, ii, 149)

O villain, villain, smiling, damned villain!
My tables—meet it is I set it down
That one may smile, and smile, and be a villain!

(Hamlet: I, v, 106)

O tiger's heart wrapp'd in a woman's hide!
How couldst thou drain the life-blood of the child?

(3 Henry VI: I, iv, 137)

The greater file of the subject held the Duke to be wise.

(Measure for Measure: III, ii, 136)

/aĭ/ before a voiceless consonant:

My wife, my wife! what wife? I have no wife.

(Othello: V, ii, 97)

Antonio, I am married to a wife
Which is as dear to me as life itself,
But life itself, my wife, and all the world,
Are not with me esteem'd above thy life.

(The Merchant of Venice: IV, i, 282)

/aĭ/ various positions:

Be silent while I write.

(Strindberg: The Father)

Why day is day, night night, and time is time.

(Hamlet: II, ii, 88)

O, sir, I find her milder than she was.

(Two Gentlemen of Verona: V, ii, 2)

In my mind's eye, Horátio.

(Hamlet: I, ii, 185)

Hath Romeo slain himself? Say thou but ay
And that bare vowel *I* shall poison more
Than the death-darting eye of cockatrice.
I am not I, if there be such an ay,
Or those eyes shut, that makes thee answer ay.
If he be slain, say ay, or if not, no.

(Romeo and Juliet: III, ii, 45)

Thou speakest aright;
I am that merry wanderer of the night.
I jest to Oberon and make him smile
When I a fat and bean-fed horse beguile.

(A Midsummer Night's Dream: II, i, 42)

That's a lie! I'm the one who broke it! Did he say that he did?
The swine!

(Strindberg: Miss Julie)

/ ɔɪ̆ / (b<u>oy</u>)

Form /ɔɪ̆/ (b<u>oy</u>) by beginning in the shape and position for the fourth back vowel /ɔ/ (<u>a</u>ll) then seamlessly blending into the short, second front vowel /ɪ/ (w<u>i</u>ll). During the blend, the jaw will close slightly, the front tongue arch will lift, the lips will unround and slightly spread.

Take care not to begin this diphthong in the more closed, lip rounded shape and position of the back vowel /ʊ/ (w<u>ou</u>ld).

Stress is on the first element of all diphthongs. The second element is rhythmically shorter as notated by / ˘ / in the IPA symbol.

AUDIO 25▶ /ɔɪ̆/ (b<u>oy</u>)

>   ɔɪ̆
> Thou lily-liver'd b<u>oy</u>!
>
> (Macbeth: V, iii, 15)
>
>   ɔɪ̆
> The King, I fear, is p<u>oi</u>son'd by a monk.
>
> (King John: V, vi, 23)
>
>   ɔɪ̆
> 'Tis safer to be that which we destr<u>oy</u>
>   ɔɪ̆
> Than by destruction dwell in doubtful j<u>oy</u>.
>
> (Macbeth: III, ii, 6)

WORDS /ɔɪ̆/ (b<u>oy</u>)

Initial	Medial	Final
ʔ oil	boil	joy
ʔ oily	coin	soy
ʔ oink	foible	ahoy
ʔ oyster	doilies	destroy
ʔ ointment	lawyer	employ

RHYTHM TRACK This sound can be categorized as long or short depending on its position in the word and the sounds that follow it.

This sound is **long /ɔˑɪ̆/** in a stressed syllable:

(a)   when it's the last sound of the word

(b)   when it's followed by a voiced consonant

This sound is **short** in all other instances.

PHRASES long /ɔˑɪ̆/

1.	avoids noise	6.	deployed Roy
2.	destroys toys	7.	enjoys St. Croix
3.	coins in tin foil	8.	conjoined in Troy
4.	recoils from boys	9.	spoiled and soiled
5.	annoyed in Illinois	10.	employed by Freud

PHRASES short /ɔɪ̆/

1.	Rolls Royce	6.	paranoid choice
2.	hoisting sails	7.	boisterous Joyce
3.	orders oysters	8.	moistened throat
4.	not boycotting	9.	voiced or voiceless
5.	stops in Detroit	10.	going to the Cloisters

Note: /ɔɪ̆/ (boy) is not marked for length from this point on.

SENTENCES /ɔɪ̆/ various lengths

1.   Boy oh boy!

2.   Joyce loves corduroy.

3.   Let's embroider in the foyer.

4.   Anoint joints with moist ointments.

5.   Is that consonant voiced or unvoiced?

6.   Join the boycott in the adjoining room.

7.   People with choices feel less exploited.

8.   Mr. Freud recoils from cleaning the toilet.

9.   Annoyingly, moist soil destroys old coins.

This sound is **long /oˑʊˑ/** in a stressed syllable:

(a)   when it's the last sound of the word

(b)   when it's followed by a voiced consonant

This sound is **short** in all other instances.

PHRASES long /oˑʊˑ/

1. stone cold
2. old clothes
3. low plateau
4. circle the globe
5. exposed his foes
6. drove home
7. cajoled loans
8. hasn't phoned
9. yoga explosion
10. proposing to Joan

PHRASES short /oʊ/

1. soaked coats
2. hope to elope
3. smoky smoke
4. revoked the vote
5. mostly unfocused
6. boasting oaf
7. woeful notes
8. hopeful folks
9. coast to coast
10. emotional vote

Note: /oʊ/ (go) is not marked for length from this point on.

SENTENCES /oʊ/ (go) various lengths

1. Who phoned, Joseph?

2. Lois played the oboe at the opening.

3. Nobody knows *Oklahoma* like Lowell.

4. No, I want to go to work even if it's snowing.

5. Rhoda was approached about taking over the role.

6. Oh no! Who in the front row is so overly verbose?

7. A video was made of the bold performance in Tokyo.

8. The opinion poll is focusing on folks from Minnesota.

9. Ms. De Soto hoped for a role in *Show Boat* in Sarasota.

10. The pony was overexposed to the cold and almost froze.

178

SOUND CHECK #1: /l/, /lt/, and /ld/ endings. Be sure to pronounce all of the consonant sounds in these combinations when they follow **/oŭ/**. The tongue tip should make contact with the hard palate behind the upper teeth and fully sound **/l/** before continuing on to the **/t/** or **/d/** sound that follows. *Read across.*

/oŭ/	/oŭl/	/oŭlt/	/oŭld/
Coe	coal	colt	cold
bow	bowl	bolt	bold
hoe	hole	holt	hold
mow	mole	molt	mold
doe	dole	dolt	doled

Thy prime of manhood daring, b<u>ol</u>d, and venturous.

(Richard III: IV, iv, 171)

PHRASES /oŭ/ before /l/, /lt/ and /ld/

1. not foret<u>ol</u>d
2. day-<u>ol</u>d s<u>ol</u>e
3. t<u>ol</u>d to ref<u>ol</u>d
4. too <u>ol</u>d to sc<u>ol</u>d
5. p<u>ol</u>ling p<u>ol</u>lsters
6. ice-c<u>ol</u>d m<u>ol</u>d
7. loves marig<u>ol</u>ds
8. twice-t<u>ol</u>d to caj<u>ol</u>e
9. reasons are twof<u>ol</u>d
10. w<u>on</u>'t withh<u>ol</u>d g<u>ol</u>d

SENTENCES /oŭ/ before /l/, /lt/ and /ld/

1. Behold the golden statue.
2. Scold Joe for undercooking the poultry.
3. They only sold shoes with hand-sewn soles.
4. Hold on a minute; that's not what I was told!
5. Members of the household revolted when blindfolded.
6. Grab ahold of the stone wall if you lose your foothold.
7. The shareholder was cajoled; then he sold to Mr. Dole.
8. The crowd was uncontrolled; we couldn't uphold the law.
9. Don't think me overbold, but I'd love the role of LEOPOLD.
10. The goalie maintained a stronghold between the goal posts.

NEUTRAL AMERICAN TEXT /oŭ/ (g**o**). *Mark the following and speak out loud.*

/oŭ/ before /l/, /lt/ and /ld/:

oŭ
And therefore fortify your h**o**ld, my lord.

(3 Henry VI: I, ii, 52)

Thy language is so bold and vicious.

(Middleton & Rowley: The Changeling)

And this, so sole and so unmatchable.

(King John: IV, iii, 52)

For here's the scroll
In which thou hast given thy soul to Lucifer.

(Marlowe: Doctor Faustus)

For many men that stumble at the threshold
Are well foretold that danger lurks within.

(3 Henry VI: IV, vii, 11)

When I desir'd him to come home to dinner,
He ask'd me for a thousand marks in gold:
"'Tis dinner-time," quoth I: "My gold!" quoth he.
"Your meat doth burn," quoth I: "My gold!" quoth he.
"Will you come?" quoth I: "My gold!" quoth he.

(The Comedy of Errors: II, i, 60)

Hold, hold! Zounds, he'll raise up a kettle of devils, I think anon.
Good my lord, entreat for me. 'Sblood, I am never able to endure
these torments.

(Marlowe: Doctor Faustus)

The bull, the primitive statue and oblique memorial of cuckolds.

(Troilus and Cressida: V, i, 54)

But he grew old—
This knight so bold—
And o'er his heart a shadow
Fell as he found
No spot of ground
That looked like Eldorado.

(Poe: Eldorado)

And by our holy Sabbath have I sworn
To have the due and forfeit of my bond.

(The Merchant of Venice: IV, i, 36)

Life is as tedious as a twice-told tale,
Vexing the dull ear of a drowsy man.

(King John: III, iv, 108)

Yet here, Laertes? Aboard, aboard, for shame!
The wind sits in the shoulder of your sail.

(Hamlet: I, iii, 55)

I have seen tempests when the scolding winds
Have riv'd the knotty oaks, and I have seen
Th' ambitious ocean swell, and rage, and foam,
To be exalted with the threat'ning clouds.

(Julius Caesar: I, iii, 5)

All that glisters is not gold,
Often have you heard that told;
Many a man his life hath sold
But my outside to behold.
Gilded tombs do worms infold.
Had you been as wise as bold,
Young in limbs, in judgment old,
Your answer had not been inscroll'd.
Fare you well, your suit is cold.

(The Merchant of Venice: II, vii, 65)

/oŭ/ various positions:

Here is a mourning Rome, a dangerous Rome,
No Rome of safety for Octavius yet;
Hie hence, and tell him so.

(Julius Caesar: III, i, 288)

O woe! O woeful, woeful, woeful day!
Most lamentable day, most woeful day
That ever, ever, I did yet behold!
O day, O day, O day, O hateful day!
Never was seen so black a day as this.
O woeful day, O woeful day!

(Romeo and Juliet: IV, v, 49)

/ aŭ / (n<u>ow</u>)

This diphthong is one of two in NAS that begins with the /a/ sound.

Form the first element /a/ by resting the tip of the tongue down behind the lower teeth, opening the jaw and flattening the tongue arch slightly more than for the fourth front vowel /æ/ (th<u>a</u>t), with the lips and cheeks neutral but energized. Then seamlessly blend in the second back vowel /ʊ/ (w<u>ou</u>ld) closing the lower jaw, lifting the back tongue arch, and rounding the lips.

Stress is on the first element of all diphthongs. The second element is rhythmically shorter as notated by / ˘ / in the IPA symbol.

AUDIO 27► /aŭ/ (n<u>ow</u>)

> aŭ
> From north to s<u>ou</u>th—
> aŭ
> Austria and France shoot in each other's m<u>ou</u>th.
> (King John: II, I, 413)
>
> aŭ aŭ aŭ aŭ
> Oh, th<u>ou</u>'rt a f<u>ou</u>l black cl<u>ou</u>d, and th<u>ou</u> dost threat
>
> A violent storm!
> (Webster: The White Devil)
>
> aŭ aŭ aŭ
> O h<u>ou</u>nd of Crete, think'st th<u>ou</u> my sp<u>ou</u>se to get?
> (Henry V: II, i, 73)

WORDS /aŭ/ (n<u>ow</u>)

Initial	Medial	Final
? out	pounds	how
? owl	without	cow
? oust	founder	thou
? ouch	rounding	brow
? ounce	mountain	chow

Take care not to begin this diphthong with the /æ/ (th<u>a</u>t) sound. This results in a diphthong that is overly tense and nasal for Neutral American, but is spoken in some Southern and Midwestern dialects.

RHYTHM TRACK This sound can be categorized as long or short depending on its position in the word and the sounds that follow it.

This sound is **long /aˑŭˑ/** in a stressed syllable:

(a)   when it's the last sound of the word

(b)   when it's followed by a voiced consonant

This sound is **short** in all other instances.

PHRASES /aˑŭˑ/

1.	l<u>ou</u>d cr<u>ow</u>ds	6.	gr<u>ou</u>nd d<u>ow</u>n
2.	f<u>ou</u>nd ar<u>ou</u>nd	7.	r<u>ou</u>nd cr<u>ow</u>ns
3.	d<u>ow</u>dy in br<u>ow</u>n	8.	surr<u>ou</u>nd s<u>ou</u>nd
4.	ar<u>ou</u>sed the t<u>ow</u>n	9.	h<u>ow</u>l and gr<u>ow</u>l
5.	w<u>ow</u>s with ch<u>ow</u>der	10.	schn<u>au</u>zers all<u>ow</u>ed

PHRASES short /aŭ/

1.	sh<u>ou</u>t ab<u>ou</u>t	6.	st<u>ou</u>t sp<u>ou</u>t
2.	what a sn<u>ou</u>t	7.	<u>ou</u>t of cl<u>ou</u>t
3.	<u>ou</u>sted sp<u>ou</u>se	8.	d<u>ou</u>se the h<u>ou</u>se
4.	gr<u>ou</u>ch on the c<u>ou</u>ch	9.	p<u>ou</u>ting boy sc<u>ou</u>ts
5.	m<u>ou</u>sy-colored bl<u>ou</u>se	10.	looking <u>ou</u>t for tr<u>ou</u>t

Note: /aŭ/ (n<u>ow</u>) is not marked for length from this point on.

SENTENCES /aŭ/ (n<u>ow</u>) various lengths

1.   Our hound 'bow-wows' to go out.

2.   Now, how many ounces in a pound?

3.   Theatre in the round can be powerful!

4.   You're grounded! How does that sound?

5.   I can't vouch for powdered clam chowder.

6.   The director shouted, "Louder, faster, funnier!"

7. What an astounding performance, take a bow!

8. "That was out of bounds," the lookout shouted.

9. We'll all meet downtown around the fountain.

10. Pouting won't increase your allowance, Howard.

SOUND CHECK #1: /aŭ/ before /l/. The tip of the tongue rests down behind the lower teeth on /aŭ/, then moves to touch the gum ridge on /l/. The middle of the tongue remains relaxed and uninvolved, and the lips remain slightly rounded, to avoid inserting /ə/ (uh) before /l/. Speak 'owl' not 'owuhl'.

/aŭl/	/aŭl/	/aŭl/	/aŭl/
owl	cowl	jowl	prowl
howl	afoul	yowl	growl
befoul	peafowl	scowl	seafowl

PHRASES /aŭ/ before /l/

1. heard yowling
2. owls downtown
3. scowling mouth
4. prominent jowl
5. something afoul
6. prowling around

SENTENCES /aŭ/ before /l/

1. The owl isn't considered a seafowl, is it?

2. Now, no howling if you don't get the part.

3. We saw thousands of Southeast Asian peafowl.

4. Scowling and growling could befoul your reputation.

5. She wore a cowl-necked evening gown to the awards.

NEUTRAL AMERICAN TEXT /aŭ/ (now). *Mark the following and speak out loud.*

/aŭ/ before /l/:

aŭ
It was the owl that shriek'd.

(Macbeth: II, ii, 3)

Howl, howl, howl! O, you are men of stones!

(King Lear: V, iii, 258)

Foul stigmatic, that's more than thou canst tell.

(2 Henry VI: V, i, 215)

O thou foul thief, where hast thou stow'd my daughter?

(Othello: I, ii, 62)

Wilt thou ever be a foul-mouth'd and ca'**lum**nious knave?

(All's Well That Ends Well: I, iii, 56)

How the knave jowls it to the ground, as if 'twere Cain's jaw-bone.

(Hamlet: V, i, 76)

Bring forth that fatal screech-owl to our house
That nothing sung but death to us and ours.

(3 Henry VI: II, vi, 56)

/aŭ/ various positions:

Now are our brows bound with victorious wreaths.

(Richard III: I, i, 5)

Methought I saw a thousand fearful wracks;
A thousand men that fishes gnaw'd upon.

(Richard III: I, iv, 24)

I wouldn't pity him; he's lived without
Concessions…free to think…and move about.

(Rostand: Cyrano de Bergerac)

But now mischance hath trod my title down,
And with dishonor laid me on the ground.

(3 Henry VI: III, iii, 8)

Until my misshap'd trunk that bears this head
Be round impaled with a glorious crown.

(3 Henry VI: III, ii, 170)

Thou wouldst be great,
Art not without ambition, but without
The illness should attend it.

(Macbeth: I, v, 18)

Thou toad, thou toad, where is thy brother Clarence?

(Richard III: IV, iv, 145)

PHRASES /eɚ/ (th<u>eir</u>)

1.	solit<u>ary</u> h<u>eir</u>	6.	Delaw<u>are</u> aff<u>air</u>
2.	b<u>are</u>ly th<u>ere</u>	7.	desp<u>air</u>ing G<u>ary</u>
3.	gl<u>ar</u>ing ch<u>air</u>man	8.	ordin<u>ar</u>ily p<u>air</u>ed
4.	million<u>aire</u>'s m<u>are</u>	9.	sp<u>are</u> earthenw<u>are</u>
5.	rep<u>air</u>ing armch<u>air</u>s	10.	decl<u>ar</u>ed a zillion<u>aire</u>

SENTENCES /eɚ/ (th<u>eir</u>)

1. Mary is gregarious.

2. Play fair and square.

3. Don't stare. It's scary.

4. They're very caring parents.

5. That's unfair and embarrassing.

6. Pierre's fairly happy anywhere.

7. Barry is now Department Chair.

8. Beware, malaria can cause despair.

9. Store all threadbare chairs upstairs.

10. Gary's music blared across the prairie.

11. Mary's allergic to various dairy products.

12. Can Karen's secretary type the questionnaire?

13. Who was paired with the debonair Fred Astaire?

14. Would you like to be an au pair somewhere, Sara?

15. There's no comparison between peaches and pears.

16. Name that fairy tale: "Who is the fairest of them all?"

17. Sharon's character is hilarious! What is she wearing?

18. Go through the square; then turn onto the thoroughfare.

19. That interview won't be aired; there's too much swearing.

20. Don't stare at my haircut. It's terrible, but will be repaired.

NEUTRAL AMERICAN TEXT /eɚ/ (th<u>ei</u>r). *Mark the following and speak aloud.*

eɚ
O, bew<u>are</u>, my lord, of jealousy!

(Othello: III, iii, 165)

Fair is foul, and foul is fair,
Hover through the fog and filthy air.

(Macbeth: I, i, 11)

Oh, it strikes, it strikes! Now body turn to air,
Or Lucifer will bear thee quick to hell.

(Marlowe: Doctor Faustus)

As waggish boys in game themselves forswear,
So the boy Love is perjur'd every where.

(A Midsummer Night's Dream: I, i, 240)

There's the promised signal! Trumpets! There—
The Marshal's men return with brazen fare!

(Rostand: Cyrano de Bergerac)

Fair sir, God save you! Where's the Princess?

(Love's Labor's Lost: V ii, 310)

Action and accent did they teach him there:
"Thus must thou speak," and "thus thy body bear".

(Love's Labor's Lost: V, ii, 99)

CAMILLO.   I dare not know, my lord.
POLIXENES. How, dare not? Do not? Do you know, and dare not?
          Be intelligent to me, 'tis thereabouts.

(The The Winter's Tale: I, ii, 376)

'Tis just like a summer bird-cage in a garden: the birds that are
without despair to get in, and the birds that are within despair and
are in a consumption for fear they shall never get out.

(Webster: The White Devil)

/ ʊɚ̆ / (p**oor**)

Form /ʊɚ̆/ (p<u>oor</u>) by beginning in position and shape for the second back vowel sound /ʊ/ (w<u>ou</u>ld), then seamlessly blending in the very short mid-vowel /ɚ/ (er). During the blend, the lips unround and the tongue tip raises from its position resting down behind the lower teeth, to point toward the hard palate for the 'r' coloring necessary in Neutral American.

Stress is on the first element of all diphthongs. The second element is rhythmically shorter as notated by / ˘ / in the IPA symbol.

AUDIO 30▶ /ʊɚ̆/ (p<u>oor</u>)

>   ʊɚ̆
> The p<u>oor</u> Vershinins had a fright.
> (Chekhov: The Three Sisters)
>
>   ʊɚ̆   ʊɚ̆
> But what would my ass<u>ur</u>ances have been worth against y<u>our</u>s?
> (Ibsen: A Doll's House)
>
>   ʊɚ̆
> But this rough magic I here abj<u>ure</u>.
> (The Tempest: V, i, 50)

WORDS /ʊɚ̆/ (p<u>oor</u>)

Initial	Medial	Final
*	fury	moor
*	sure	contour
*	mural	insecure
*	during	pedicure
*	insurance	caricature

jʊɚ̆
Y<u>our</u>e a peach!

(Chekhov: The Cherry Orchard)

The strong form of 'your' is pronounced /jʊɚ̆/ as in the quote above. The weak form of 'your' can be /jʊ/ or /jɚ/ as in the selection at the top of the next page.

ʊɚ̆   jʊ *(or* jɚ *)*
Ass<u>ur</u>ance bless y<u>our</u> thoughts!

(Timon of Athens: II, ii, 180)

The /ʊɚ̆ / (p<u>oor</u>) diphthong should be used for speakers of classic text. It is often mispronounced as /ɔɚ̆ / (sp<u>or</u>ts) or /ɝ / (<u>ER</u>)—as in the contemporary pronunciation of 'sure' as '*sherr*'.

abjure	allure	amour	assure
boorish	bourse	brochure	bureau
bureaucrat	caesura	contour	cure
curious	demure	detour	dour
duration	during	endure	ensure
fury	gourd	gourmet	impure
insecure	insurance	injurious	inure
jury	Lourdes	lures	lurid
luxurious	mature	moor	mural
obscure	plural	poor	procure
prurient	pure	rural	secure
spoor	tour	velour	Zurich

PHRASES /ʊɚ̆ / (p<u>oor</u>)

1.	sec<u>ur</u>ity lapse	6.	y<u>our</u>s for sure
2.	an obsc<u>ure</u> t<u>our</u>	7.	all<u>ur</u>ing j<u>ur</u>ies
3.	b<u>oor</u>ish for s<u>ure</u>	8.	imp<u>ure</u> and l<u>ur</u>id
4.	needs ins<u>ur</u>ance	9.	c<u>ur</u>ious in L<u>our</u>des
5.	proc<u>ur</u>es a C<u>oor</u>s	10.	an obsc<u>ure</u> broch<u>ure</u>

SOUND CHECK #1: The first element of this diphthong begins with the back vowel /ʊ/ (w<u>ou</u>ld), which requires lip-rounding. The rounded lips are released as the second element, the short mid-vowel /ɚ̆/ (er) is blended. *Read across.*

/ʊ/	/ʊɚ̆/	/ʊ/	/ʊɚ̆/
put	poor	look	lure
shook	sure	took	tour
book	boor	cook	Coors
sugar	insure	Sputnik	spoor
should	assure	should	brochure

/ ɔɚ̆ / (sp<u>or</u>ts)

Form /ɔɚ̆ / (sp<u>or</u>ts) by beginning in the position and shape for the fourth back vowel sound /ɔ/ (<u>a</u>ll), then seamlessly blending in the very short mid-vowel /ɚ/ (<u>er</u>). During the blend, the jaw closes slightly, the lips unround and the tongue tip raises from its position resting down behind the lower teeth, to point toward the hard palate for the 'r' coloring necessary in NAS.

Stress is on the first element of all diphthongs. The second element is rhythmically shorter as notated by / ˘ / in the IPA symbol.

AUDIO 31▶ /ɔɚ̆/ (sp<u>or</u>ts)

>   ɔɚ̆   ɔɚ̆
> The purest treasure m<u>or</u>tal times aff<u>or</u>d
>
> Is spotless reputation.
> > (Richard II: I, i, 177)
>
>   ɔɚ̆   ɔɚ̆
> The m<u>or</u>e I hate, the m<u>or</u>e he follows me.
>   ɔɚ̆   ɔɚ̆
> The m<u>or</u>e I love, the m<u>or</u>e he hateth me.
> > (A Midsummer Night's Dream: I, i, 198)
>
>   ɔɚ̆
> To leave my Julia—shall I be forsw<u>or</u>n?
>   ɔɚ̆
> To love fair Silvia—shall I be forsw<u>or</u>n?
>   ɔɚ̆
> To wrong my friend, I shall be much forsw<u>or</u>n.
> > (The Two Gentlemen of Verona: II, vii, i)

WORDS /ɔɚ̆/ (sp<u>or</u>ts)

Initial	Medial	Final
ʔ orbit	sword	war
ʔ order	report	shore
ʔ organic	horses	abhor
ʔ ordinary	former	adore
ʔ orchestra	toward	ignore

PHRASES /ɔɚ/ (sp<u>or</u>ts)

1.	div<u>or</u>ce c<u>our</u>t	6.	n<u>or</u>mal c<u>or</u>ks
2.	ad<u>ore</u>s metaph<u>or</u>s	7.	c<u>or</u>porate rep<u>or</u>ts
3.	troubad<u>our</u> of y<u>ore</u>	8.	landl<u>or</u>d's disc<u>or</u>d
4.	Singap<u>ore</u> sophom<u>ore</u>	9.	waterb<u>or</u>ne st<u>or</u>ks
5.	transf<u>or</u>ms the m<u>or</u>gue	10.	inf<u>or</u>ming disc<u>our</u>ses

SENTENCES /ɔɚ/ (sp<u>or</u>ts)

1. Encore, encore!

2. *H.M.S. Pinafore* is adored.

3. Are all dinosaurs carnivores?

4. Soaring organ music fortifies.

5. Morgan's an authority on Horton Foote.

6. Who orchestrated the score for *West Side Story*?

7. The restored first floor auditorium looks gorgeous.

8. Theodore played the part of TORVALD in Singapore.

9. More and more people gathered outside the stage door.

10. Those reports distort the effect of morphine on hornets.

SOUND CHECK #1: Compare /ʊɚ/ (p<u>oor</u>) and /ɔɚ/ (sp<u>or</u>ts). The /ʊɚ/ diphthong is initiated with the jaw slightly more closed, the back tongue arch slightly higher, and the lips slightly more rounded and energized than for the /ɔɚ/ diphthong. Feel this small but important difference in shape when speaking the following words, phrases, and sentences out loud. *Read across.*

/ʊɚ/	/ɔɚ/	/ʊɚ/	/ɔɚ/
poor	pore	tour	tore
you're	yore	boor	bore
fury	fjord	lure	lore
moor	more	rural	roar
jury	George	dour	door

ʊɚ   ɔɚ   ɔɚ

Alas, poor Y<u>or</u>ick! I knew him, H<u>or</u>atio.

(Hamlet: V, i, 184)

SOUND CHECK #1: The first element of the /ɔɚ/ (sp<u>or</u>ts) diphthong requires lip-rounding, or sinking of the cheeks, while /ɑɚ/ (c<u>ar</u>) does not. Notice this difference when speaking the following words and phrases. *Read across.*

/ɔɚ/	/ɑɚ/	/ɔɚ/	/ɑɚ/
for	far	tore	tar
pour	par	bore	bar
lord	lard	dork	dark
cored	card	horde	hard
gored	guard	stork	stark

PHRASES /ɔɚ/ and /ɑɚ/

1. torn t<u>ar</u>ps
2. boring b<u>ar</u>s
3. rem<u>ar</u>kable encore
4. c<u>ar</u>peted with corks
5. m<u>ar</u>ching in formation
6. more m<u>ar</u>velous
7. pours in the p<u>ar</u>k
8. gorgeous g<u>ar</u>dens
9. no more n<u>ar</u>cotics
10. h<u>ar</u>d-he<u>ar</u>ted whores

NEUTRAL AMERICAN TEXT /ɑɚ/ (c<u>ar</u>). *Mark the following and speak out loud.*

  ɑɚ   ɑɚ
P<u>ar</u>don me, p<u>ar</u>don me.

               (Troilus and Cressida: I, ii, 83)

I hate the Moor. My cause is hearted.

               (Othello: I iii, 366)

I humbly do beseech you of your pardon.

               (Othello: III, iii, 212)

And I, the mistress of your charms,
The close contriver of all harms,
Was never call'd to bear my part,
Or show the glory of our art?

               (Macbeth: III, v, 6)

Oh gentle Faustus, leave this damned art,
This magic, that will charm thy soul to hell,
And quite bereave thee of salvation.

               (Marlowe: Doctor Faustus)

Mischief, thou art afoot.

(Julius Caesar: III, ii, 260)

Gentlemen, importune me no farther,
For how I firmly am resolv'd you know.

(The Taming of the Shrew: I, i, 48)

Remember March, the ides of March remember.

(Julius Caesar: IV iii, 18)

We here discharge your Grace from being Regent
I' th' parts of France, till term of eighteen months
Be full expir'd.

(2 Henry VI: I, i, 66)

And if I were thy nurse, thy tongue to teach,
"Pardon" should be the first word of thy speech.
I never long'd to hear a word till now,
Say "pardon," King, let pity teach thee how.
The word is short, but not so short as sweet,
No word like "pardon" for kings' mouths so meet.

(Richard II: V, iii, 113)

Put on this nightcap sir, 'tis charmed—and now
I'll show you by my strong commanding art
The circumstance that breaks your duchess' heart.

(Webster: The White Devil)

K. RICHARD.   Harp not on that string, madam, that is past.
Q. ELIZABETH.   Harp on it still shall I till heart-strings break.

(Richard III: IV, iv, 364)

Romeo, come forth, come forth, thou fearful man:
Affliction is enamor'd of thy parts,
And thou art wedded to calamity.

(Romeo and Juliet: III, iii, 1)

Ah, less—less bright
The stars of night
Than the eyes of the radiant girl!

(Poe: Eulalie)

TRIPHTHONGS OF 'R'

See Overview pages 18-26

/ aĭə̆ / (f<u>ire</u>)

Form the triphthong /aĭə̆/ (f<u>ire</u>) by seamlessly blending the /aĭ/ (m<u>y</u>) diphthong with the very short mid-vowel /ə̆/ (<u>er</u>) to sound as one sound. During the blend, the tongue tip raises from its position resting down behind the lower teeth and points toward the hard palate for the 'r' coloring necessary in Neutral American. Lip rounding is not required for any element of this triphthong.

Rhythmically, this sound can also be blended as a diphthong, followed immediately by the unstressed vowel /ə̆/ (<u>er</u>), which would be represented as /aĭ ə̆/ instead of /aĭə̆/. In any case, the first element is stressed, while the second and third elements are unstressed.

AUDIO 33▶ /aĭə̆/ or /aĭ ə̆/ (f<u>ire</u>)

Think'st thou that I will leave my kingly throne,
　　　　　　　aĭə̆
Wherein my grands<u>ire</u> and my father sat?

(3 Henry VI: I, i, 124)

Thou art too ugly to attend on me.
　　　　　　　aĭ ə̆
Go and return an old Franciscan fr<u>iar</u>.

(Marlowe: Doctor Faustus)

And love shall play the wanton on your lip,
　　aĭə̆　　aĭə̆
Meet and ret<u>ire</u>, ret<u>ire</u> and meet again.

(Middleton & Rowley: The Changeling)

WORDS /aɪɚ/ or /aɪ ɚ/ (fire)

Initial	Medial	Final
? ire	fiery	pyre
? iron	friars	wire
? irony	attired	choir
? ironed	desiring	squire
? ironing	enquired	expire

ADDITIONAL WORDS /aɪɚ/ or /aɪ ɚ/ (fire)

admire	tire	hire	dire
inspire	afire	entire	mire
acquire	squire	bemire	retire
esquire	inquire	perspire	suspire
transpire	hellfire	Maguire	conspire

PHRASES /aɪɚ/ or /aɪ ɚ/ (fire)

1. enquiring minds
2. admired empires
3. conspiring to hire
4. undesired wildfires
5. requires new wiring
6. fires the buyer
7. the entire choir
8. aspires to retire
9. prior to expiring
10. desires new attire

SOUND CHECK #1: The back of the tongue should remain relaxed and uninvolved, so the /j/ (you) sound is not inserted before the /ɚ/, whatever the rhythmic pronunciation of this sound. For example, speak: 'tire' not 'tiyyre'.

---

tire	fire	hire	dire
liar	wire	spire	mire
pyre	crier	buyer	retire

PHRASES /aɪ/ and /aɪɚ/

1. fights fires
2. right to enquire
3. perspiring pipes
4. sighted the squire
5. might be inspired
6. lying liars
7. wise to hire
8. denies desires
9. high church spire
10. finding Ms. Myer

SENTENCES /aɪ̆/ and /aɪ̆ɚ/

1. The temperature climbed higher and higher.

2. The children called, "Liar, liar pants on fire!"

3. Does the party require certain attire, Ms. Meyer?

4. The entire chain of events conspired against him.

5. I admire people who can change their own flat tires.

NEUTRAL AMERICAN TEXT /aɪ̆ɚ/ or /aɪ̆ ɚ/ (**fire**). *Mark the following and speak out loud.*

But most miserable
aɪ̆ɚ
Is the de<u>sire</u> that's glorious.

(Cymbeline: I, vi, 7)

I have within mine eye all my desires.

(Middleton & Rowley: The Changeling)

Ha, majesty! How high thy glory tow'rs
When the rich blood of kings is set on fire!

(King John: II i, 350)

Belike he means,
Back'd by the power of Warwick, that false peer,
To aspire unto the crown and reign as king.

(3 Henry VI: I, i, 51)

Why should a man, whose blood is warm within,
Sit like his grandsire cut in alabaster?

(The Merchant of Venice: I, i, 83)

It was your duty to bear with humility the cross which a Higher
Power had, in its wisdom, laid upon you.

(Ibsen: Ghosts)

DE FLORES. I'll set some part a-fire
    Of Diaphanta's chamber.
BEATRICE. How? Fire, sir?
    That may endanger the whole house.
DE FLORES. You talk of danger when your fame's on fire.

(Middleton & Rowley: The Changeling)

/ aŭɚ / (power)

Form the triphthong /aŭɚ/ (power) by seamlessly blending the /aŭ/ (now) diphthong with the very short mid-vowel /ɚ/ (er) as one sound. During the blend, the lips unround as the tongue tip raises from its position resting down behind the lower teeth, and points toward the hard palate for the 'r' coloring required in Neutral American.

Rhythmically, this sound can also be blended as a diphthong followed immediately by the unstressed vowel /ɚ/ (er), which would be represented as /aŭ ɚ/ instead of /aŭɚ/. In any case, the first element is stressed, while the second and third elements are unstressed.

AUDIO 34▶ /aŭɚ/ or /aŭ ɚ/ (power)

aŭɚ
One writ with me in sour misfortune's book!
(Romeo and Juliet: V, iii, 82)

aŭɚ
I never can see him but I am heart-burn'd an hour after.
(Much Ado About Nothing: II i, 3)

aŭɚ   aŭɚ
That same cowardly, giant-like ox-beef hath devour'd many a
aŭ
gentleman of your house.
(A Midsummer Night's Dream: III, i, 192)

WORDS /aŭɚ/ or /aŭ ɚ/ (power)

Initial	Medial	Final
ʔ our	soured	sour
ʔ ours	powerful	scour
ʔ hour	glowered	cower
ʔ hours	flowering	devour
ʔ hourly	deflowered	shower

SOUND CHECK #1: Do not over-round or over-energize the l[...] moving between the /aŏ/ and /ə/, or a distinct /w/ sound will be in[...] Speak the practice words on the previous page again, with this in mind.

PHRASES /aŏə/ or /aŏ ə/ (power)

1.	cowers for hours	4.	ours soured
2.	powerful scouring	5.	flowers in towers
3.	showers on flowers	6.	glowering (brooding) look

SENTENCES /aŏə/ or /aŏ ə/ (power)

1. Why do you look so sour?

2. They called every hour on the hour.

3. What a powerful scouring detergent.

4. The cowering hound devoured doggie treats.

5. We scoured the woods looking for wildflowers.

NEUTRAL AMERICAN TEXT /aŏə/ or /aŏ ə/ (power). *Mark the following and speak out loud.*

aŏə
The heavens do low'r upon you for some ill.

(Romeo and Juliet: IV, v, 94)

ALIBIUS. What hour is't, Lollio?
LOLLIO. Towards belly-hour sir.
ALIBIUS. Dinner time?

(Middleton & Rowley: The Changeling)

Larded all with sweet flowers,
Which bewept to the ground did not go
With true-love showers.

(Hamlet: IV, v, 38)

Within the infant rind of this weak flower
Poison hath residence and medicine power.

(Romeo and Juliet: II, iii, 23)

CONSONANTS

WARM-UPS

Speak the speech, I pray you, as I pronounc'd it to you, trippingly on the tongue, but if you mouth it, as many of our players do, I had as lief the town-crier spoke my lines.

(Hamlet: III, ii, 1)

Tip of the Tongue
/ n / / d / / t / / l /

Four consonants: /t, d, n, l/ require that the tip of the tongue make contact with the upper gum ridge, just *behind* the upper front teeth, during articulation. The tongue blade should not be involved, and the tongue tip should have no contact with the upper front teeth.

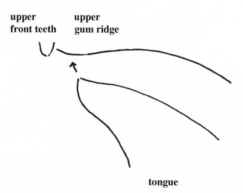

upper front teeth   upper gum ridge

tongue

There is a strong tendency for actors to speak with unnecessary tension in the jaw, throat, and tongue, especially during moments of high emotion, in order to compensate for a weak tongue tip or improper placement. The following warm-ups will help develop strength and precision of contact.

WARM-UP 1

Look in a mirror. Relax your lower jaw open with the body of the tongue relaxed and flat and the tongue tip gently touching the back of the *bottom* teeth. This is both the 'start' and 'finish' position. Breathe.

Touch the upper gum ridge directly behind your upper front teeth with your fingertip, feeling the bumpy surface of the gum ridge, also known as the alveolar ridge. This is the 'target'.

(a)   Begin in the 'start' position, looking in a mirror. Breathe in. Lift the tongue tip up to touch the 'target'. Breathe out, releasing the tongue back down to rest in the 'finish' position. Repeat 3X.

(b)   Breathe in. Touch the tongue tip up to the 'target', sound '**n**', push-off on 'aahhh', and release the tongue back to 'finish'. The 'word' spoken is 'naaaaah' or **/na/**. Repeat on: '**d**aaaaah', 't**aaaaah**', '**l**aaaaah', **/da, ta, la/** in IPA.

TARGET PRACTICE

(a)   Speak the 'words' in lines 1-5 below in the same manner, observing in a mirror. The tongue should be the active articulator, not the jaw, which remains relaxed. If you begin to feel tense, take a moment to massage your face, jaw, and neck. Work slowly, breathing between each word.

				IPA
nah	**d**ah	tah	lah	/nɑ, dɑ, tɑ, lɑ/
nuh	**d**uh	tuh	luh	/nʌ, dʌ, tʌ, lʌ/
nae	**d**ae	tae	lae	/næ, dæ, tæ, læ/
nie	die	tie	lie	/naɪ̆, daɪ̆, taɪ̆, laɪ̆/
nay	**d**ay	tay	lay	/neɪ̆, deɪ̆, teɪ̆, leɪ̆/

(b)   Repeat, without looking in the mirror, trying to duplicate the feel and placement of the tongue tip on the start/target/finish positions.

(c)   Pinch the tongue tip lightly between each phrase that follows in order to increase tip of the tongue awareness.

		IPA
breathe	**n**ah **d**ah	/nɑ, dɑ/
breathe	**n**ah **d**ah tah	/nɑ, dɑ, tɑ/
breathe	**n**ah **d**ah tah lah	/nɑ, dɑ, tɑ, lɑ/

breathe	nuh duh	/nʌ, dʌ/
breathe	nuh duh tuh	/nʌ, dʌ, tʌ/
breathe	nuh duh tuh luh	/nʌ, dʌ, tʌ, lʌ/
breathe	nie die	/naĭ, daĭ/
breathe	nie die tie	/naĭ, daĭ, taĭ/
breathe	nie die tie lie	/naĭ, daĭ, taĭ, laĭ/

(d)   Tap the tongue tip on the 'target' three times, before fully releasing the tongue tip back down to the 'finish' position on the following.

breathe	t, t, t, tah	/tʰ, tʰ, tʰ, tʰɑ/
breathe	t, t, t, tuh	/tʰ, tʰ, tʰ, tʰʌ/
breathe	t, t, t, tae	/tʰ, tʰ, tʰ, tʰæ/
breathe	t, t, t, tie	/tʰ, tʰ, tʰ, tʰaĭ/
breathe	t, t, t, tay	/tʰ, tʰ, tʰ, tʰeĭ/

(e)   Repeat the previous exercise substituting /d/ for /t/.

WORDS tip of the tongue placement. The following words begin and end with the tip of the tongue consonants /n, d, t, l/. Speak these words with, then without, the aid of a mirror. Remember to breathe, keep the jaw relaxed, and stop to massage the jaw if you begin to tense. If pinching the tongue helps you to focus attention onto the tongue tip, then add that also.

none	dine	ton	nod	dean	dull	led
Tate	done	dad	den	Ned	net	lend
tied	teen	dud	dead	teed	deed	lied
Dan	gnat	Tad	tan	ten	let	tend
diet	dial	dale	lad	dill	tail	lean

(f)   Consult a dictionary for practice words with initial /n, d, t, l/.

AUDIO 35▶ /n, d, t, l/ **tip of tongue placement**

And let us **not** be **dainty** of leave-**taking**.

(Macbeth: II, iii, 144)

Your wit's too hot, it speeds too fast, 'twill tire.

(Love's Labor's Lost: II, i, 119)

So full of dismal terror was the time.

(Richard III: I, iv, 7)

PHRASES tip of the tongue placement. Notice unstressed /d/ between two vowels tends to be lighter, as in the word 'dedicated' in phrase three.

1.	dull lead weight	11.	identifies intent
2.	tender teenagers	12.	delicate day today
3.	dedicated to dad	13.	deleted a done deal
4.	time to talk today	14.	topsy-turvy tonight
5.	tinted tomato red	15.	tend to defend Tom
6.	loved real gold	16.	toiled for oil
7.	filled ten pools	17.	loaded with pulp
8.	gulped cold milk	18.	held less holdings
9.	boiled and broiled	19.	milled around sulking
10.	told it's too moldy	20.	hulky, bulky sculpture

SENTENCES tip of the tongue placement

1. Tackle it today, Teddy.

2. Take Tina to tennis, Tad.

3. Don't talk until Act Two ends.

4. Terry decided to go to town Tuesday.

5. You can take out a tail light tailgating.

6. Did Derrick treat Dad to dinner downtown?

7. You can count on Daniel to do a good deed.

8. Day-to-day work has delicate Donna dead tired.

9. Dana delighted in cooking delicious tandoori at night.

10. Our director decided to delete a scene during rehearsal.

EXERCISE Speak the following sound combinations *slowly* first, to establish accuracy, then speak more quickly. Remember, the tongue tip contacts the gum ridge on 't', 'd', 'n', 'l'.

			IPA
Breathe	puh, tuh, kuh	*(3X fast!)*	/pʌ tʌ kʌ/
Breathe	buh, duh, guh	*(3X fast!)*	/bʌ dʌ gʌ/
Breathe	buh, nuh, guh	*(3X fast!)*	/bʌ nʌ gʌ/
Breathe	buh, luh, guh	*(3X fast!)*	/bʌ lʌ gʌ/

EXERCISE

Step 1. Stand in front of a mirror. Place the tip of your tongue down behind your lower front teeth, and drop your lower jaw open so there is at least ½ inch of space between your lips. Remember to breathe.

Step 2. Protrude your lips slightly forward. Place your index fingers vertically at the corners of your lips. Slide your fingers toward the tips of your protruding lips, catching the tips of your lips between your fingers and pulling them slightly out from your teeth.

There should be enough space to breathe easily through your mouth, and to slide the tongue out between the corner of your mouth and fingers. If not, begin again.

Step 3. Step away from the mirror and look back to your book, page 211. Read sentences 1-10 again (yes, with your lips held 'out of commission' between your fingers) emphasizing the tip of the tongue consonants and trying to be clearly understood.

Continue reading even though sounds that require lip involvement or rounding will be awkward; this exercise is not for them. Remember to breathe through your mouth whenever you need to and breathe between each sentence.

Step 4. Now, release your fingers and speak the sentences again. Hopefully, you will notice an increased clarity, dexterity, and ease on the tip of the tongue consonants.

This exercise is useful in auditioning emergencies: to wake up the tip of the tongue sounds before last minute auditions, or to supplement a warm-up done earlier on in the day.

ADDITIONAL PRACTICE *Try the previous exercise on the following lines, or on a memorized selection of text, a monologue, or a nursery rhyme.*

I do see
Danger and disobedience in thine eye.

(1 Henry IV: I, iii, 15)

All's cheerless, dark, and deadly.
Your eldest daughters have foredone themselves,
And desperately are dead.

(King Lear: V, iii, 291)

EXERCISE Speak the following. Stronger/longer utterances are indicated by the use of capital letters. Remember to breathe!

LAH lah lah—LAH lah lah—LAH lah lah—LAH   breathe
LAH lay lee LIE low loo,
LAH lay lee LIE low loo,
LAH lay lee LIE low loo loo.   breathe

TAH tah tah—TAH tah tah—TAH tah tah—TAH   breathe
TAH tay tee TIE toe too,
TAH tay tee TIE toe too,
TAH tay tee TIE toe too too.   breathe, etc.

DAH dah dah—DAH dah dah—DAH dah dah—DAH
DAH day dee DIE doe doo,
DAH day dee DIE doe doo,
DAH day dee DIE doe doo doo.

NAH nah nah—NAH nah nah—NAH nah nah—NAH
NAH nay nee NIE no noo,
NAH nay nee NIE no noo,
NAH nay nee NIE no noo noo.

PAH pah pah—PAH pah pah—PAH pah pah—PAH
PAH pay pee PIE po poo,
PAH pay pee PIE po poo,
PAH pay pee PIE po poo poo.

BAH bah bah—BAH bah bah—BAH bah bah—BAH
BAH bay bee BIE bo boo,
BAH bay bee BIE bo boo,
BAH bay bee BIE bo boo boo.

MAH mah mah—MAH mah mah—MAH mah mah—MAH
MAH may mee MIE mo moo,
MAH may mee MIE mo moo,
MAH may mee MIE mo moo moo.

also:

     KAH kah kah—KAH kah kah—KAH kah kah—KAH (etc.)

     GAH gah gah—GAH gah gah—GAH gah gah—GAH (etc.)

     NGAH ngah ngah—NGAH ngah ngah—NGAH ngah ngah—NGAH (etc.)

and consonant combinations:
     SPAH—SKAH—SLAH—STAH—STRAH (etc.)

TONGUE TWISTERS

Speak the following slowly for accuracy, then three times *FAST!*

/ w l j /   Will you William?

/ l /   He is literally literary.

/ r l /   Red leather, yellow leather.

/ d j /   Did you, would you, could you?

/ s n l /   Cinnamon, aluminum, linoleum.

/ d /   Don't you dare to do damaging deeds.

/ t /   A tidy tiger tied a tie tighter to tidy her tiny tail.

/ t d n l /   What a to-do to die today at a minute or two to two;
               A thing distinctly hard to say but harder still to do.
               For they'll beat a tattoo at twenty-to-two
               A ra-ta-ta-ta-ta-ta-ta-ta-too
               [A ra-da-da-da-da-da-da-da-da-doo]   [bracketed text added
               [A ra-na-na-na-na-na-na-na-noo]   for warm-up]
               [A ra-la-la-la-la-la-la-la-loo]
               And the dragon will come when he hears the drum
               At a minute or two to two today,
               At a minute or two to two.

                                                       (Anonymous)

/ t /   Tommy and Tina were tattooed in total, but Tanny was only tattooed on
         her toe; so Tommy told Tina where Tanny was tattooed, but Tina said
         Tanny's tattoo wouldn't show.

/ t ʃ / Charlie is choosy when checking his cheeses, and cheese is a challenge
         when Charlie arrives. But Charlie is charming and chooses a cheddar,
         then chills it and chips it and chops in some chives.

/ t θ / Tom threw Terrence three thumbtacks. Three thumbtacks were thrown
         to Terrence by Tom. Why did Tom throw Terrence three thumbtacks?

/ s θ / Theophilus Thistle, the successful thistle-sifter, in sifting a sieve full of
         unsifted thistles, thrust three thousand thistles through the thick of his
         thumb. See that thou, in sifting a sieve full of unsifted thistles, thrust
         not three thousand thistles through the thick of thy thumb. Success to
         the successful thistle-sifter!

TONGUE TWISTERS[1]

/ t b /   Toy boat.

/ j n /   Unique New York.

/ ð θ /   That thick thatched roof.

/ r l /   Upper roller, lower roller.

/ n l /   Eleven benevolent elephants.

/ ð θ /   They thanked them thoroughly.

/ r ʃ /   Rush the washing, Russell Rusk.

/ ð l t /   The lips, the teeth, the tip of the tongue—
               The tip of the tongue, the lips, the teeth.

MULTIPLE   To sit in solemn silence in a dull, dark dock,
               In a pestilential prison, with a life-long lock,
               Awaiting the sensation of a short, sharp shock,
               From a cheap and chippy chopper on a big black block!
               A dull, dark dock,
               A life-long lock,
               A short, sharp shock,
               A big black block!
               To sit in solemn silence
               In a pestilential prison,
               And awaiting the sensation
               From a cheap and chippy chopper on a big black block!
                                   (W.S. Gilbert: The Mikado)

/ p /   Peter Piper picked a peck of pickled peppers, a peck of pickled peppers did Peter Piper pick. If Peter Piper picked a peck of pickled peppers, where is the peck of pickled peppers that Peter Piper picked?

/ ʃ s /   Sheila is selling her shop by the seashore, for shops by the seashore are so sure to lose. She's not so sure just what she should be selling; should Sheila sell shell fish or should she sell shoes?

/ w tʃ / How much wood would a woodchuck chuck if a woodchuck could chuck wood, Chuck?

---

[1] See Ken Parkin's *Anthology of British Tongue Twisters*: New York: Samuel French, 1969, *Mother Goose*, and the works of *Dr. Seuss* for additional fun, challenging material.

WARM-UP 2

Same Consonant Blends

The following is covered in each individual consonant chapter. Actors may choose not to incorporate well-articulated same consonant blends for all characters, but practicing provides a good warm-up, regardless.

When the same consonant sound ends a word and also begins the next word, initiate the second word with a slight rhythmic pulse of energy while maintaining the contact of the articulators.

CONSONANTS

	Voiceless		Voiced
/t‚t/	hurt‚ toes	/dd/	bad day
	felt‚ terror		dared dad
	not‚ timely		hid dough
	that‚ teenager		dead drunk
/p‚p/	lap‚ pool	/bb/	rob banks
	help‚ people		job baking
	shop‚ patiently		Rob Benson
	ship‚ pineapples		lob basketballs
/k‚k/	black‚ cape	/gg/	beg girls
	pick‚ cabbage		hug Gary
	walk‚ carefully		big guest
	sack‚ crumpled		bag groceries
/ff/	stiff foam	/vv/	love variety
	roof falling		leave vacant
	leaf fluttered		have visitors
	half famished		revive Victor
/θθ/	fifth thief	/ðð/	mouth that
	bath Thursday		breathe this
	uncouth theory		soothe them
	mammoth theatre		bathe themselves

Guidelines

Connecting Stop-Plosives with Other Sounds

Because they contain two rhythmic elements, a 'stop' and an 'explosion' or release, there are special considerations when speaking and connecting these six stop-plosives to other sounds, especially for well-pronounced characters and/or classical text.

1. When stop-plosives are followed immediately by a pause or silence, either within, or at the end of a sentence, there are two possible options for contemporary speech:

   (a) the final plosive is not released, and the 'stop' element ends the word. This is common in casual speech.

   (b) the 'stop' element is quickly released and finishes the word or phrase. This is slightly more clear and well-spoken, and should be used in classical texts.

   Try the following examples below, both ways.

   > That's i**t**. No goo**d**. Mess u**p**.

   Phonetic markings are used in IPA to notate whether the breath is released (aspirated) or not released (unaspirated) on voiceless plosives. The same principle of release applies to the voiced plosives, though there are no special IPA markings used for notation. The following words are marked with phonetic symbols for demonstration.

   > Aspirating the voiceless plosive: See that^h
   >
   > Not aspirating the voiceless plosive: See that$_|$

2. When followed immediately by a vowel or diphthong sound, the 'plosive' element releases into the sound that follows:

   > Step^h in. Paint^h it. Pick^h actors.
   >
   > Dub Ann. Brad is. Drag on.

222

3.   When followed immediately by another consonant sound, a clear 'stop' is required, which should be rhythmically noticeable. The plosive is not released before beginning the next consonant sound.

Stop₁ yelling.	Don't₁ fly.	Pick₁ Sue.
Bob said.	Pad those.	Tag this.

SUMMARY of GUIDELINES

Well-Pronounced Neutral American:

(a) make a clear stop then release the plosive before a pause, silence, vowel or diphthong

(b) make a clear stop, but do not release the plosive before a consonant

Voiceless stop-plosives before *Read across.*

a pause	a vowel or diphthong	another consonant
pʰ tʰ kʰ	pʰ tʰ kʰ	p₁ t₁ k₁
grip	grip it	grip lock
flop	flop over	flop down
sleep	sleep in	sleep well
hot	hot evening	hot date
pack	pack earrings	pack shoes
wait	wait a while	wait there
great	great afternoon	great meal

Voiced stop-plosives before *Read across.*

a pause	a vowel or diphthong	another consonant
dig	dig up	dig there
Bob	Bob ate	Bob left
big	big elephant	big mess
hide	hide outside	hide carefully
grab	grab apples	grab bananas
had	had everything	had nothing
child	child eating	child screaming

Additional practice exercises and sound checks follow.

> **SOUND CHECK #1a: voiceless /tʰ, pʰ, kʰ/ before pause or silence.** Release the final plosive when playing well-pronounced characters or speaking more formal, poetic, or classical text. It can be useful to notate text with /ʰ/ as shown.

AUDIO 36 A ▶ voiceless /tʰ, pʰ, kʰ/ before a pause or silence

They have a plentiful lack of witʰ.

(Hamlet: II, ii, 199)

I shall drop this very minuteʰ... Ah, I shall dropʰ.

(Chekhov: The Cherry Orchard)

Malcolm, awakeʰ!

(Macbeth: II, iii, 75)

PHRASES /tʰ, pʰ, kʰ/ before a pause or silence

1.	just a bitʰ	6.	a big slipʰ
2.	heard a popʰ	7.	what a fitʰ
3.	a little packʰ	8.	not shippedʰ
4.	looking for Jackʰ	9.	needs to pickʰ
5.	searched for a hatʰ	10.	puts butter on itʰ

Remember: in Neutral American Speech, when 't' is spoken in an unstressed syllable between two vowel sounds, it is pronounced as a very light 'd', as in **but**ter (number 10, above). This is represented phonetically by a little *carat* under the symbol: /t̬/. Medial 't' remains /t/ in a stressed syllable between two vowel sounds, as in a **tt**ached and a **tt**ainted.

> *My father was a'**tt**ached, not a'**tt**ainted,*
> *Condemn'd to die for treason, but no traitor.*
>
> (1 Henry VI: II, iv, 96)

When 'ed' is added to the end of a verb (sometimes abbreviated **'d** in classic texts, as in **dispatch'd**), the 'ed' ending is pronounced as /t/ if the sound directly preceding the 'ed' is a voiceless consonant sound, as in the following:

/ftʰ/	/ʃtʰ/	/t̩ʃtʰ/	/stʰ/
ruffed	dished	pitched	iced
doffed	cashed	coached	raced
staffed	washed	marched	passed
briefed	refreshed	thatched	rejoiced

/k̩tʰ/	/sk̩tʰ/	/p̩tʰ/	/sp̩tʰ/
licked	asked	dipped	lisped
racked	risked	rapped	rasped
packed	basked	cupped	clasped
clucked	husked	shopped	grasped

t̩ʃtʰ
A bloody deed, and desperately dispatch'd!

(Richard III: I, iv, 271)

SENTENCES voiceless /tʰ, pʰ, kʰ/ before a pause or silence

1. Take your pick.

2. May I have a sip?

3. They were shocked.

4. Will you please give that back?

5. I checked; they did what you asked.

6. The music has stopped; should we clap?

7. It's fantastic; she got the part she wished!

8. It slipped and was chipped when shipped.

9. You need a vocal warm up; that note is flat.

10. The audience was in tears at the end of the first act.

SOUND CHECK #1b: Voiced /d, b, g/ are released before a pause or silence. When releasing final voiced plosives, a short /ɪ/ (w<u>i</u>ll) vowel sound may be heard as part of the voiced release. Do not allow the /ə/ (<u>uh</u>) sound, known as an 'off-glide'. Voiced endings before a pause or silence are marked with a double underline in the audio selections and practice phrases that follow.

AUDIO 36 B▶ voiced /d, b, g/ before a pause or silence

O, thou art decei<u>v'd</u>.

(Romeo and Juliet: II, iv, 97)

It boots not to resist both wind and ti<u>de</u>.

(3 Henry VI: IV, iii, 59)

O, well be<u>gg'd</u>!

(Coriolanus: I, ix, 87)

When 'ed' is added to the end of a verb, **/d/** is spoken, unless the sound previous to the 'ed' is a voiceless consonant.

/bd/	**/gd/**	**/ld/**	**/md/**
ribbed	tugged	filed	filmed
fibbed	pegged	doled	steamed
robbed	bragged	felled	schemed
clubbed	mugged	mauled	thumbed

/nd/	**/ðd/**	**/vd/**	**/zd/**
fanned	writhed	saved	raised
chained	soothed	halved	buzzed
resigned	breathed	grieved	amazed
shunned	smoothed	resolved	quizzed

/ʒd/	**/dʒd/**	**vowel/diph/triphthong + /d/**	
garaged	lodged	faired	fired
barraged	fudged	purred	toured
massaged	engaged	cheered	poured
camouflaged	emerged	mothered	cowered

There is another element to this guideline. When 'ed' is added to the end of a verb that ends in 'd' or 't', the 'ed' ending becomes a separate syllable, as in: "They pain<u>ted</u> the wall but the color fa<u>ded</u>." In this case, voiced **/ɪ/** is the sound that comes before the final 'd', so the ending remains voiced **/d/**.

PHRASES voiced /d, b, g/ before a pause or silence

1.	naughty chi<u>ld</u>	6.	hurt by the co<u>ld</u>
2.	politely wor<u>ded</u>	7.	brazenly snu<u>bbed</u>
3.	defending Doug	8.	watching the ba<u>gs</u>
4.	incredibly relie<u>ved</u>	9.	beautifully inscri<u>bed</u>
5.	passing every gra<u>de</u>	10.	rightfully bequea<u>thed</u>

SENTENCES voiced /d, b, g/ before a pause or silence

1.   Hey, that's my cab!

2.   That's it; you're grounded.

3.   You are exceptionally rude.

4.   They should have been told.

5.   Is that your answer, a shrug?

6.   I've never seen such an unruly mob.

7.   Do you mean my document can't be found?

8.   When they were young, they were very wild.

9.   Stand up, turn around, and don't make a sound.

10.   Yesterday, you swore my contract was finalized!

See also SONNET 27 and SONNET 50 by William Shakespeare, pages 316 and 317, for additional practice text with voiced plosive endings.

SOUND CHECK #2: Stop-plosives are released before a vowel or diphthong sound. This is not generally a problem for native English speakers.

PHRASES stop-plosives followed by a vowel or diphthong:

1.	shipped^h it	6.	led on
2.	slipped^h up	7.	job over
3.	leapt^h over it	8.	bag open
4.	caught^h in the heat	9.	begged off
5.	packed^h everything	10.	required a break

SOUND CHECK #3: Stop-plosives are not released before another consonant sound. A clear stop is required, which should be rhythmically noticeable, before beginning the consonant sound of the word that follows the stop-plosive, below.

AUDIO 36 C▶ **final voiceless /t, p, k/, voiced /d, b, g/ before a consonant**

Rude, in sooth, in good sooth, very rude.

(Troilus and Cressida: III, i, 56)

Now in good time, here comes the Duke[1] of York.

(Richard III: III, i, 95)

If every trick were told that's dealt by night,

There are few here that would not blush outright.

(Tourneur: The Revenger's Tragedy)

PHRASES final voiceless /t, p, k,/ before another consonant

1.	what fun	6.	hot coffee
2.	might rain	7.	not finished
3.	pick fights	8.	stop shaking
4.	peanut butter	9.	back stabbing
5.	leap tall buildings	10.	help someone

PHRASES final voiced /d, b, g/ before another consonant

1.	made supper	6.	wild thing
2.	paid the price	7.	rag sullied
3.	big promotion	8.	compiled files
4.	prime rib restaurant	9.	good riddance
5.	had second thoughts	10.	grabbed something

SOUND CHECK #4: stop-plosives before the same stop-plosive. When the same stop-plosive sound ends a word and also begins the next word, the stop between the two may be held slightly longer than usual before continuing. In any case, there should be a noticeable stop before beginning the 2nd word.

ship **p**ens	curt **t**alk	think **k**indly
rob **b**anks	dad **d**id	bag **g**roceries

PHRASES voiceless /t, p, k,/ before the same stop-plosive

1.	hurt **t**oes	6.	lap **p**ool
2.	felt **t**error	7.	not **t**imely
3.	black **c**abbage	8.	that **t**eenager
4.	bought **t**abloids	9.	sack **c**rumpled
5.	hot **t**omato soup	10.	stopped **t**alking

---

[1] The title 'Duke' may also be pronounced /djuk/ with a liquid ju (you).

PHRASES voiced /d, b, g/ before the same stop-plosive. Be sure to make a clear stop on the first voiced plosive and begin the second with a new impulse of energy.

1.	big **g**uest	6.	beg **G**ary
2.	hi**d d**ough	7.	ba**d d**ope
3.	dea**d d**runk	8.	dare**d d**ad
4.	Ro**b B**enson	9.	jo**b b**aking
5.	date**d D**aniel	10.	fe**d d**emonstrators

God match me with a good dancer!

(Much Ado About Nothing: II, i, 107)

SOUND CHECK #5: /d/, /t/ before /j/ (you). Make a clear stop using the tongue tip to contact the upper gum ridge on final /d/ and /t/ when followed directly by a word beginning with /j/ (you). If the blade or front of the tongue is used, /dʒ/ will be spoken instead of /d/, and /t͡ʃ/ instead of /t/, resulting in: 'would jew' instead of 'would you', and 'get chure' instead of 'get your'.

---

woul**d** you	coul**d** you	di**d** you
pu**t** your	sa**t** your	le**t** your

SENTENCES /d/ and /t/ before /j/

1.	Di**d** you eat?	6.	Di**d** you know?
2.	Woul**d** you go?	7.	Be**t** your brother.
3.	Shoul**d** you ask?	8.	Di**d** your dad stay?
4.	Pu**t** your sox on.	9.	Le**t** your hair down.
5.	We me**t** your parents.	10.	Se**t** your things there.

MORE SENTENCES /d/ and /t/ before /j/

1. Did you get it?

2. Could you run lines?

3. Shouldn't you audition?

4. Didn't you like the play?

5. Did you do a vocal warm-up?

6.   Would your character do that?

7.   Couldn't you produce it yourself?

8.   Didn't your agent give you the sides?

9.   Could you change our rehearsal time?

10.   Did you let your hair grow for the part?

11.   Should you take the job for that money?

12.   Did your lawyer negotiate your contract?

13.   Would you mind if we put your check in the mail?

14.   Did you want to know who was in the audience tonight?

15.   Sorry, kid. We ate your snacks while you were on stage.

SOUND CHECK #6: /d, t/ before /θ, ð/. When speaking /d, t, n, l/ before a 'th', the tip of the tongue generally moves forward onto the teeth in anticipation of the 'th' position. This is represented phonetically by placing a little 'tooth' underneath the IPA symbol, which signifies dentalization: / n̪, d̪, t̪, l̪ /.

PHRASES /d̪/ and /t̪/ before 'th'

1.	fanned̪ the flames	6.	what̪ thinking
2.	planted̪ them here	7.	thought̪ that over
3.	not̪ the bad̪ things	8.	had̪ that for dinner
4.	extended̪ the width	9.	hated̪ the bad traffic
5.	brought̪ those to work	10.	acted̪ that out̪ Thursday

NEUTRAL AMERICAN TEXT stop-plosives. *Mark the following and speak out loud.*

voiceless plosives before a pause or silence:

Is this a trap[h]?

(Strindberg: The Father)

You lie in your throat!

(2 Henry IV: I, ii, 85)

A hit, a very palpable hit.

(Hamlet: V, ii, 281)

Don't do that! I hate when you do that.

(Strindberg: Miss Julie)

I for a Clarence weep, so doth not she;
These babes for Clarence weep, and so do I;
I for an Edward weep, so do not they.

(Richard III: II, ii, 83)

But each Saturday, he says with such conceit:
Again, this Friday, sister, I ate…meat!

(Rostand: Cyrano de Bergerac)

voiced plosives before a pause or silence:

I'll be reveng'd.

(Cymbeline: II, iii, 155)

What, you egg!

(Macbeth: IV, ii, 83)

A second time I kill my husband dead,
When second husband kisses me in bed.

(Hamlet: III, ii, 184)

He's dead, he's dead, he's dead!
We are undone, lady, we are undone!
Alack the day, he's gone, he's kill'd, he's dead!

(Romeo and Juliet: III, ii, 37)

You have never known how to endure any bond.

(Ibsen: Ghosts)

voiced/voiceless plosives before a vowel or diphthong:

Piteous predicament! Even so lies she,
Blubb'ring and weeping, weeping and blubb'ring.

(Romeo and Juliet: III, iii, 86)

Why brand they us
With base? with baseness? bastardy? base, base?

(King Lear: I, ii, 9)

KATHERINE. What is your crest? a coxcomb?
PETRUCHIO. A combless cock, so Kate will be my hen.
KATHERINE. No cock of mine, you crow too like a craven.
(The Taming of the Shrew: II, i, 225)

To die, to sleep—
To sleep, perchance to dream—ay, there's the rub,
For in that sleep of death what dreams may come,
When we have shuffled off this mortal coil,
Must give us pause.
(Hamlet: III, i, 63)

Believe me, sir, had I such venture forth,
The better part of my affections would
Be with my hopes abroad. I should be still
Plucking the grass to know where sits the wind,
Peering in maps for ports and piers and roads.
(The Merchant of Venice: I, i, 15)

DUKE. Hath he borne himself penitently in prison? How seems
he to be touch'd?
PROVOST. A man that apprehends death no more dreadfully but as
a drunken sleep, careless, reckless, and fearless of what's
past, present, or to come; insensible of mortality, and
desperately mortal.
(Measure for Measure: IV, ii, 140)

ANTONY. For Brutus' sake, I am beholding to you.
4 PLEBEIAN. What does he say of Brutus?
3 PLEBEIAN. He says, for Brutus' sake
He finds himself beholding to us all.
4 PLEBEIAN. 'Twere best he speak no harm of Brutus here!
(Julius Caesar: III, ii, 65)

/d/ and /t/ before /j/:

I won't allow it! I forbid you!
(Ibsen: A Doll's House)

Could you oblige me...with a loan of 240 rubles...?
(Chekhov: The Cherry Orchard)

Mend your speech a little,
Lest you may mar your fortunes.
(King Lear: I, i, 94)

CONTINUANTS

See Overview pages 13-17

Continuants hold their position through the duration of the sound, and thus are capable of 'lingering'. This elongation offers rhythmic contrast with the abruptness of the previous group, the stop-plosives.

Continuants have three sub-groups: Nasal, Lateral, and Fricative.

Nasal Continuants
/ m /　　/ n /　　/ ŋ /
(mom)　　(on)　　(sing)

These are the only three sounds in English that are released through the nose, not the mouth. All three are voiced and do not have voiceless partners.

/ m / (mom)

Form /m/ by closing the lips and directing sound through the nose.

AUDIO 37▶ /m/ (mom)

But how now, Sir John Hume?
Seal up your lips, and give no words but mum.

(2 Henry VI: I, ii, 88)

It is so delicious to lie and dream.

(Ibsen: The Master Builder)

And tell fair Hero I am Claudio,
And in her bosom I'll unclasp my heart.

(Much Ado About Nothing: I, i, 322)

PHRASES voiced /n/ endings

1.	very lean	6.	what fun
2.	downtown	7.	how serene
3.	missed train	8.	weighs a ton
4.	before dawn	9.	Mister Lennon
5.	new black van	10.	rehearsing a scene

SOUND CHECK #2 Rhythm Highlighter: syllabic /ŋ/. Eliminate the vowel sound in the last, unstressed syllable, allowing the /n/ sound to resonate in its place, as in the word 'wooden'. Syllabics are notated in IPA by a small line under the resonating consonant, which can be represented / ŋ̩ | m̩ /. Text is marked with the phonetic symbol throughout for demonstration purposes.

AUDIO 38 B▶ **syllabic /ŋ̩/**

He hath 'eaten̩ me out of house and home.

(2 Henry IV: II, i, 74)

Contempt, farewell, and 'maiden̩ pride, adieu!

(Much Ado about Nothing: III, i, 109)

The smallest worm will turn, being 'trodden̩ on.

(3 Henry VI: II, ii, 17)

The difference in rhythm and pitch between the stressed (first) and the unstressed (usually last) syllable is accentuated by the total absence of a vowel sound in the unstressed ending. This can be represented rhythmically as:

LONGshort   (*or*)   **TUM**tuh

WORDS syllabic /dŋ̩ / words ending in the spelling

den/don: 'ardent, 'bidden, 'broaden, 'burden, 'garden, 'gladden, 'golden, 'harden, 'hidden, 'maiden, 'olden, 'prudence, 'ridden, 'rodent, 'sadden, 'strident, 'student, 'sudden, 'widen, 'wooden, 'Gordon, 'pardon

dn't: 'couldn't, 'didn't, 'hadn't, 'shouldn't, 'wouldn't

EXERCISE for speaking syllabic /dņ/ (wooden)

1.   Speak the word 'wood'. Bring the tip of the tongue up to the gum ridge for the final 'd' and maintain that position. Do not release the final 'd' sound; feel the tip of the tongue making solid contact with the upper gum ridge.

2.   Speak the word 'wooden'. Maintain contact between the tip of the tongue and upper gum ridge throughout the entire second, unstressed syllable, eliminating the vowel sound and speaking it as if spelled 'dn'. The entire word is spoken as if spelled: 'woodn'.

Speak the following:

Would you know if this wood is wooden?

No, I wouldn't know if it's wooden.

Wouldn't it be nice if it were wooden!

Why this obsession with things wooden?

Well, wouldn't you like to know!

Tush, that's a 'wooden thing!

(1 Henry VI: V, iii, 89)

3.   Speak the word 'wouldn't'. Maintain contact of the tip of the tongue against the gum ridge throughout the 'dnt' ending. Release the 't' when the word is finished.

PHRASES syllabic /dņ/ (wooden)

1.	'didņ't drive	6.	ten 'students
2.	'couldņ't you	7.	they 'wouldņ't
3.	in the 'gardeņ	8.	'didņ't want to
4.	received a 'pardoņ	9.	good 'riddaņce
5.	'hadņ't thought of it	10.	'shouldņ't buy that

SENTENCES syllabic /dņ/ (wooden)

1.   Wouldn't Gordon enjoy playing that part!

2.   We couldn't imagine where they found the hidden treasure.

3. Didn't anyone tell you?

4. Couldn't I play both parts?

5. I shouldn't have answered my phone.

6. It would be better to meet later, wouldn't it?

7. Didn't you get your ticket at the student rate?

8. They couldn't have been nicer at the audition.

9. He couldn't wait to widen all the wooden floors.

10. I'm an ardent admirer and was saddened by his death.

11. Prudence felt gardening every weekend was a burden.

12. That was a strident warning; couldn't you tone it down?

13. Pardon me; did he suddenly say that laughing is forbidden?

14. In olden times, young maidens were forbidden many things.

15. I didn't anticipate all the hidden charges on my phone service.

Goldeṇs' Rodeṇts

Rodney and Gordoṇ Goldeṇ entered the rodeṇt control business after discovering their overly strideṇt voices were capable of rooting out rodeṇts from gardeṇs and under woodeṇ floors. Their parents hadṇ't foreseen this talent, but are happy to bid good riddaṇce to the burdeṇ of paying for college tuitioṇ.

WORDS syllabic /t̩ṇ/ words ending in the spelling

ten: 'batten, 'beaten, 'bitten, 'brighten, 'eaten, en'lighten, 'flatten, 'frighten, 'heighten, 'kitten, 'lighten, 'mitten, 'smitten, 'sweeten, 'tighten, 'wheaten, 'whiten, 'written

ton: 'button, 'cotton, 'Keaton, 'mutton, 'Newton

tant: 'blatant, com'batant, im'portant, 'mutant

The tip of the tongue contacts the gum ridge for unaspirated /t̩/, which is followed immediately (without moving the tongue tip) by voiced /ṇ/, which resonates and releases through the nose. The throat remains open throughout the entire word, including the syllabic ending, so no glottal is formed.

SENTENCES syllabic /t̩ n̩/ endings

1. She dislikes mutton.

2. He's originally from Manhattan.

3. Mr. Whitney dislikes impoliteness.

4. Brighten up! Don't be disheartened.

5. Did Richard Burton ever play Satan?

6. When flattened, the rotten eggs smelled.

7. It's important to sweeten Mrs. Keaton's tea.

8. I've forgotten; do they make cotton buttons?

9. Don't be frightened; show us what you've written.

10. I was bitten by that kitten, right through my mittens.

Something is rotten in the state of Denmark.

(Hamlet: I, iv, 90)

WORDS additional syllabic /n̩/

/fn̩/	fen, fin, fon	'deafen, 'muffin, 'griffon
/vn̩/	ven	'driven, e'leven, en'liven
/sn̩/	sen, son, cen	'loosen, 'mason, 'recent, 'decent
/zn̩/	sin, sen, son, zon	'cousin, 'chosen, 'reason
/ʃn̩/	tion, sion, ian	'action, 'passion, lo'gician
/ʒn̩/	sion, sian	de'rision, sub'mersion, 'Asian

SOUND CHECK #3: same consonant blends /n n/. When the same consonant sound ends one word and also begins the next, very well-pronounced characters can use a slight rhythmic pulse of breath and energy to connect them, while maintaining the shape and contact of the articulators.

1.	one name	6.	won nachos
2.	ten knives	7.	Maine nights
3.	seen kneeling	8.	lemon noodles
4.	even numbers	9.	nine neighbors
5.	eleven nations	10.	fine knowledge

PHRASES medial /ŋ/ (ng) alone

1.	winging it	6.	longed to belong
2.	slinging hash	7.	singing youngster
3.	clingy clothes	8.	catching gangsters
4.	stinging remarks	9.	ringed by strangers
5.	unstringing lights	10.	hanging up hangers

PHRASES medial /ŋg/ (ng/g) combinations

1.	bilingual class	6.	angry language
2.	mangled finger	7.	lingering anguish
3.	jingled triangles	8.	bungled strangling
4.	mingling singles	9.	longer and stronger
5.	hungry for Pringles	10.	distinguished English

PHRASES medial /ŋ/ /ŋg/ /ŋk/

1.	inky fingers	6.	single singer
2.	jingle jangle	7.	youngest uncle
3.	singing jingles	8.	stronger thinker
4.	thankful banker	9.	instinctive things
5.	meringue filling	10.	blinks when thinking

SENTENCES /ŋ/ /ŋg/ /ŋk/ various positions and combinations

1. The singer made that long song famous.

2. We're anxious to learn the English language.

3. Hank fell off the donkey and broke his ankle.

4. What's playing at Lincoln Center in the spring?

5. Think about bringing along something to drink.

6. That distinguished gentleman is from Hong Kong.

7. I'm ironing a few things before traveling to Long Island.

8. The lizard blinked, winked, and thrust out its long tongue.

9. Use the wooden hanger. It's stronger than the plastic hanger.

10. The swing hung from a long rope and banged into the house.

SOUND CHECK #2: voiced /ŋ/ endings. Maintain contact of the articulators and vocal fold vibration until the word and thought are finished. Otherwise, an off-glide or short /ə/ (uh) vowel sound may be added after the final /ŋ/.

See also pages 100-102 for 'ing' endings, and the poem on page 312.

1.	ding dong	6.	nothing doing
2.	strong gang	7.	earning a living
3.	beautiful ring	8.	developing a song
4.	charming king	9.	nothing remaining
5.	spring gardening	10.	bringing everything

NEUTRAL AMERICAN TEXT /ŋ/ (sing). *Mark the following and speak out loud.*

voiced /ŋ/ endings

You are too much mistaken in this king.

(Henry V: II, iv, 30)

How can the authorities tolerate such things!

(Ibsen: Ghosts)

The ears are senseless that should give us hearing.

(Hamlet: V, ii, 369)

If the Prince be too important, tell him there is measure
in every thing.

(Much Ado About Nothing: II, i, 70)

Whom should we match with Henry, being a king,
But Margaret, that is daughter to a king?

(1 Henry VI: V, v, 66)

Is whispering nothing?
Is leaning cheek to cheek? Is meeting noses?
Kissing with inside lip? ...
Is this nothing?
Why then the world and all that's in't is nothing,
The covering sky is nothing, Bohemia nothing,
My wife is nothing, nor nothing have these nothings,
If this be nothing.

(The The Winter's Tale: I, ii, 284)

/ŋ/ various positions

I have been feasting with mine enemy.

(Romeo and Juliet: II, iii, 49)

Ambassadors from Harry King of England.

(Henry V: II, iv, 65)

What's this but libelling against the Senate,
And blazoning our unjustice every where?

(Titus Andronicus: IV, iv, 17)

I kept a-hallowing and whooping in his ears, but all could not
wake him. I, seeing that, took him by the leg and never rested
pulling, till I had pulled me his leg quite off.

(Marlowe: Doctor Faustus)

I feel as though I had been born long, long ago; I trail my life
along like an endless train... And often I have not the slightest
desire to go on living.

(Chekhov: The Seagull)

A whoreson cold, sir, a cough, sir, which I caught with ringing
in the King's affairs upon his coronation-day, sir.

(2 Henry IV: III, ii, 181)

Some wine ho!
"And let me the canakin clink, clink;
And let me the canakin clink.
A soldier's a man;
O, man's life's but a span;
Why then let a soldier drink."

(Othello: II, iii, 68)

ROSENCRANTZ.
    My lord, you must tell us where the body is, and go with us
    to the King.
HAMLET.
    The body is with the King, but the King is not with the body.
    The King is a thing—
GUILDENSTERN.
    A thing, my lord?
HAMLET.
    Of nothing, bring me to him.

(Hamlet: IV, ii, 25)

Lateral Continuant

There is only one lateral continuant. This particular voiced sound has no voiceless partner, and is represented by the phonetic symbol:

/ l / (lily)

Form /l/ by gently touching the tip of the tongue to the gum ridge and allowing sound to release over the sides of the tongue and through the mouth. The tongue tip should not slide onto, or protrude between, the teeth. The sides of the tongue may be felt gently pressing against the insides of the upper molars.

AUDIO 40 A▶ /l/ (lily)

I love long life better than figs.
>   (Antony and Cleopatra: I, ii, 32)

There is not yet so ugly a fiend of hell
As thou shalt be, if thou didst kill this child.
>   (King John: IV, iii, 123)

You're a spoilt soft creature, Dunyasha.
>   (Chekhov: The Cherry Orchard)

WORDS /l/ (lily)

Initial	Medial	Final
leg	apply	tall
life	Paula	will
late	wilder	foul
lease	foolish	coal
lunch	spilling	smell

Note: Additional practice material on vowels and diphthongs before consonant /l/ is available in all of the vowel and diphthong sections.

NEUTRAL AMERICAN TEXT /l/ (<u>lily</u>). *Mark the following, including IPA notations on syllabic endings, if useful, and speak out loud.*

syllabic / |̯ /:

A pox of wrinkļes!

(Timon of Athens: IV, iii, 148)

Double, double, toil and trouble;
Fire burn, and cauldron bubble.

(Macbeth: IV, i, 10)

HAMLET.   Methinks it is like a weasel.
POLONIUS. It is back'd like a weasel.

(Hamlet: III, ii, 379)

Fair isle, that from the fairest of all flowers
     Thy gentlest of all gentle names dost take!
How many memories of what radiant hours
     At sight of thee and thine at once awake!

(Poe: To Zante)

RAGUENEAU. Have you met with trouble?
CYRANO.   No; no trouble.
LISE.   You're telling us a lie!
CYRANO.   Did my nose double?

(Rostand: Cyrano de Bergerac)

voiced /l/ in various positions and in consonant combinations:

Two househo<u>lds</u>, both a<u>l</u>ike in dignity.

(Romeo and Juliet: Prologue)

Whereat, with blade, with bloody blameful blade,
He bravely broach'd his boiling bloody breast.

(A Midsummer Night's Dream: V, i, 146)

Thou art a bile,
A plague-sore, or embossed carbuncle,
In my corrupted blood. But I'll not chide thee,
Let shame come when it will.

(King Lear: II, iv, 223)

A heavy summons lies like lead upon me.

(Macbeth: II, i, 6)

Banners yellow, glorious, golden,
  On its roof did float and flow,
(This—all this—was in the olden
  Time long ago,)
And every gentle air that dallied,
  In that sweet day,
Along the ramparts plumed and pallid,
  A winged odor went away.

(Poe: The Haunted Palace)

Such an exploit have I in hand, Ligarius,
Had you a healthful ear to hear of it.

(Julius Caesar: II, i, 318)

There fell a silvery-silken veil of light,
With quietude, and sultriness, and slumber,
Upon the upturn'd faces of a thousand
Roses that grew in an enchanted garden.

(Poe: To Helen)

Villainy, villainy, villainy!
I think upon't, I think—I smell't—O villainy!
I thought so then—I'll kill myself for grief—
O villainy! villainy!

(Othello: V, ii, 190)

My uncle's will in this respect is mine.
If he see aught in you that makes him like,
That any thing he sees, which moves his liking,
I can with ease translate it to my will;
Or if you will, to speak more properly,
I will enforce it eas'ly to my love.

(King John: II, i, 510)

To-morrow night look that thou lie alone,
Let not the nurse lie with thee in thy chamber.
Take thou this vial, being then in bed,
And this distilling liquor drink thou off,
When presently through all thy veins shall run
A cold and drowsy humor; for no pulse
Shall keep his native progress, but surcease;
No warmth, no breath shall testify thou livest.

(Romeo and Juliet: IV, i, 91)

Fricative Continuants

Releasing air between two articulators that are close enough together to cause a friction sound produces the fricatives **f** (leaf), **v** (leave), **θ** (bath), **ð** (bathe), **s** (bus), **z** (buzz), **ʃ** (rush), **ʒ** (rouge), and **h** (he).

/ f / (leaf)   / v / (leave)

Form **/f, v/** by resting the tip of the tongue down behind the lower front teeth, gently placing the bottom edge of the upper teeth on the lower lip, and releasing air (or air and sound) through the mouth between these two articulators.

AUDIO 41▶ **/f/ (leaf) and /v/ (leave)**

A fool, a fool! I met a fool i' th' forest.

(As You Like It: II, vii, 12)

Forgive me, Alsemero, all forgive:
'Tis time to die, when 'tis a shame to live.

(Middleton & Rowley: The Changeling)

Give me thy fist, thy fore-foot to me give.

(Henry V: II, i, 67)

WORDS /f/ (leaf) and /v/ (leave)

	Initial	Medial	Final
/f/	fee	prefer	leaf
	find	defiled	half
	form	refined	wife
	finish	roofing	strife
	fashion	stuffiest	cough

/v/	vow	travels	save
	very	starved	have
	vote	heaven	leave
	verse	hovering	nerve
	vixen	revealing	prove

SOUND CHECK #1: consonant combinations containing voiceless /f/. Be sure to include all of the sounds in the consonant combinations that follow.

/sf/	/fs/	/ftʰ/	/ftₗs/
sphere	briefs	craft	lifts
sphenoid	muffs	cuffed	lofts
sphincter	proofs	roughed	thefts

SENTENCES consonant /f/ and combinations

1. Draft Jeff.
2. They left no proof.
3. Be rough and tough.
4. Sift through the gifts.
5. She's bereft of beliefs.
6. The chiefs laughed.
7. Mr. Wolf triumphed.
8. That's the thief's stuff.
9. Leaf through the drafts.
10. Kids sniffed cream puffs.

SOUND CHECK #2: final consonant combinations containing voiced /v/[1]. Speak all of the sounds in the following combinations. Voice through the end of the last consonant without adding an off-glide, or short /ə/ (uh) vowel sound.

/lv/	/vz/	/vd/	/vlz/
delve	lives	loved	revels
solve	halves	moved	novels
valve	perceives	grieved	travels

PHRASES voiced /v/ endings

1. can't save
2. ten loaves
3. freed captives
4. vigorously loved
5. vacations dissolved
6. big graves
7. well loved
8. not behaved
9. badly received
10. worried executives

---

[1] 'Have' /hæv/ is usually pronounced /hæf/ before an infinitive: 'I have to see'.

PHRASES /θ, ð/ *vs.* /t, d/

1.	nothing doing	6.	hotter than that
2.	without telling	7.	throngs downtown
3.	two dry throats	8.	good whether today
4.	dandy birthday	9.	smattering of thunder
5.	dead Elizabethan	10.	determined to breathe

SOUND CHECK #2: consonant combinations. Include all of the consonant sounds in the following combinations. Remember, / n̪, d̪, t̪, l̪ / are usually dentalized when they occur directly before 'th'. *Read down the columns.*

/θs/	/l̪θ/	/d̪θ *and* t̪θ/	/ðd/	/ðz/
baths	health	width	teethed	bathes
births	wealth	eighth	breathed	loathes
heaths	stealth	breadth	mouthed	soothes

PHRASES consonant combinations

1.	tooth's root	6.	stealth sleuths
2.	Ruth's breath	7.	bathes another
3.	the earth's myths	8.	teething pythons
4.	the youth's wealth	9.	width and breadth
5.	healthy southerners	10.	Elizabeth breathed

SOUND CHECK #3: Compare /f/ with /θ/ *and* /v/ with /ð/. The flattened tip of the tongue should be placed against the underside of the upper teeth when speaking /θ or ð/, otherwise /f or v/ will be spoken instead. This is evident in Cockney pronunciation of 'think' as 'fink' and 'breathing' as 'breaving'.

PHRASES voiceless /f/ *vs.* /θ/

1.	fifth floor lifts	6.	finally thinking
2.	twelfth triumph	7.	breathless sphinx
3.	half their wealth	8.	spiffy Elizabethan
4.	left in the depths	9.	deciphers anthems
5.	engulfed by warmth	10.	monthly certificates

PHRASES voiced /v/ *vs.* /ð/

1.	nor<u>th</u>ern revels	6.	leveled altoge<u>th</u>er
2.	eleven hea<u>th</u>ens	7.	five others ba<u>th</u>ing
3.	smoo<u>th</u>ed graves	8.	disheveled clo<u>th</u>ing
4.	you<u>th</u>s disapprove	9.	relieved of wri<u>th</u>ing
5.	believed unwor<u>th</u>y	10.	grieving and soo<u>th</u>ing

SOUND CHECK #4: same consonant blends / θ θ / *and* / ð ð /. When the same consonant sound ends one word and also begins the next word, then very well-pronounced characters can use a slight rhythmic pulse of breath and energy to connect them, while maintaining the shape and contact of the articulators.

1.	fif**th th**ief	6.	mou**th th**at
2.	mou**th th**irsty	7.	brea**the th**is
3.	ba**th Th**ursday	8.	smoo**th th**em
4.	uncou**th th**eory	9.	wri**the th**ereafter
5.	mammo**th th**eatre	10.	ba**the th**emselves

NEUTRAL AMERICAN TEXT /θ/ (ba<u>th</u>) and /ð/ (ba<u>the</u>). *Mark the following and speak out loud.*

    θ   θ
Forsoo<u>th</u>, a great ari<u>th</u>metician.

(Othello: I, i, 19)

Our thunder from the south
Shall rain their drift of bullets on this town.

(King John: II, i, 411)

His health was never better worth than now.

(1 Henry IV: IV, i, 27)

He's awfully clever, and he plays the violin!

(Chekhov: Three Sisters)

Hast thou not spoke like thunder on my side?

(King John: III, i, 124)

A man so breathed, that certain he would fight.

(Love's Labours Lost: V, ii, 653)

Grim death, how foul and loathsome is thine image!

(The Taming of the Shrew: Ind. i. 35)

I do defy
The tongues of soothers, but a braver place
In my heart's love hath no man than yourself.

(1 Henry IV: IV, i, 6)

What shall I say to thee, Lord Scroop, thou cruel,
Ingrateful, savage, and inhuman creature?
Thou that didst bear the key of all my counsels,
That knew'st the very bottom of my soul,
That almost mightst have coin'd me into gold,
Wouldst thou have practic'd on me, for thy use?

(Henry V: II, ii, 94)

AUSTRIA.   O, that a man should speak those words to me!
BASTARD.   And hang a calve's-skin on those recreant limbs.
AUSTRIA.   Thou dar'st not say so, villain, for thy life.
BASTARD.   And hang a calve's-skin on those recreant limbs.
K. JOHN.   We like not this, thou dost forget thyself.

(King John: III, i, 130)

ZANCHE.   You remember your oaths?
FLAMINEO.   Lovers' oaths are like mariners' prayers, uttered
In extremity.

(Webster: The White Devil)

SAMUEL.   I will bite my thumb at them, which is disgrace to them
if they bear it.
ABRAHAM.   Do you bite your thumb at us, sir?
SAMUEL.   I do bite my thumb, sir.
ABRAHAM.   Do you bite your thumb at us, sir?

(Romeo and Juliet: I, i, 42)

Death, that hath suck'd the honey of thy breath,
Hath had no power yet upon thy beauty:
Thou art not conquer'd, beauty's ensign yet ·
Is crimson in thy lips and in thy cheeks,
And death's pale flag is not advanced there.
Tybalt, liest thou there in thy bloody sheet?
O, what more favor can I do to thee,
Than with that hand that cut thy youth in twain
To sunder his that was thine enemy?

(Romeo and Juliet: V, iii, 92)

Fricative Continuants

/ ʃ / (ru<u>sh</u>) / ʒ / (rou<u>ge</u>)

Form /ʃ/ and /ʒ/ by raising the blade of the tongue up toward the back of the gum ridge, anchoring the sides of the tongue against the insides of the upper molars, and releasing air over the tongue blade and through the mouth.

The tongue is pulled slightly further back in the mouth than for /s/ and /z/, and the blade is involved rather than the tip, which makes the groove of the tongue wider for /ʃ/ and /ʒ/. Lip rounding is unnecessary.

AUDIO 43▶ /ʃ/ (ru<u>sh</u>) and /ʒ/ (rou<u>ge</u>)

    ʃ   ʒ

Leave <u>sh</u>all you have to court her at your plea<u>s</u>ure.

(The Taming of the Shrew: I, i, 54)

                ʃ

He was not born to <u>sh</u>ame:

       ʃ   ʃ

Upon his brow <u>sh</u>ame is a<u>sh</u>am'd to sit.

(Romeo and Juliet: III, ii, 91)

                           ʃ

But why speak you in this strange halting fa<u>sh</u>ion?

     ʃ   ʃ

Has your wit grown <u>sh</u>ort of breath? or pa<u>ss</u>ion?

(Rostand: Cyrano de Bergerac)

WORDS /ʃ/ (ru<u>sh</u>) and /ʒ/ (rou<u>ge</u>)

	Initial	Medial	Final
/ʃ/	shun	special	dish
	shop	passion	bash
	shine	anxious	mesh
	sheep	wishing	relish
	shame	machine	marsh

	Initial.	**Medial**	**Final**
/ʒ/	*	usual	loge
	*	Asian	rouge
	*	lesion	garage
	*	vision	prestige
	*	measure	massage

PHRASES /ʃ/ and /ʒ/

1.	shiny beige shift	6.	unconscious wish
2.	precious freshness	7.	Russian vacations
3.	ensures succession	8.	treasured pleasures
4.	rushes to conclusions	9.	occasionally shaky
5.	spacious shoe shelves	10.	diminished seizures

SENTENCES /ʃ/ and /ʒ/

1. Shrill shrieks shocked the gendarmes.

2. Who's the most gracious shellfish chef?

3. We occasionally treasure hunt in Persia.

4. She envisions planting unusual rosebushes.

5. Sheila unleashed her vicious dog on Frazier.

6. Sharon expressed her displeasure in the garage.

7. The camouflaged espionage team remains cautious.

8. Gigi is on vacation, so her fashionable shoe shop is closed.

A little lip-rounding on these sounds is fine. But, many people use excessive lip-rounding to overcompensate for inaccurate alignment and coordination of the tongue and breath release on /ʃ/ and /ʒ/.

SOUND CHECK #1: same consonant blends / ʃ ʃ / and / ʒ ʒ /. When the same consonant sound ends one word and also begins the next word, very well-pronounced characters can use a slight rhythmic pulse of breath and energy to connect them, while maintaining the shape and contact of the articulators.

1.	dish shop	6.	flesh shook
2.	wish shyly	7.	wash shoes
3.	posh shawls	8.	harsh shouts
4.	push sharply	9.	massage Zsa Zsa
5.	fresh showers	10.	camouflage gendarmes

NEUTRAL AMERICAN TEXT /ʃ/ (ru<u>sh</u>), /ʒ/ (rou<u>ge</u>). *Mark the following and speak out loud.*

ʃ ʃ
<u>Sh</u>allow, <u>sh</u>allow.

(As You Like It: III, ii, 57)

Have leave and leisure to make love to her.

(The Taming of the Shrew: I, ii, 136)

Petruchio, shall I then come roundly to thee,
And wish thee to a shrewd ill-favor'd wife?

(The Taming of the Shrew: I, ii, 59)

You owe me no subscription. Then let fall
Your horrible pleasure.

(King Lear: III, ii, 18)

There's but three furies found in spacious hell,
But in a great man's breast three thousand dwell.

(Webster: The White Devil)

First, mighty liege, tell my your Highness' pleasure.

(Richard III: IV, iv, 447)

Urge neither charity nor shame to me.
Uncharitably with me have you dealt,
And shamefully my hopes, by you, are butcher'd.
My charity is outrage, life my shame,
And in that shame still live my sorrow's rage!

(Richard III: I, iii, 273)

GLO'STER. She should have stay'd in France, and starv'd in France,
   Before—
CARDINAL.   My Lord of Gloucester, now ye grow too hot:
   It was the pleasure of my lord the King.

(2 Henry VI: I, i, 136)

Fricative Continuant

/ h / (h**e**)

Form **/h/** by releasing air through the glottis, or space between the vocal folds, through a relaxed throat, and out the mouth.

AUDIO 44▶ /h/ (h**e**)

But **h**e! why, **h**e **h**ath a **h**orse better than the Neapolitan's.
(The Merchant of Venice: I, ii, 58)

I wonder at this **h**aste, that I must wed
Ere **h**e that should be **h**usband comes to woo.
(Romeo and Juliet: III, v, 118)

Hold, take my sword. There's **h**usbandry in **h**eaven.
(Macbeth: II, i, 4)

WORDS /h/ (h**e**)

Initial	Medial	Final
he	ahoy	*
how	yahoo	*
who	inherit	*
heave	behind	*
whore	inhabit	*

Several common words contain **/hju/** sounds including **h**uman, **h**umid, **h**umiliation, **h**umor, **h**uge. Do not drop the **/h/** from these words in Neutral American. There are also a few words with 'h' in the spelling that have no **/h/** in American pronunciation, for example: herb, heiress and honor.

PHRASES /h/ (h**e**)

1.	**h**appy **h**oliday	6.	**h**as **h**igh **h**opes
2.	**h**alf way **h**ome	7.	**h**and **h**eld **h**ammer
3.	**h**ardly **h**abitual	8.	**h**ypothermic Henry
4.	**wh**olly **h**elpless	9.	**h**ow **h**ot and **h**umid
5.	**h**ospitalized **h**ere	10.	**h**armonious and **h**oly

SENTENCES /h/ (h<u>e</u>)

1. Holly is happiest when rehearsing.

2. Henry is humorless when it's humid.

3. The humanitarian hails from Houston.

4. Hurry up. Hospitalize him for hypothermia.

5. Have you heard if the hurricane is headed here?

NEUTRAL AMERICAN TEXT /h/ (h<u>e</u>). *Mark the following and speak out loud.*

<u>He</u> comes to you so <u>h</u>elplessly, accusing <u>h</u>imself and confessing <u>h</u>is own weakness.

(Ibsen: Ghosts)

Because he hath a half-face like my father!
With half that face would he have all my land—
A half-fac'd groat five hundred pound a year!

(King John: I, i, 92)

Hast thou, according to thy oath and band,
Brought hither Henry Herford thy bold son,
Here to make good the boist'rous late appeal,
Which then our leisure would not let us hear?

(Richard II: I, i, 2)

Go, horse these traitors on your fiery backs,
And mount aloft with them as high as heaven;
Thence pitch them headlong to the lowest hell.

(Marlowe: Doctor Faustus)

SALISBURY. What other harm have I, good lady, done,
But spoke the harm that is by others done?
CONSTANCE. Which harm within itself so heinous is
As it makes harmful all that speak of it.

(King John: III, i, 38)

MARIA. Sir, I have not you by th' hand.
AGUECHEEK. Marry, but you shall have—and here's my hand.

(Twelfth Night: I, iii, 65)

PHRASES tip-of-the-tongue placement and awareness

1.	hat₁ stayed still	6.	lid still stuck
2.	made Stacy stay	7.	had stuff stuffed
3.	band still standing	8.	did sting Stanley
4.	hot₁ steaming steam	9.	bad stock statements
5.	debt₁ stays stationary	10.	bet₁ stagehand stayed

PHRASES tip-of-the-tongue placement and awareness

had zinc	hid zeal	need Zen	mad zap
bad zipper	need zing	feed zealots	sad Zane
dead zebra	did zigzag	spied zenith	paid zilch
ten seats	can see	mean zit	fun still
tan zebra	fan sitting	man says	non-stick
tin zipper	nine sides	mean sun	pin some
yell zinc!	he'll sell	file says	bill Sam
feel sorry	tell zealots	dull stuff	fill seats
till Sunday	deal zapped	mail Sandy	chill some

SOUND CHECK #2: side edges of the tongue—placement and awareness.
The sides of the tongue can press or anchor against the inner edges of the upper
teeth, offering stability when forming /s/ and /z/. This pressing can often be
felt more acutely when forming 'sh' /ʃ/ and 'ch' /t͡ʃ/. Therefore, the following
exercise compares /ʃ/ /t͡ʃ/ and /s/ words to help identify the pressing feeling.

Speak the first two words in the row below with an awareness of the
positioning and feeling of the side edges of the tongue. Try to maintain some
contact of the sides of the tongue with the inside of the upper teeth during the
initial /s/ of the third word in the row. The tongue may flatten and move
slightly forward as air shoots out over the tip on 's'. *Read across.*

/ʃ/	/t͡ʃ/	/s /		/ʃ/	/t͡ʃ/	/s/
shin	chin	sin		shine	china	sign
shill	chill	sill		ship	chip	sip
shy	chai	sigh		Shea	change	say
Shane	chain	sane		sheep	cheap	seep

SENTENCES side edges of the tongue placement and awareness

1.	Shine china signs.	6.	Shift Chuck's status.
2.	Shake cheap stilts.	7.	Shake chicken soup.
3.	She'll change seats.	8.	Shane, change seats.
4.	Ship chipped statues.	9.	Share Chan's sneaks.
5.	Shock Chuck on stage.	10.	Shun cheese Sunday.

SOUND CHECK #3: back of tongue placement and awareness. The back of the tongue should be raised toward the soft palate when forming **/s/** and **/z/**. When speaking **/g/** and **/k/**, the back of the tongue raises to touch the front of the soft palate. Therefore, back of tongue awareness when speaking **/g/** and **/k/** may help the speaker's awareness of back of tongue positioning on **/s/** and **/z/**.

Raise the back of the tongue to touch the soft palate on final **/g/** and **/k/** of the first word of the pair, below. Keep the back of the tongue raised toward the soft palate while positioning the tip for initial **/s/** that begins the second word of the pair. *Read down the columns.*

Column 1	Column 2	Column 3
pack₁ some	pick₁ some	big state
pack₁ steak	pick₁ Steve	big stake
pack₁ steel	pick₁ sage	big stain
pack₁ snakes	pick₁ season	big stein
pack₁ staples	pick₁ Simon	big snap
pack₁ samples	pick₁ singer	big sneak

SENTENCES back of the tongue placement and awareness

1.	Pick₁ Stan.	6.	Hug Stan.
2.	Pick₁ Stacey.	7.	Hug Stacey.
3.	Pick₁ Steven.	8.	Hug Steven.
4.	Pick₁ starlets.	9.	Hug starlets.
5.	Pick₁ somebody.	10.	Hug somebody.

SOUND CHECK #4: /s, z/ in combination with sounds that require lip rounding. Round only for the sounds that require it, and do not allow this rounding to draw the tongue tip forward onto the teeth on **/s/** and **/z/**.

	Initial	**Medial**	**Final**
/s/	sue	assume	juice
	soil	forcing	horse
	soap	assorted	sauce
	sawing	roasting	across
	soothe	resource	choice
/z/	zoo	frozen	rose
	zone	noises	doze
	zoom	pauses	pews
	zodiac	abused	poise
	zounds	choosing	views

PHRASES /s, z/ with rounded vowels

1.	Zorro's horses	6.	Zodiac zone
2.	soothing snoring	7.	zucchini soup
3.	roasted soy sauce	8.	owns used suits
4.	soaring forcefully	9.	confused closing
5.	Susan's sore voice	10.	zooms through zoos

WORD PAIRS unrounded/rounded vowels *Read across.*

see	sue	seep	soup	sit	soot
zebra	zoo	zip	zone	say	soy
sigh	saw	sick	soak	sire	sore

PHRASES /s, z/ with unrounded and rounded vowels

1.	sitting in soot	6.	soiled snails
2.	sawing outside	7.	so, so sea sick
3.	snoring sleeper	8.	soon to see him
4.	seen with Susan	9.	storks stay soaked
5.	saving soy sauce	10.	store forks at Stella's

Softly, silently, the scythe
Slithered through the thick sweet sward;
Seething, sweating, sad serfs writhe,
Slicing swaths so straight and broad.

(Anonymous)

SOUND CHECK #5: consonant combinations and clusters (three back-to-back consonants) beginning with /s/. Pronounce all of the sounds listed.
Note: /str/ instruction and practice appears on pages 297-299 with /r/.

/sf/	/sk^h/	/sl/	/sm/
sphinx	scold	sled	smug
sphere	skimp	slime	smile
sphincter	scamp	slope	smooth

/sn/	/sp^h/	/st^h/	/sw/
snuff	spat	stay	sway
snows	speed	stoke	sweat
snakes	spool	stoned	swoon

/sp،r/	/st،r/	/sk،r/	/sk،w/
sprain	street	scraps	squid
spring	strive	scrawl	squall
spruce	strokes	scream	squire

PHRASES consonant combinations with initial /s/

1. snaking streets
2. sneak previews
3. strategic squeeze
4. slanderous scandal
5. spoonful of sweets
6. smug speakers
7. six suave swindlers
8. inexplicable spying
9. scrambled switches
10. sleek smelly sneakers

PHRASES initial /st/ (aspirating the 't' depends on what comes after the 't')

1. steamy stairs
2. standing still
3. stainless steel
4. stepping stones
5. stimulating style
6. stiff stitching
7. still stigmatized
8. stammering stars
9. staying in steerage
10. starched stationary

PHRASES initial /sk/ (aspirating the 'k' depends on what comes after the 'k')

1. skipper's skiff
2. skates and skis
3. skillful sketches
4. skin-tight ski masks
5. squashed mosquitoes
6. skidding skiers
7. skinny skinflint
8. sketch skeletons
9. squarely miscast
10. skin care skeptic

PHRASES final /st/ (aspirating the 't' depends on what comes after the 't')

1.	best dressed	6.	held in trust
2.	worst colorist	7.	kindest finalist
3.	deceased ghost	8.	cheeriest contest
4.	lost in Budapest	9.	unsurpassed cast
5.	feminist journalist	10.	outclassed in the past

PHRASES final /sk/ (aspirating the 'k' depends on what comes after the 'k')

1.	risky to ask	6.	a flashy flask
2.	musk bisque	7.	statuesque desk
3.	grotesque mask	8.	masked asterisk
4.	flask in Basque	9.	tusk in a mosque
5.	burlesque at dusk	10.	picturesque kiosk

SOUND CHECK #6: consonant combinations and clusters ending with /s/.
Pronounce all of the sounds listed. Be careful in the following instances.

(a)   When a voiceless stop-plosive is followed directly by another consonant, a definite unaspirated 'stop' is required prior to the second consonant, notated in IPA: **/ k$_1$s   p$_1$s   t$_1$s /**.

(b)   When a voiceless stop-plosive is between two continuants in the same syllable, speak the first consonant, make the definite 'stop' of the second, followed by the last consonant sound, as in: **/ lp$_1$s   mp$_1$s   ft$_1$s   sk$_1$s   sp$_1$s   st$_1$s /**.

/fs/	/k$_1$s/	/p$_1$s/	/t$_1$s/
cuffs	fix	leaps	hats
beefs	packs	ships	fights
whiffs	hawks	soups	shoots

/lfs/	/lp$_1$s/	/mfs/	/mp$_1$s/
elf's	gulps	lymph's	lumps
gulfs	scalps	nymphs	skimps
wolfs	whelps	harrumphs	mumps

/ft$_1$s/	/sk$_1$s/	/sp$_1$s/	/st$_1$s/
lifts	asks	lisps	tests
tufts	husks	gasps	fasts
crafts	whisks	wasps	rusts

278

WORDS final /sk^h/ and /k$_i$s/ comparison *Read across.*

/sk^h/	/k$_i$s/	/sk^h/	/k$_i$s/
risk	Rick's	Fisk	fix
ask	ax	bask	backs
flask	flax	task	tacks
desk	decks	disk	Dick's
brisk	bricks	dusk	ducks

When speaking /sk$_i$t/ combinations, remember to make a definite 'stop' on the 'k' before continuing on to the 't'. Aspirating the final 't' or not depends on the sound that comes immediately after it.

SENTENCES final /sk/ and /sk$_i$t/ in the words 'ask' / 'asked'

1.	Ask about it.	6.	I asked you.
2.	Don't ask me.	7.	Ask him again.
3.	Ask Mr. Rusk.	8.	Ask me anything.
4.	Ask a question.	9.	What did you ask?
5.	Who asked you?	10.	I've asked you before.

PHRASES final /st$_i$s/ /sp$_i$s/ /sk$_i$s/ /lfs/ /lp$_i$s/ /mfs/ /mp$_i$s/ /ft$_i$s/

1.	past reque**sts**	6.	takes ri**sks**
2.	li**sps** the least	7.	worst pe**sts**
3.	cla**sps** his fi**sts**	8.	cla**sps** for ma**sks**
4.	he**lps** the ca**sts**	9.	thu**mps** on de**sks**
5.	ski**mps** on cra**fts**	10.	e**lf's** loud harru**mphs**

> *Amid__st__ the mi__sts__ and colde__st__ fro__sts__,*
> *With __stout__e__st__ wri__sts__ and loude__st__ boa__sts__,*
> *He thru__sts__ his fi__sts__ again__st__ the po__sts__,*
> *And __still__ insi__sts__ he sees the gho__sts__.*

(Anonymous)

SENTENCES final /st$_i$s/ /sp$_i$s/ /sk$_i$s/ /lfs/ /lp$_i$s/ /mfs/ /mp$_i$s/ /ft$_i$s/

1. Are egoists realists?

2. Pianists need strong wrists.

3. Will the essayists be missed?

4.   Chris resists chips and crisps.

5.   *The Duellists* was not to be missed.

6.   The book's antagonists slit their wrists.

7.   Wasps were seen eating crusts at dusk.

8.   Bicyclists, stay to the right of motorists.

9.   He asks that you finish your tasks, at last.

10.   The scientist insists the cysts pose no risks.

11.   The elephant thrusts, then adjusts his tusks.

12.   Violinists playing for the vocalists are pacifists.

13.   When pissed, the linguist lisps and twists his fists.

14.   Perhaps mystics think ghosts float over the coasts.

15.   The accompanists pressed their wrinkled costumes.

16.   When they flashed, the powder flasks were trashed.

17.   He hoists the posts to his chest, but it exhausts him.

18.   Priests were distressed by the results of the contests.

19.   Guests detest pests performing arabesques on desks.

20.   Journalists are at risk of losing their computer disks.

21.   The stout anthropologist was stuck amidst the stones.

22.   They gasped when the mask's clasps came unclasped.

23.   Statistics state stardom can elude even the best actors.

24.   When asked, beasts stop in their tracks, or so he attests.

25.   Little nymphs and elves gave the accompanists the mumps.

SOUND CHECK #7: same consonant blends /s s/. When the same consonant sound ends one word and also begins the next, very well-pronounced characters can use a slight rhythmic pulse of breath and energy to connect them, while maintaining the shape and contact of the articulators.

PHRASES same consonant blends /s s/

1.	hurts sales	6.	bus station
2.	loose scarf	7.	cents saved
3.	nice students	8.	peace sought
4.	niece singing	9.	this Saturday
5.	sauce spilling	10.	nurse sighing

PHRASES same consonant blends /st͵ st/

1.	best stage	6.	dust storm
2.	cast stranded	7.	must sting
3.	protest stories	8.	inquest started
4.	worst strategy	9.	decreased stench
5.	best stationary	10.	least stifling state

SOUND CHECK #8: /θ, s/ combinations. Feel the movement of the tip of the tongue from between the teeth on /θ/, up to point toward the gum ridge on /s/.

1.	bath Sunday	6.	both singing
2.	path seekers	7.	wealth secured
3.	Beth staying	8.	stealth security
4.	math solutions	9.	breath spraying
5.	growth stabilized	10.	mouth screaming

SOUND CHECK #9: plural, possessive, third-person /z/ endings. When an 's' is added to the end of a noun making it plural or possessive, or to the end of a third-person singular verb, the 's' is pronounced /z/ when the sound directly preceding it is voiced, as in: dogs, ribs, cows, Phil's, Brad's, Sue's, runs, plays.

/bz/	/dz/	/gz/	/lz/
curbs	lads	kegs	piles
babes	buds	bags	Bill's
Rob's	Jude's	Meg's	pencils

/mz/	/nz/	/vz/	/dʒɪz/
teams	fins	caves	cages
dimes	pines	leaves	ridges
Kim's	Ken's	Dave's	judge's

Since vowels, diphthongs and triphthongs are <u>voiced</u>:

bees	furs	laws	rows
eyes	brother's	Fay's	Roy's
fleas	Martha's	glues	dramas

PHRASES voiced /z/ endings

1.	Hazel's things	6.	Paul's pizzas
2.	bathes squirrels	7.	has ten tables
3.	loves bold films	8.	those zany cousins
4.	the wolves' howls	9.	thousands of grizzlies
5.	eggs with cheeses	10.	appetizing vegetables

SOUND CHECK #10: When a word ends in /s, z, t͡ʃ, or d͡ʒ/ and 'es' is added to make the word plural or possessive, a separate syllable ending in /ɪz/ is formed. For example: 'batch' becomes 'batches' and 'quiz' becomes 'quizzes'.

PHRASES voiced /ɪz/ endings

1.	urges marches	6.	Liz's curses
2.	races to places	7.	poses with roses
3.	Marge's revenges	8.	bunches of riches
4.	fizzes and whizzes	9.	presses and passes
5.	pitches and catches	10.	smudges on judges

Three little ghostesses,
Sitting on postesses,
Eating buttered toastesses,
Greasing their fistesses,
Up to their wristesses.
Oh, what beastesses
To make such feastesses!

(Mother Goose: Three Ghostesses)

See also THE TIDE RISES, THE TIDE FALLS by Henry Wadsworth Longfellow, page 318, for additional practice text with voiced /z/ endings.

SOUND CHECK #11: /ð, z/ combinations. Feel the tip of the tongue moving from the position for forming /ð/, with the flattened tip of the tongue between the teeth, to /z/, with the tip of the tongue pointing up toward the gum ridge.

282

1.	bathes	6.	soothe Zoe
2.	teethes	7.	breathe Zen
3.	sheathes	8.	loathes zoos
4.	loathe zinc	9.	mouths zilch
5.	sunbathe zestfully	10.	bathe zombies

SOUND CHECK #12: same consonant blends /z z/. When the same consonant sound ends one word and also begins the next, very well-pronounced characters can use a slight rhythmic pulse of breath and energy to connect them, while maintaining the shape and contact of the articulators.

1.	his zebra	6.	is zany
2.	raise Zoe	7.	has zero
3.	praise Zen	8.	ooze zeal
4.	people's zoo	9.	his xylophone
5.	curses Czars	10.	loves zucchini

NEUTRAL AMERICAN TEXT /s/ (sue) and /z/ (zoo). *Mark the following and speak out loud.*

voiced /z/ endings and consonant combinations:

Ay, in the catalogue ye go for men,
As hounds and greyhounds, mongrels, spaniels, curs,
Shoughs, water-rugs, and demi-wolves are clept
All by the name of dogs.

(Macbeth: III, i, 91)

Hath not a Jew eyes? Hath not a Jew hands, organs, dimensions, senses, affections, passions...

(The Merchant of Venice: III, i, 59)

NORTHUMBERLAND. Think not that Henry shall be so depos'd.
WARWICK.   Depos'd he shall be, in despite of all.

(3 Henry VI: I, i, 153)

voiceless /s/ consonant combinations:

Skipper, stand back.

(The Taming of the Shrew: II, i, 339)

Let the offender stand forth.

(Tourneur: The Revenger's Tragedy)

O Cassius, I am sick of many griefs.

(Julius Caesar: IV, iii, 144)

O, 'twas the foulest deed to slay that babe.

(Richard III: I, iii, 182)

Thou toldst me thou didst hold him in thy hate.

(Othello: I, i, 6)

Recounts most horrid sights seen by the watch.

(Julius Caesar: II, ii, 16)

Be bright and jovial among your guests to-night.

(Macbeth: III, ii, 28)

What says my sweet queen, my very very sweet queen?

(Troilus and Cressida: III, i, 80)

Ask for me to-morrow, and you shall find me a grave man.

(Romeo and Juliet: III, i, 97)

At the dance tonight, she snapped the gamekeeper away from
Anna—no waiting to be asked.

(Strindberg: Miss Julie)

And he requires your haste-post-haste appearance,
Even on the instant.

(Othello: I, ii, 37)

Madam, the guests are come, supper serv'd up, you call'd, my
young lady ask'd for.

(Romeo and Juliet: I, iii, 100)

My lips, two blushing pilgrims, ready stand
To smooth that rough touch with a tender kiss.

(Romeo and Juliet: I, v, 95)

I am not sick, if Brutus have in hand
Any exploit worthy the name of honor.

(Julius Caesar: II, i, 316)

Strike as thou didst at Caesar; for I know,
When thou didst hate him worst, thou lovedst him better
Than ever thou lovedst Cassius.

(Julius Caesar: IV, iii, 105)

They are as sick that surfeit with too much as they that starve
with nothing.

(The Merchant of Venice: I, ii, 5)

O, it came o'er my ear like the sweet sound
That breathes upon a bank of violets,
Stealing and giving odor.

(Twelfth Night: I, i, 5)

Oh mighty Caesar! dost thou lie so low?
Are all thy conquests, glories, triumphs, spoils,
Shrunk to this little measure? Fare thee well!

(Julius Caesar: III, i, 148)

Doubly divorc'd! Bad men, you violate
A twofold marriage—'twixt my crown and me,
And then betwixt me and my married wife.—
Let me unkiss the oath 'twixt thee and me;
And yet not so, for with a kiss 'twas made.

(Richard II: V, i, 71)

VITTORIA. O, ye dissembling men!
FLAMINEO.   We sucked that, sister,
        From women's breasts, in our first infancy.

(Webster: The White Devil)

Rebellious subjects, enemies to peace,
Profaners of this neighbor-stainéd steel—
Will they not hear?— What ho, you men, you beasts!
That quench the fire of your pernicious rage
With purple fountains issuing from your veins—
On pain of torture, from those bloody hands
Throw your mistempered weapons to the ground.

(Romeo and Juliet: I, i, 81)

Thou orb aloft full-dazzling! thou hot October noon!
Flooding with sheeny light the gray beach sand,
The sibilant near sea with vistas far and foam,
And tawny streaks and shades and spreading blue;
O sun of noon refulgent! my special word to thee.

(Walt Whitman: Thou Orb Aloft Full-Dazzling)

AFFRICATES

See Overview pages 13-17

There is only one affricate cognate pair, which consists of a stop-plosive and fricative sound seamlessly blended to sound as one.

/ t͡ʃ / (ri<u>ch</u>)   / dʒ / (ri<u>dge</u>)

Form voiceless /t͡ʃ/ by putting the tongue tip against the upper gum ridge, making firm contact for the initial stop element /t/, then quickly releasing into /ʃ/. No lip rounding is necessary.

Form voiced /dʒ/ by putting the tongue tip against the upper gum ridge, making firm contact for the initial stop element /d/, then quickly releasing into the /ʒ/ sound. No lip rounding is necessary.

AUDIO 46▶ /t͡ʃ/ (ri<u>ch</u>) /dʒ/ (ri<u>dge</u>)

>   t͡ʃ
> The air hath starv'd the roses in her <u>ch</u>eeks,
>   t͡ʃt   t͡ʃ
> And pin<u>ch</u>'d the lily-tin<u>c</u>ture of her face.
> > (The Two Gentlemen of Verona: IV, iv, 154)
>
>   dʒ
> Bravo! Now my boot, kiss it—and pay me homa<u>ge</u>!
> > (Strindberg: Miss Julie)
>
>   t͡ʃ
> Tremble, thou wre<u>tch</u>
>   dʒ
> That hast within thee undivul<u>ged</u>[1] crimes
>   dʒ
> Unwhipt of <u>j</u>ustice!
> > (King Lear: III, ii, 51)

---

1 The word 'undivulged' may be pronounced with four syllables, especially if written: undivulgéd.

WORDS /t͡ʃ/ (ri<u>ch</u>) /d͡ʒ/ (ri<u>dge</u>)

	Initial	Medial	Final
/t͡ʃ/	chin	inched	rich
	cheap	ratchet	patch
	chimes	culture	hutch
	chance	watching	coach
	chapter	miniature	bunch

	Initial	Medial	Final
/d͡ʒ/	gym	rejoice	rage
	Jack	bridged	edge
	joke	merging	lodge
	joint	graduated	judge
	juggle	degenerate	visage

PHRASES /t͡ʃ/ and /d͡ʒ/

1. whi<u>ch ch</u>eap wa<u>tch</u>
2. <u>j</u>agged e<u>dg</u>ed gor<u>ge</u>
3. ri<u>ch ch</u>ocolate <u>ch</u>ips
4. <u>ch</u>unky <u>ch</u>erry fu<u>dge</u>
5. <u>ch</u>ecking ea<u>ch</u> ba<u>dge</u>
6. ma<u>t</u>ure fea<u>t</u>ures
7. gigantic <u>ch</u>ickens
8. <u>ch</u>ecking messa<u>ge</u>s
9. dis<u>ch</u>arging <u>G</u>eorge
10. stran<u>ge</u> <u>J</u>une <u>j</u>ourney

SENTENCES /t͡ʃ/ (ri<u>ch</u>) /d͡ʒ/ (ri<u>dge</u>)

1. Chet sketched with chalk.

2. That's wretched cheesecake.

3. Marge chose to change agents.

4. What strange and tempestuous weather.

5. The roads merge after the bridge, Jason.

6. The judge convicted Jonathan of perjury.

7. Jill switched her jury duty to July from June.

8. If I stay on a rigid budget maybe I'll become rich.

9. Which chapter challenges your imagination, Jackie?

10. Our coach has us jumping rope. We actually enjoy it.

SOUND CHECK #1: tip-of-the-tongue placement on /t t͜ʃ/ and /d dʒ/. The tongue tip contacts the gum ridge when initiating these sounds. *Read across.*

tin	chin	din	gin
Tad	Chad	dad	Jack
tug	chug	dug	jug
two	chew	dew	juice
talk	chalk	dawn	Jaw

SOUND CHECK #2: connecting final stop-plosives and initial affricates. Stop the final plosive of the first word completely, before initiating the second.

	/t͜ t͜ʃ/		/d dʒ/
1.	hat͜ check	6.	bad jump
2.	cut͜ cheese	7.	fired John
3.	not͜ chosen	8.	plaid jersey
4.	what͜ children	9.	glad journey
5.	great͜ chocolate	10.	read journals

SOUND CHECK #3: voiced /dʒ/ endings. Maintain vocal fold vibration through the end of the last word without adding an off-glide, or /ə/ (uh) sound.

1.	no ju<u>dge</u>	6.	over indu<u>lge</u>
2.	great on sta<u>ge</u>	7.	off the bri<u>dge</u>
3.	had him pa<u>ged</u>	8.	need for reve<u>nge</u>
4.	became enra<u>ged</u>	9.	everything cha<u>nged</u>
5.	shouldn't be ca<u>ged</u>	10.	must not be divu<u>lged</u>

SOUND CHECK #4: same consonant blends /t͜ʃ t͜ʃ/ and /dʒ dʒ/. When the same consonant sound ends one word and also begins the word that follows, a slight rhythmic pulse of breath (and energy) is used to connect them. The articulators do move slightly within the formation of these sound combinations.

1.	pat**ch ch**airs	6.	huge **j**ump
2.	rea**ch Ch**ina	7.	**J**udge **J**ason
3.	sear**ch Ch**uck	8.	large **j**ackets
4.	mu**ch ch**eering	9.	barge **j**unked
5.	whi**ch ch**ocolates	10.	strange **g**erms

NEUTRAL AMERICAN TEXT /tʃ/ (ri<u>ch</u>) /dʒ/ (ri<u>dge</u>). *Mark the following and speak out loud.*

voiced /dʒ/ endings:

dʒ
What is your parenta<u>ge</u>?

(Twelfth Night: I, v, 277)

The King is in high rage.

(King Lear: II, iv, 296)

You're like to have a swift and pleasant passage.

(Middleton & Rowley: The Changeling)

Gentle Lucetta, fit me with such weeds
As may beseem some well-reputed page.

(The Two Gentlemen of Verona: II, vii, 42)

Oh! So simple, really, how I managed!
I continued where I saw the country ravaged,
Torn, with horrors—ah! such wasteful siege!
Messieurs, if this be service to your liege,
I believe a woman could do better!

(Rostand: Cyrano de Bergerac)

/tʃ/ and /dʒ/ in various positions

No, no, they do but jest, poison in jest.

(Hamlet: III, ii, 234)

O me, the word choose! I may neither choose who I would, nor refuse who I dislike.

(The Merchant of Venice: I, ii, 22)

Then take him up, and manage well the jest.
Carry him gently to my fairest chamber,
And hang it round with all my wanton pictures.

(The Taming of the Shrew: Ind. i, 45)

ELEANOR.   Come to thy grandame, child.
CONSTANCE. Do, child, go to it grandame, child,
            Give grandame kingdom, and it grandame will
            Give it a plum, a cherry, and a fig.

(King John: II, i, 159)

GLIDES

See Overview pages 13-17

There are three voiced 'glide' sounds in Neutral American Speech, none of which have voiceless partners:

/ w / (<u>w</u>e)   / j / (<u>y</u>ou)   / r / (<u>r</u>ed)

Glides all begin by forming the shape for a vowel sound, but rather than holding that shape and producing the vowel sound, the articulators are released from this shape and flow or 'glide' into the vowel sound that always follows. The three glides do not fit neatly into the definition of consonants, and are sometimes referred to as 'semi-vowels'.

/ w / (<u>w</u>e)

Form **/w/** by resting the tip of the tongue down behind the lower teeth and rounding the lips, as if speaking the back vowel **/u/** (wh<u>o</u>). While voicing sound, immediately release this shape into the vowel sound that always comes after, or **/u/** might be spoken instead of **/w/**.

AUDIO 47 ▶ **/w/** (<u>w</u>e)

And in a <u>w</u>ord, but even now <u>w</u>orth this,
And now <u>w</u>orth nothing?

(The Merchant of Venice: I, i, 35)

A <u>w</u>ill! A <u>w</u>icked <u>w</u>ill,
A <u>w</u>oman's <u>w</u>ill, a cank'red grandam's <u>w</u>ill!

(King John: II, i, 193)

<u>Wh</u>y should I <u>w</u>ar <u>w</u>ithout the <u>w</u>alls of Troy,
That find such cruel battle here <u>w</u>ithin?

(Troilus and Cressida: I, i, 2)

WORDS /w/ (<u>we</u>)

Initial	Medial	Final
we	away	*
went	equal	*
wild	bewail	*
watch	rewind	*
wonder	language	*

PHRASES /w/ (<u>we</u>)

1.	<u>w</u>ire s<u>w</u>ing set	6.	<u>wh</u>at questions
2.	<u>w</u>ild <u>w</u>ilderness	7.	<u>w</u>ell, <u>w</u>ell, <u>w</u>ell
3.	<u>w</u>orse and <u>w</u>orse	8.	<u>w</u>orsening <u>w</u>eather
4.	<u>wh</u>ispering <u>w</u>illows	9.	<u>wh</u>en <u>W</u>illiam s<u>w</u>ore
5.	some<u>wh</u>ere s<u>w</u>anky	10.	s<u>w</u>eaty ac<u>qu</u>aintances

SENTENCES /w/ (<u>we</u>)

1. Why not wear it?

2. Twyla is always misquoted.

3. Which one do you want, Wanda?

4. Wow, you're wearing a Swiss watch.

5. We love winter walks in white snow.

6. Do squirrels squeak or are they quiet?

7. William was sworn in, then questioned.

8. Will you water the flowers on Wednesday?

9. Wacky Wendell wants whiskey with wine.

10. I'm not sure whether the weather will worsen or not.

The voiceless partner **/hw/** is *not* spoken in Neutral American, though it is used in Classical American and, occasionally, in Standard British (RP). It is covered with these dialects.

NEUTRAL AMERICAN TEXT /w/ (<u>w</u>e). *Mark the following and speak out loud.*

But <u>w</u>ill you <u>w</u>oo this <u>w</u>ild-cat?

(The Taming of the Shrew: I, ii, 196)

If I be waspish, best beware my sting.

(The Taming of the Shrew: II, i, 210)

Why, what wouldst thou do there before I go?

(Richard III: IV, iv, 454)

Some word there was, worser than Tybalt's death.

(Romeo and Juliet: III, ii, 108)

Women, being the weaker vessels, are ever thrust to the wall;
therefore I will push Montague's men from the wall, and thrust
his maids to the wall.

(Romeo and Juliet: I, i, 15)

We were so sorry we couldn't give you a seat in the carriage.

(Ibsen: Hedda Gabler)

DUKE. Why, you are nothing then: neither maid, widow, nor wife?
LUCIO. My lord, she may be a punk; for many of them are neither
maid, widow, nor wife.

(Measure for Measure: V, i, 177)

Read the will, we'll hear it, Antony.
You shall read us the will, Caesar's will.

(Julius Caesar: III, ii, 147)

JULIET. "Romeo is banished"!
There is no end, no limit, measure, bound,
In that word's death, no words can that woe sound.
Where is my father and my mother, nurse?
NURSE. Weeping and wailing over Tybalt's corse.
Will you go to them? I will bring you thither.
JULET. Wash they his wounds with tears? Mine shall be spent,
When theirs are dry, for Romeo's banishment.

(Romeo and Juliet: III, ii, 124)

Glide
/ j / (you)

Form /j/ by beginning in almost the same shape as for the front vowel /i/ (we), with the lower jaw nearly closed, the tip of the tongue down behind the lower teeth, and the front and middle[1] of the tongue arched high and forward toward the hard palate.

Immediately release this shape into the vowel sound that always comes after, or /i/ might be spoken instead of /j/.

AUDIO 48▶ /j/ (you)

       j   j   j
O Cupid, Cupid, Cupid!

                            (Troilus and Cressida: III, i, 111)

     j   j   j   j
Be you his eunuch, and your mute I'll be.

                            (Twelfth Night: I, ii, 62)

                      j
They that have the yellow jaundice think all objects they
          j
look on to be yellow.

                            (Webster: The White Devil)

WORDS /j/ (you)

Initial	Medial	Final
yes	fuse	*
use	cute	*
yell	beyond	*
yawn	opinion	*
yesterday	reunion	*

---

[1] The vowel /i/ (we) requires *front* tongue arching only.

PHRASES /j/ (you)

1.	musical revue	6.	yellow onions
2.	yammer at you	7.	miniscule feuds
3.	young and beautiful	8.	yogurt for youth
4.	yelling your excuses	9.	yearly arguments
5.	yearning for Yankees	10.	yoo-hoo, yourself

NEUTRAL AMERICAN TEXT /j/ (you). *Mark the following and speak out loud.*

   j   j
Yonder comes my master, your brother.
(As You Like It: I, i, 26)

To yourself; why, she woos you by a figure.
(The Two Gentlemen of Verona: II, i, 148)

Oh you abuse me, you abuse me, you abuse me!
(Webster: The White Devil)

Farewell to you, and you, and you, Voluminus.
(Julius Caesar: V, v, 31)

Yet he's gentle, never school'd and yet learned.
(As You Like It: I, i, 166)

See you yond coign a' th' Capitol, yond cornerstone?
(Coriolanus: V, iv, 1)

Off with his head, and set it on York gates,
So York may overlook the town of York.
(3 Henry VI: I, iv, 179)

"Will you walk a little faster?" said a whiting to a snail,
"There's a porpoise close behind us, and he's treading on my tail.
See how eagerly the lobsters and the turtles all advance!
They are waiting on the shingle—will you come and join the dance?
Will you, won't you, will you, won't you, will you join the dance?
Will you, won't you, will you, won't you, won't you join the dance?"
(Lewis Carroll: Alice in Wonderland)

Glide
/ r / (<u>r</u>ed)

Form /r/ by relaxing the jaw half open, arching the middle of the tongue high near the hard palate, and pointing the tip of the tongue up behind the alveolar ridge. While voicing sound, immediately release this shape into the vowel sound that always comes after, dropping the tongue tip down behind the lower teeth.

The back of the tongue and throat remain relaxed throughout, or /ɝ/ (ER) may be spoken instead of /r/. More or less lip rounding is involved, depending on the shape of the vowel sound that follows. Compare: '<u>r</u>ed' to '<u>r</u>oom'.

Some friction is involved during the production of consonant /r/ (<u>r</u>ed), which is why it can be classified as both a glide *and* a fricative sound.

AUDIO 49 A ▶ /r/ (<u>r</u>ed)

I <u>pr</u>ay come and <u>cr</u>ush a cup of wine.

(Romeo and Juliet: I, ii, 80)

Sir, spare your <u>thr</u>eats.
The bug which you would <u>fr</u>ight me with, I seek.

(The The Winter's Tale: III, ii, 91)

I will here <u>shr</u>oud till the <u>dr</u>egs of the storm be past.

(The Tempest: II, ii, 40)

WORDS /r/ (<u>r</u>ed)

Initial	Medial	Final
red	bereft	*
raft	erased	*
rust	drafted	*
rival	derelict	*
rescue	strained	*

PHRASES consonant /r/

1.	racing Ryan	6.	raging roosters
2.	rough and ready	7.	removing risks
3.	ruffles and ridges	8.	wrinkled rabbits
4.	rowdy roughhousing	9.	ridiculous reasons
5.	reasonable restaurant	10.	really, really right

Consonant and vowel sounds spelled with 'r'. An 'r' in the spelling of a word can represent a vowel *or* a consonant. If you are uncertain which is which, look at the sound that comes *after* the 'r', and remember the following:

A vowel spelled with 'r' is always followed by a consonant sound, as in 'bird' and 'hurt', or by nothing—when it is the last sound of a word—as in 'mother' and 'sister'. Five diphthongs and two triphthongs contain the vowel of 'r'.

A consonant spelled with 'r' is always followed by a vowel sound, as in 'around' and 'arrest', and is often the first sound of a word, as in 'red' and 'right'. It is often preceded by other consonant sounds in consonant combinations, as in the words tree, drive, three, street, prime, scream.

SOUND CHECK #1: consonant /r/ and combinations. Make sure the back of the tongue remains relaxed and uninvolved when forming the consonant, so /ɝ/ (ER) is not inserted before, or spoken instead of, consonant /r/. This is what happens when Tony the Tiger says: "It's GERRRRATE!". Transcribed: **gɝ-reɪt.**

WORDS consonant /r/ and combinations

read	rap	room	riot
rip	run	rookie	ride
rash	rush	raw	rage
prim	prime	practice	press
brash	brief	breath	bride
crash	crave	create	crunch
grave	grumpy	grime	grunt
freed	fraction	frenetic	fresh
thread	three	through	throw
shriek	shrill	shrank	shrew
sprayed	spry	sprung	spruce
scream	scratch	scramble	scrim
stray	street	strangle	strip
strength	striated	structure	straws

PHRASES consonant /r/ and combinations

1.	pricey promotions	6.	scraped screens
2.	brings bright brass	7.	springy sprinters
3.	crooning crocodiles	8.	shrieking shrapnel
4.	great green groceries	9.	Fred framing Frank
5.	radical remembrance	10.	throws three thrones

SOUND CHECK #2: /dr/ and /tr/ combinations. Feel the tip of the tongue contact the gum ridge before releasing into the consonant /r/. If the blade of the tongue is used, 'tr' will sound like 'chr' /tʃr/ and 'dr' will sound like 'jr' /dʒr/.

See the tip of the tongue warm-ups on pages 209-218.

AUDIO 49 B▶ /dr/ and /tr/ combinations

I have had a dream, past the wit of man to say what dream it was.
(A Midsummer Night's Dream: IV, i, 205)

I'll prove more true
Than those that have more cunning to be strange.
(Romeo and Juliet: II, ii, 100)

Truly, the tree yields bad fruit.
(As You Like It: III, ii, 116)

WORDS /dr/ and /tr/ combinations

drill	drastic	treble	drape
dread	dredge	drifter	trigger
tripped	trimmed	treason	transfer

PHRASES /dr/ and /tr/ combinations

1.	trades tractors	6.	dried droplets
2.	tranquil trance	7.	dreadful dress
3.	trampled trails	8.	dripping drain
4.	treasonous trap	9.	drunken drivel
5.	trouble trusting	10.	droning druggist

SENTENCES /dr/ and /tr/ combinations

1. What's in the truck's trunk?

2. Drinking and driving don't mix.

3. Drew dreaded the drudgery of the draft.

4. Tracy's playing the trendsetting stock trader.

5. The trio rode the tricycle in the drizzling rain.

6. The translation is tremendous—very dramatic.

7. Trampolines were transported via tractor trailer.

8. Tracy, trim the trees before they droop into traffic.

9. Clever Trevor Trump was cast as COUNT DRACULA.

10. Try trick-or-treating on the train tracks; trust me, trouble!

SOUND CHECK #3: /str/. Make certain to begin this combination of consonants with 'st' **/st/**, which requires that air release over the tip of the tongue, not 'sh' **/ʃ/**, which requires that air release over the sides of the tongue.

AUDIO 49 C▶ /str/ combinations

Destruction straight shall dog them at the heels.

(Richard II: V, iii, 139)

How strange it is to see a famous actress cry.

(Chekhov: The Seagull)

But must my sons be slaughtered in the streets
For valiant doings in their country's cause?

(Titus Andronicus: I, i, 112)

WORDS comparing /st/ and /str/ combinations. Maintain the initial **/st/** in the following word pairs **/st str/** *Read across.*

stay/stray	stack/strap	sty/stride	sty/stripe
steep/street	sting/string	stick/strict	step/strep
stuck/struck	stung/strung	stay/straight	sty/astride

EXERCISES   **(1)** Elongate initial **/s/** in the previous word pairs. Make sure to say 's' and not 'sh'. Then, repeat without elongating.

(2) Pulse initial **/st/** twice in the previous word pairs, then finish the word (for example: 'st'..'st'..'stay' / 'st'..'st'..'stray'). Repeat without pulsing.

If the above exercises were helpful, use them with the following:

WORDS /str/

strict	stray	strut	strobe
street	stride	strip	straws
strum	strode	stroll	strikes
strong	stretch	stroke	stringy
strewn	strudel	distract	struggle

When **/s/** is followed by a sound that requires lip-rounding, initiate the **/s/** before rounding the lips for the sound that comes after. This pertains to several words in the columns above.

PHRASES /str/

1. strategic strokes
2. astride a stroller
3. strapping strangers
4. strenuous stretches
5. strident red streamers
6. straight-faced
7. strained straps
8. obstructed street
9. strutting strumpet
10. structured strategy

ADDITIONAL PHRASES /str/

1. stringy straps
2. strange stripes
3. strong structure
4. stressed strippers
5. strained strawberries
6. stricken strikers
7. strategic stretches
8. strengthened streets
9. struggling strummers
10. straightened streamers

SENTENCES /str/

1. I'm a straphanger.

2. Comedy is her strong suit.

3. Three strikes—you struck out!

4. They were stressed out when stranded.

5. Strenuous workouts can strain muscles.

6. Could you straighten that; it's not straight.

7. Still typecast as the strutting strong-man?

8. The strained strawberries are in the strainer.

9. Unstring my straitjacket; it's a bit restrictive.

10. We strive to yawn and stretch when stressed.

11. Strange screams rang out from Screech Street.

12. What a unique strain of streptococcus bacteria.

13. Drew's offspring adore fresh strawberry strudel.

14. She looks straight-laced in that strange costume.

15. Astral sightings distressed the strong astronomer.

16. Her straight shiny shift with the red stripes shrank.

17. Last spring, strikers threatened to halt construction.

18. Three structures were constructed in a straight line.

19. You're strong; could you string up the strobe lights?

20. A strolling string quartet at a street fair? What a treat!

21. They strove to streamline production of the astringent.

22. She kept a straight face with a straight flush in her hand.

23. That stray streaked straight into the street and was struck.

24. That's strange. Why wasn't it structured in a straight line?

25. Here come the Stratford triplets: Trevor, Tracy and Trina.

Stratford Triplets

Trevor, Tracy, and Trina, the strapping little Stratford triplets, adore freshly strained strawberries. Their parents' strenuous struggle to produce a continuous stream of freshly strained strawberry compote saps all their strength. The stricken parents are determined to streamline production, stretch out current supplies, and drastically restrict their offspring's consumption.

> **SOUND CHECK #4: 'linking' consonant /r/.** When vowel or diphthong of 'r' is followed directly by another vowel or diphthong sound, consonant /r/ can be inserted between the two to insure that they are smoothly linked, and to prevent the second sound from being initiated with a glottal attack.

The addition of a linking consonant /r/ is often automatic, for example:

Mother is here in the dining room.

Taken word by word, there is only one consonant /r/ in the sentence above: 'room'. But when smoothly speaking the sentence, linking consonant /r/ is added after the vowel of 'r' in moth<u>er</u>, and after the diphthong of 'r' in h<u>ere</u>.

Words are not usually linked with the consonant /r/ if linking results in the formation of another word, as in:

Do you know 'A Flea In Her Ear' by Feydeau?

Words are never linked with consonant /r/ in Neutral American Speech if there is no 'r' in the spelling of the word.

PHRASES linking consonant /r/

1.	for a while	6.	paying for it
2.	fear of flying	7.	sneer at them
3.	no particular area	8.	whether or not
4.	bear in the woods	9.	gather everything
5.	hear everyone else	10.	brother advised him

O for a horse with wings!

(Cymbeline: III, ii, 48)

Note. Intrusive *vowel* of 'r': Speaking an 'er' sound when there is no 'r' in the spelling is called adding an intrusive 'r'. This can be heard, for example, in the pronunciation of sofa as 'sofer' and saw as 'sawr'.

Intrusive 'r' correction is addressed on pages 129-130 and 153-154.

NEUTRAL AMERICAN TEXT /r/ (<u>red</u>). *Mark the following and speak out loud.*

/r/ alone and in various combinations:

Holy <u>Fr</u>anciscan f<u>r</u>iar! b<u>r</u>other, ho!

(Romeo and Juliet: V, ii, 1)

The sea's more rough and raging than calm rivers.

(Webster: The White Devil)

By all the gods that Romans bow before,
I here discard my sickness! Soul of Rome!
Brave son, deriv'd from honorable loins!

(Julius Caesar: II, i, 320)

I will not do them wrong; I rather choose
To wrong the dead, to wrong myself and you,
Than I will wrong such honorable men.

(Julius Caesar: III, ii, 125)

Arthur, that great forerunner of thy blood,
Richard, that robb'd the lion of his heart,
And fought the holy wars in Palestine,
By this brave duke came early to his grave;
And for amends to his posterity,
At our importance hither is he come
To spread his colors, boy, in thy behalf,
And to rebuke the usurpation
Of thy unnatural uncle, English John.
Embrace him, love him, give him welcome hither.

(King John: II, i, 2)

/dr/ and /tr/ combinations:

The drink, the drink! I am pois'ned.

(Hamlet: V, ii, 310)

Give me my bed by stealth, there's true delight
What breeds a loathing in't, but night by night?

(Tourneur: The Revenger's Tragedy)

Of fantasy, of dreams, and ceremonies.

(Julius Caesar: II, i, 197)

There's no more faith in thee than in a stew'd prune, nor no
more truth in thee than in a drawn fox.

(1 Henry IV: III, iii, 112)

I used to have fine dreams and great thoughts, and the present
and the future were bright with hope.

(Chekhov: Three Sisters)

/str/ combinations:

Is it not strange? and strange?

(Measure for Measure: V, i, 42)

I cannot strike, I see his brother's wounds.

(Middleton & Rowley: The Changeling)

He that strikes the first stroke, I'll run him up to the hilts.

(Henry V: II, i, 63

I see you stand like greyhounds in the slips,
Straining upon the start.

(Henry V: III, i, 31)

If ever you disturb our streets again
Your lives shall pay the forfeit of the peace.

(Romeo and Juliet: I, i, 96)

She swore, in faith 'twas strange, 'twas passing strange;
'Twas pitiful, 'twas wondrous pitiful.

(Othello: I, iii, 160)

linking consonant /r/:

Horatio—or I do forget myself.

(Hamlet: I, ii, 161)

Only most people don't formulate it to themselves, or else keep
quiet about it.

(Ibsen: Ghosts)

You will not do't for all the world, I hope.

(Pericles: IV, i, 84)

PRACTICE TEXT

Fill in the blank lines with the appropriate IPA marking for well-pronounced Neutral American. Voiced endings before a (possible) pause have been double-underlined, syllabic endings have been marked, and consonant /r/ and consonant combinations have been underlined. See the key on page 320 and the Shakespeare monologues on pages 321-325 for samples of other marked text. Speak the selections aloud.

Example:

       ɪ   tʰ

The swifte<u>st tr</u>aveler is he that goes afoot.

(Thoreau: Walden, 1, Economy)

1.
          –   – –   –   –

Beware of all e<u>nterpr</u>ises that <u>r</u>equire new clothe<u>s</u>.

(Thoreau: Walden, 1, Economy)

2.
               –   –

I love a <u>br</u>oad margin to my life.

(Thoreau: Walden, 4, Sounds)

3.
          –   –   –

The ge<u>nt</u>leman has not seen how to <u>r</u>eply to this.

(Webster: Second Speech on Foote's Resolution)

4.
              –   – – –

She was a pha<u>nt</u>om of delight

                         –   –

When fir<u>st sh</u>e gleamed upon my sight.

(Wordsworth: She Was a Phantom of Delight)

5.
          – –   –   –

Belike some no<u>bl</u>e ge<u>nt</u>leman that mea<u>ns</u>

        –   –

<u>Tr</u>aveling some journey to <u>r</u>epose him here.

(The Taming of the Shrew: Ind. i, 75)

6.
        –   –   –

She might lie by an empe<u>r</u>or's side and command him ta<u>sks</u>.

(Othello: IV, i, 184)

7.   She dwelt among the untrodden ways

Beside the springs of Dove.
(Wordsworth: She Dwelt Among the Untrodden Ways)

8.
Sweet childish days, that were as long

As twenty days are now.
(Wordsworth: To a Butterfly)

9.
Be not as extreme in submission as in offense.
(The Merry Wives of Windsor: IV, iv, 11)

10.
The deep of night is crept upon our talk.
(Julius Caesar: IV, iii, 226)

11.
O, let me stay, befall what may befall!
(2 Henry VI: III, ii, 402)

12.
As Tammie glowered, amazed and curious,

The mirth and fun grew fast and furious.
(Robert Burns: Tam O'Shanter)

13.
He said fever…the brain…if I heard right…

If you could see him! Ah! his head bound tight!
(Rostand: Cyrano de Bergerac)

14.
Death is my son-in-law, Death is my heir,

My daughter he hath wedded. I will die,

And leave him all; life, living, all is Death's.
(Romeo and Juliet: IV, v, 38)

From **IOLANTHE**

WHEN YOU'RE LYING AWAKE
(The Nightmare Song)

Gilbert and Sullivan

When you're lying awake with a dismal headache,
    and repose is taboo'd by anxiety,

I conceive you may use any language you choose
    to indulge in, without impropriety;

For your brain is on fire—the bedclothes conspire
    of usual slumber to plunder you:

First your counterpane goes, and uncovers your toes,
    and your sheet slips demurely from under you;

Then the blanketing tickles—you feel like mixed pickles—
    so terribly sharp is the pricking,

And you're hot, and you're cross, and you tumble and toss
    till there's nothing 'twixt you and the ticking.

Then the bedclothes all creep to the ground in a heap,
    and you pick 'em all up in a tangle;

Next your pillow resigns and politely declines
    to remain at its usual angle!

Well, you get some repose in the form of a doze,
    with hot eye-balls and head ever aching,

But your slumbering teems with such horrible dreams
    that you'd very much better be waking!

From **THE TELL-TALE HEART**

Edgar Allan Poe

True!—nervous—very, very dreadfully nervous I had been and am; but why *will* you say that I am mad? The disease had sharpened my senses—not destroyed—not dulled them. Above all was the sense of hearing acute. I heard all things in the heaven and in the earth. I heard many things in hell. How, then, am I mad? Hearken! And observe how healthily—how calmly I can tell you the whole story.

It is impossible to say how first the idea entered my brain; but once conceived, it haunted me day and night. Object there was none. Passion there was none. I loved the old man. He had never wronged me. He had never given me insult. For his gold I had no desire. I think it was his eye! Yes, it was this! One of his eyes resembled that of a vulture—a pale blue eye, with a film over it. Whenever it fell upon me, my blood ran cold; and so by degrees—very gradually—I made up my mind to take the life of the old man, and thus rid myself of the eye forever.

Now this is the point. You fancy me mad. Madmen know nothing. But you should have seen *me*. You should have seen how wisely I proceeded—with what dissimulation I went to work! I was never kinder to the old man than during the whole week before I killed him. And every night, about midnight, I turned the latch of his door and opened it—oh, so gently! And then, when I had made an opening sufficient for my head, I put in a dark lantern, all closed, closed, so that no light shone out, and then I thrust in my head. Oh, you would have laughed to see how cunningly I thrust it in! I moved it slowly—very, very slowly, so that I might not disturb the old man's sleep.

A FRAGMENT

H. W. Longfellow

Awake! arise! the hour is late!
Angels are knocking at thy door!
They are in haste and cannot wait,
And once departed come no more.

Awake! arise! the athlete's arm
Loses its strength by too much rest;
The fallow land, the untilled farm
Produces only weeds at best.

From **THE SPHINX**

Edgar Allan Poe

During the dread reign of the Cholera in New York, I had accepted the invitation of a relative to spend a fortnight with him in the retirement of his *cottage ornée* on the banks of the Hudson. We had here around us all the ordinary means of summer amusement; and what with rambling in the woods, sketching, boating, fishing, bathing, music, and books, we should have passed the time pleasantly enough, but for the fearful intelligence which reached us every morning from the populous city. Not a day elapsed which did not bring us news of the decease of some acquaintance. Then, as the fatality increased, we learned to expect daily the loss of some friend. At length we trembled at the approach of every messenger. The very air from the South seemed to us redolent with death. That palsying thought, indeed, took entire possession of my soul. I could neither speak, think, nor dream of any thing else. My host was of a less excitable temperament, and, although greatly depressed in spirits, exerted himself to sustain my own. His richly philosophical intellect was not at any time affected by unrealities. To the substances of terror he was sufficiently alive, but of its shadows he had no apprehension.

From THE CATARACT OF LODORE

Robert Southey

How does the water come down at Lodore?

Rising and leaping,
Sinking and creeping,
Eddying and whisking,
Spouting and frisking,
Turning and twisting,
Around and around
With endless rebound!
Dividing and gliding and sliding,
And falling and brawling and sprawling,
And driving and riving and striving,
And sprinkling and twinkling and wrinkling,
And sounding and bounding and rounding,
And bubbling and troubling and doubling,
And grumbling and rumbling and tumbling,
And clattering and battering and shattering;
Retreating and beating and meeting and sheeting,
Delaying and straying and playing and spraying,
Advancing and prancing and glancing and dancing,
Recoiling, turmoiling and toiling and boiling,
And gleaming and streaming and steaming and beaming,
And rushing and flushing and brushing and gushing,
And flapping and rapping and clapping and slapping,
And curling and whirling and purling and twirling,
And thumping and plumping and bumping and jumping,
And dashing and flashing and splashing and clashing;
And so never ending, but always descending,
Sounds and motions for ever and ever are blending
All at once, and all o'er, with a mighty uproar,—
And this way, the water comes down at Lodore.

HOPE

Emily Dickinson

XXXII

HOPE is the thing with feathers
That perches in the soul,
And sings the tune without the words,
And never stops at all,

And sweetest in the gale is heard;
And sore must be the storm
That could abash the little bird
That kept so many warm.

I've heard it in the chillest land,
And on the strangest sea;
Yet, never, in extremity,
It asked a crumb of me.

From **MOBY-DICK**

Herman Melville

Call me Ishmael. Some years ago—never mind how long precisely—having little or no money in my purse, and nothing particular to interest me on shore, I thought I would sail about a little and see the watery part of the world. It is a way I have of driving off the spleen, and regulating the circulation. Whenever I find myself growing grim about the mouth; whenever it is a damp, drizzly November in my soul; whenever I find myself involuntarily pausing before coffin warehouses, and bringing up the rear of every funeral I meet; and especially whenever my hypos get such an upper hand of me, that it requires a strong moral principle to prevent me from deliberately stepping into the street, and methodically knocking people's hats off— then, I account it high time to get to sea as soon as I can.

From **CYRANO DE BERGERAC**

Edmond Rostand

CHRISTIAN
Get me that kiss!

CYRANO   No!

CHRISTIAN   Now, or later...

CYRANO   True!
That heady moment comes, when both of you—
Your lips inevitably touching, close!
Yours, the lion's whiskers...hers, the rose!

THE SHUTTERS OPEN. CHRISTIAN HIDES UNDER THE BALCONY.

Would that it were otherwise...

ROXANE (ABOVE)   Is it you?
We spoke of a...

CYRANO   ...a kiss, and sweet word, too!
You shy from forming it upon your lips.
If that word burn, how you must fear eclipse
Of mine, on yours, in one consuming fire!
And yet, tonight, you recklessly conspire,
And gracefully slip, almost denying fears,
From mockery, to smiles, from sighs, to tears...
You need only slip once more from tears to this
One word, one trembling word away...a kiss!

ROXANE
Be still—!

CYRANO A kiss, and what is that? A contract
Signed and sealed, a promise more exact...
A desire that longs to be confirmed...the blush of
The embracing 'o' within the verb "to love"...
A secret whisper drawing lips as ears...
Infinity...the music of the spheres...
As bees hum in communion with the flower...
A way to touch a heartbeat...and the power,
As you taste one lingering instant of the soul!

HENRY V: Prologue

William Shakespeare

O for a Muse of fire, that would ascend
The brightest heaven of invention!
A kingdom for a stage, princes to act,
And monarchs to behold the swelling scene!
Then should the warlike Harry, like himself,
Assume the port of Mars, and at his heels
(Leash'd in, like hounds) should famine, sword, and fire
Crouch for employment. But pardon, gentles all,
The flat unraised spirits that hath dar'd
On this unworthy scaffold to bring forth
So great an object. Can this cockpit hold
The vasty fields of France? Or may we cram
Within this wooden O the very casques
That did affright the air at Agincourt?
O, pardon! since a crooked figure may
Attest in little place a million,
And let us, ciphers to this great accompt,
On your imaginary forces work.
Suppose within the girdle of these walls
Are now confin'd two mighty monarchies,
Whose high, upreared, and abutting fronts
The perilous narrow ocean parts asunder.
Piece out our imperfections with your thoughts;
Into a thousand parts divide one man,
And make imaginary puissance;
Think, when we talk of horses, that you see them
Printing their proud hoofs i' th' receiving earth;
For 'tis your thoughts that now must deck our kings,
Carry them here and there, jumping o'er times,
Turning th' accomplishment of many years
Into an hour-glass: for the which supply,
Admit me Chorus to this history;
Who, Prologue-like, your humble patience pray,
Gently to hear, kindly to judge, our play.

KEY TO MARKING NEUTRAL AMERICAN MONOLOGUES

Rhythm Highlighters	Marking
Stressed syllables (all marked for awareness)	ˈpurchase
Noun verb variations (stressed syllable marked)	ˈdiscourse
Weak forms (marked sparingly, actor's choice)	ə ə i a, the (vs.) the
/ɪ/ (will) prefixes and suffixes	ɪ ɪ reˈpeat, ˈcloset
/ə/ (uh) schwa suffixes	ə ˈstatement
Syllabic endings marked: /n̩ l m̩/	ˈwooden̩, ˈlittl̩e, ˈprism̩,
Vowel Sound Considerations	**Marking**
Linking words (marked sparingly, actor's choice)	here‿it‿is
/e/ (get) before 'm', 'n' (in a stressed syllable)	e e e them, when, sent
/æ/ (that) vowel (relaxed vowel, not a nasal diphthong)	æ æ æ cast, sand, man
/ɔ/ (all) (marked to distinguish from father sound)	ɔ ɔ ɔ fall, often, song
/ʊɚ/ (poor) diphthong (not /ɝ/ ER or /ɔɚ/ sports)	ʊɚ ʊɚ aˈssure, tour
/aɪ/ (my) diphthong (marked before a voiceless consonants in the same word)	aɪ aɪ aɪ white, pipe, wife
Consonant Sound Considerations	**Marking**
Voiceless stop-plosive endings (aspirated before a pause or silence)	hitʰ, packʰ, lipʰ
Voiced consonant ends (clearly voiced—especially before a pause or silence)	dead, found, king
Consonant /r/ and combinations (clear—especially tr, dr, and str combinations)	trap, dread, street

The /æ/ (that) sound is generally unmarked in ALL monologues in words that can be spoken with either a weak OR strong form, as in the words: and, that, an, than, shall, etc.

          æ ɪ   ɪ

That 'banish what they sue for. Re'deem thy 'brother

By 'yielding‿up thy 'body to my wi<u>ll</u>,

                               ə

Or‿else he must not‿'only die the death,

                     ɪ   ɔ

But thy‿un'kindness shall his death <u>draw</u>‿out[h]

              ɪ   ə   æ

To 'ling'ring 'suffe<u>r</u>ance. 'Answer me to-'mor<u>r</u>ow,

                    i

Or by the‿a'ffectio<u>n</u> that now guides me most[h],

æɪ   ə

I'll <u>p</u><u>r</u>ove‿a 'ty<u>r</u>ant to hi<u>m</u>. As for you,

                     æ   ɔ

Say what you can: my false‿o'er'weighs your <u>tr</u>ue.

                                (Measure for Measure: II, iv, 154)

CLASSICAL AMERICAN DIALECT

AUDIO SELECTIONS▶
Patricia Fletcher

SUMMARY CHECKLIST

It may be useful to read the Introduction, pages 1-4, for an overview and comparison with Neutral American and Standard British, before continuing.

When switching from Neutral American to Classical American dialect, the following adjustments and sound changes are necessary.

CONSONANTS

Aspirated medial / t^h /

In Neutral American, when /t/ occurs in an unstressed syllable between two vowel sounds, it is actually said as a very light 'd', represented phonetically by /t̬/, for example:

butter = / 'bʌt̬ɚ / or budder

In Classical American, the light 'd' sound is not spoken, a lightly aspirated /t^h/ is used instead. This is sometimes called a 'flutter t'. The tip of the tongue touches the gum ridge and voiceless 't' is released on a puff of breath.

The small phonetic marking / ^{h} / written in one's script can provide a useful reminder to speak a flutter 't'.

AUDIO 53▶ **lightly aspirated medial /t^h/**

Methinks nobody should be sad but^h I.

(King John: IV, i, 13)

It^h is the law, not^h I, condemn your brother.

(Measure for Measure: II, ii, 80)

Yes, I hear people talk of that^h; but^h it^h is utt^{h}erly impossible.

(Ibsen: The Master Builder)

Highlight the vowel in the stressed syllable, and pronounce the 'flutter t' as part of the unstressed syllable. If the /t/ seems too sharp or intrusive, try releasing it on a little more breath.

butter: →'bʌt^{h}ɚ	litter: →'lɪt^{h}ɚ
batter: →'bæt^{h}ɚ	bitter: →'bɪt^{h}ɚ
better: →'bet^{h}ɚ	bit of: →'bɪt^h əv

WORDS with lightly aspirated medial /tʰ/

ˈwittʰy	ˈpitʰy	ˈkittʰy	ˈcitʰy
ˈfattʰer	ˈdittʰy	aˈbilitʰy	ˈsnottʰy
ˈsanitʰy	ˈlittʰer	ˈmightʰy	ˈwritʰer
ˈprettʰy	ˈvanitʰy	ˈcheatʰer	ˈfittʰing
ˈlightʰing	ˈseatʰing	adˈmittʰing	ˈsweetʰest

PHRASES with lightly aspirated medial /tʰ/

1.	hittʰing the lottʰery	6.	whatʰ itʰ is
2.	thatʰ everyone did	7.	stop hatʰing
3.	whatʰ Alan thought	8.	whitʰe as snow
4.	whatʰever you want	9.	waitʰing outside
5.	votʰing his conscience	10.	a little[1] fightʰing

SENTENCES with lightly aspirated medial /tʰ/

1. Your shirt is dirty.

2. Where are you sitting?

3. She's my favorite aunt.

4. Katie isn't permitted to go.

5. We'll meet in the waiting room.

6. You danced a fine minuet on stage.

7. She's waiting until there's available seating.

8. My flashlight isn't working, it needs batteries.

9. The bitter chocolate cookies need a sugar coating.

10. People with no sense of gratitude have bad attitudes.

11. I bet everyone will wait in line to get into the audition.

12. I'll have a little bit of butter on my lettuce and tomatoes.

13. How can you think of fighting on a beautiful autumn day?

---

[1] Syllabic endings spelled with a 't' as in beetle, little, bottle, are pronounced /tļ/ in Classical American, not /dļ/ as in Neutral American.

14. He tried to get out of it without[1] hurting anyone's feelings.

15. The meeting was cancelled when the heating system broke.

Eat^{h}ing Keat^{h}ing's

Sweet^{h}ie, it^h is bett^{h}er to butt^{h}er your biscuit^h and toast^h
With the very best butt^{h}er from Keat^{h}ing's.
If you cheat^h and use butt^{h}er from Kat^{h}ie's or Kroft's,
You will never be sure what you're eat^{h}ing.

Betty Botta bought some butter.
"But," said she, "this butter's bitter.
If I put it in my batter,
It will make my batter bitter.
But a bit of better butter
Will make my bitter batter better."
So she bought a bit of butter
Better than the bitter butter
And it made her bitter batter better.
So, 'twas better Betty Botta
Bought a bit of better butter.

(Anonymous)

See the patter trio by Gilbert and Sullivan on page 400 for additional 'flutter t' practice.

CLASSICAL AMERICAN TEXT lightly aspirated medial /t^h/. *Mark the following for 'flutter t' and speak out loud.*

It^h isn't money that matt^{h}ers.

(Chekhov: The Seagull)

Arm me audacity from head to foot.

(Cymbeline: I, vi, 19)

That is very nice and dutiful of him.

(Ibsen: Ghosts)

---

[1] Use voiced 'th' /ð/ when speaking 'with' in all forms (without, within, etc.).

Lay breath so bitter on your bitter foe.

(A Midsummer Night's Dream: III, ii, 44)

When we are both accoutered like young men,
I'll prove the prettier fellow of the two.

(The Merchant of Venice: III, iv, 63)

She was brought up in a milieu of equality and women's rights,
and all that.

(Strindberg: Miss Julie)

I'm through with ghosted letters, borrowed wit,
And acting roles I know I just don't fit!

(Rostand: Cyrano de Bergerac)

It's carnival week, and the servants are so excited about it.

(Chekhov: Three Sisters)

I am so used to frequent flattery,
That, being alone, I now flatter myself.

(Webster: The White Devil)

I pray you let us satisfy our eyes
With the memorials and the things of fame.

(Twelfth Night: III, iii, 22)

She better would have fitted me or Clarence;
But in your bride you bury brotherhood.

(3 Henry VI: IV, i, 54)

Saturday, the twenty-sixth—while supper waited—
M'sieur de Bergerac died. Assassinated.

(Rostand: Cyrano de Bergerac)

Well, wait a moment, Mrs. Alving. Let us look into the matter
a little more closely.

(Ibsen: Ghosts)

Leave it all behind! Tell me you love me, or else—what am I, what?

(Strindberg: Miss Julie)

But you know someone ought to write a play on how we poor
teachers live, and get it acted.

(Chekhov: The Seagull)

Voiceless / hw / (<u>wh</u>y)

spelled 'wh'

When the /w/ sound is represented by 'wh' in the spelling, voiceless or whispered /hw/ is spoken instead of voiced /w/. An exception to the spelling guideline occurs when the 'wh' spelling represents /h/ as in 'who' and 'whore'.

Voiceless /hw/ should not involve friction or tension in the throat. Release a little puff of breath through gently rounded lips and continue on to the vowel sound that always follows.

AUDIO 54► voiceless /hw/ (<u>wh</u>y)

                                     hw

Let's sit down here for a <u>wh</u>ile.

(Chekhov: Three Sisters)

          hw   hw

Go to bed <u>wh</u>en I was dressed—damnation! <u>Wh</u>at have you

done to me?

(Strindberg: The Father)

             hw   hw   hw

Aye, sir, and <u>wh</u>ere'fore; for they say, every <u>wh</u>y hath a <u>wh</u>ere'fore.

(The Comedy of Errors: II, ii, 43)

WORDS /w/ (<u>we</u>) *vs.* /hw/ (<u>wh</u>y) *Read across.*

/w/	/hw/	/w/	/hw/
wet	whet	we'll	wheel
wig	Whig	wail	whale
witch	which	wear	where
wacky	whack	well	whelp
weather	whether	wine	whine

PHRASES using voiceless /hw/ (<u>why</u>)

1.	w<u>h</u>at I know	6.	w<u>h</u>ich one
2.	any<u>wh</u>ere else	7.	well, <u>wh</u>y not
3.	heard <u>wh</u>irring	8.	<u>wh</u>ittling away
4.	<u>wh</u>imsical note	9.	asking Mr. W<u>h</u>ite
5.	<u>wh</u>enever you wish	10.	going every<u>wh</u>ere

Let there be no honor
  hw   hw
<u>Wh</u>ere there is beauty; truth, <u>wh</u>ere semblance; love,
  hw
<u>Wh</u>ere there's another man.

(Cymbeline: II, iv, 108)

SENTENCES using voiceless /hw/ (<u>why</u>)

1. Where's Mr. White?

2. What's that whirring noise?

3. Which witch was with you?

4. Is whiskey made from wheat?

5. Wait awhile for Mr. Whatling.

6. Why are you doing cartwheels?

7. I don't know whether or not he went.

8. Stop whining about spilling the wine.

9. What's that whinnying and wheezing?

10. When whipped, the wild beast whinnied.

11. Why, oh why, can't I whistle when I want?

12. Do white whales swim off the coast of Wales?

13. The whitecaps overwhelmed those in the waves.

14. Why, she heard whispering and whimpering everywhere.

15. Where are you going, when are you going, and with whom?

Whirling Wheat

<pre>
hw   hw   hw   hw
</pre>
<u>Wh</u>y not lay a<u>wh</u>ile amidst the <u>wh</u>irling <u>wh</u>eat,
<pre>
hw   hw   hw   hw
</pre>
<u>Wh</u>irring, <u>wh</u>istling, <u>wh</u>ispering <u>wh</u>ile we sleep?

Whether the weather be fine
Or whether the weather be not
Whether the weather be cold
Or whether the weather be hot
We'll weather the weather
Whatever the weather
Whether we like it or not.

(Anonymous)

CLASSICAL AMERICAN TEXT voiceless /hw/ (<u>why</u>). *Mark the following and speak out loud.*

<pre>
hw   hw
</pre>
<u>Wh</u>y <u>wh</u>isper you, my lords, and answer not?

(3 Henry VI: I, i, 149)

What amorous whirlwind hurried you to Rome?

(Webster: The White Devil)

Here burns my candle out; ay, here it dies,
Which whiles it lasted, gave King Henry light.

(3 Henry VI: II, vi, 1)

What plagues and what portents, what mutiny!
What raging of the sea, shaking of earth!

(Troilus and Cressida: I, iii, 96)

Theses are but wild and whirling words, my lord.

(Hamlet: I, v, 133)

We mourn in black, why mourn we not in blood?

(1 Henry VI: I, i, 17)

What noise is this? What traitors have we here?

(1 Henry VI: I, iii, 15)

336

What, are my deeds forgot?

(Troilus and Cressida: III, iii, 144)

Tend to th' master's whistle.

(The Tempest: I, i, 6)

My salad days,
When I was green in judgment.

(Antony and Cleopatra: I, iv, 73)

Be frank! where did I fall?
Hold nothing back! what place, and on what site
Have I come tumbling like an asterite?

(Rostand: Cyrano de Bergerac)

In sooth, I know not why I am so sad;
It wearies me, you say it wearies you;
But how I caught it, found it, or came by it,
What stuff 'tis made of, whereof it is born,
I am to learn;
And such a want-wit sadness makes of me,
That I have much ado to know myself.

(The Merchant of Venice: I, i, 1)

Had women navigable rivers in their eyes,
They would dispend them all. Surely I wonder
Why we should wish more rivers to the city,
When they sell water so good cheap.

(Webster: The White Devil)

And yet, to me, what is this quintessence of dust?

(Hamlet: II, ii, 308)

When didst thou sleep when such a deed was done?

(Richard III: IV, iv, 24)

Then may I set the world on wheels, when she can spin for
her living.

(Two Gentlemen of Verona: III, i, 315)

VOWELS & DIPHTHONGS

The short, slightly lip-rounded back vowel /ɒ/, often referred to as the 'honest' sound, is added in Classical American dialect. The symbol can be found in the right column of the vowel chart that follows, between /ɔ/ (a̲ll) and /ɑ/ (f̲a̲ther). Also added is the use of liquid /ju/ (y̲o̲u̲) in certain circumstances.

In addition, several adjustments are made to vowel and diphthong sounds previously covered in Neutral American.

Front	Mid or Central	Back
Lips slightly spread	**Lips neutral**	**Lips most rounded**
Lower jaw most closed	**Lower jaw most closed**	**Lower jaw most closed**
High i w̲e̲		**u** wh̲o̲ **High**
↓ ɪ wi̲ll		**ʊ** wo̲u̲ld ↓
	ɝ **ER**	
Mid e g̲e̲t	**ɚ** e̲r	**o** o̲'mit **Mid**
↓	**ə** u̲h	↓
	ʌ **UH**	
↓		**ɔ** a̲ll ↓
æ th̲a̲t		**ɒ** h̲o̲nest
Low (a* l̲a̲ugh[1])		**ɑ** f̲a̲thers **Low**
Lips neutral	**Lips neutral**	**Lips unrounded on /ɑ/**
Lower jaw most open	**Lower jaw most open**	**Lower jaw most open**

---

[1] The most open front vowel sound represented by the symbol /a/, which is the most low, open front vowel on the chart, is spoken on certain words in the Mid-Atlantic dialect. This and other sound changes and adjustments that need to be made to *Classical American* in order to speak the more formal *Mid-Atlantic* dialect are covered briefly on pages 417-433.

/ ɒ / (h<u>o</u>nest)

In certain words, this short, slightly lip-rounded back vowel sound is spoken instead of /ɔ/ (<u>a</u>ll) *or* /ɑ/ (f<u>a</u>ther). It is also used occasionally instead of /ʌ/ (<u>UH</u>), which adds additional rhythmic variation to Classical American.

The same sound, slightly more rounded, energized, and clipped, is spoken in Standard British in words such as 'top' and 'stop', which may sound familiar.

AUDIO 55 ▶ /ɒ/ (h<u>o</u>nest)

                  ɒ   ɒ
Who's that kn<u>o</u>cking <u>o</u>n the floor?

(Chekhov: Three Sisters)

               ɒ   ae
For Brutus is an h<u>o</u>norable man.

(Julius Caesar: III, ii, 82)

            ɒ
Why, wh<u>a</u>t a candy deal of courtesy
                       ɒ
This fawning greyhound then did pr<u>o</u>ffer me!

(1 Henry IV: I, iii, 251)

The /ɒ/ (h<u>o</u>nest) sound is used:

(a)   in words spelled with 'o' and pronounced with the /ɑ/ (f<u>a</u>ther) sound in Neutral American, as in:

                not, hot, on, box, top, stop, job, shopping, probably, Tom

(b)   in words spelled with 'qua' or 'wa' and pronounced with the /ɑ/ (f<u>a</u>ther) sound in Neutral American including:

                kumquat, quad, quaff, squab, squad, squalid, squalor, squash, squat, swaddling, swallow, swamp, wad, wallet, wallow, Wally, wan, wand, wander, want, wash, wasp, wast, wassail, watch, watt, yacht

(c)   in words spelled with 'o' and pronounced with the /ɔ/ (a̱ll) sound in Neutral American, as in:

cloth, moth, cross, boss, dog, office, often, song, belong

Exception: words spelled 'ought' as in bought, fought, and sought, are spoken with /ɔ/ in both Neutral and Classical.

(d)   in strong forms of a few words pronounced with the /ʌ/ (U̱H) sound in Neutral American, including:

from, of, 'twas, was, wasn't, what, whatnot, whereof

This alteration should be subtle to avoid sounding like the Standard British dialect. The jaw and back of the tongue are relaxed and the sinking of the cheeks is slight, as is the corresponding rounding of the lips.

WORDS /ɒ/ (ho̱nest)

on	tot	dot	job
God	mob	slob	Tom
jolly	bond	from	what
body	knob	office	soften
jostle	strong	model	follow
fondle	doctor	sobbing	robbery
holiday	Robert	monster	modern
popular	promise	Holland	contents
obvious	voluntary	response	stomped
comment	chocolate	nominate	common

               ɒ   ɒ   ɒ

The swine wa̱sn't worth the love I squa̱ndered o̱n him.

(Strindberg: Miss Julie)

If it is difficult to find the right shape for /ɒ/, begin by relaxing the jaw open for the long /ɑ/ (fa̱ther) sound. Then, slightly sink in the cheeks and corners of the lips, which makes the small alteration in shape needed for the open, slightly rounded /ɒ/ (ho̱nest) sound. The back of the tongue arch may lift slightly, but placing too much focus on this element can result in the more tense, clipped sound associated with Standard British pronunciation.

Follow this procedure while reading the samples below. *Read across.*

/hɑ/	/hɒ/	hot, hospital, hop, hockey, hollow
/tɑ/	/tɒ/	top, Tom, tock, topic, Todd, tolerant
/dɑ/	/dɒ/	Don, dot, dock, docile, doctor
/bɑ/	/bɒ/	box, bottle, bond, bomb, Bob, body
/pɑ/	/pɒ/	possible, posture, posh, pop, pomp
/stɑ/	/stɒ/	stop, stock, stodgy, stocking
/ʃɑ/	/ʃɒ/	shot, shop, shock, shoddy, shopping

ɒ　　　　　　　ɒ
In truth, fair Montague, I am too fond.

(Romeo and Juliet: II, ii, 98)

It may help to think of /ɒ/ (honest) as a shorter, more relaxed /ɔ/ (all) sound. With this in mind, try speaking the previous words and the phrases that follow.

PHRASES /ɒ/ (honest)

1.	wasn't honest	6.	lost her wallet
2.	costly donkey	7.	wants tolerance
3.	not the opposite	8.	speaks too softly
4.	the longest song	9.	spotted ten dollars
5.	slobbering stopped	10.	hears the clock tock

SENTENCES /ɒ/ (honest)

1. Rob cannot[1] stop sobbing.

2. The actors want hot coffee.

3. Todd's office is off the lobby.

4. Was he in Washington or wasn't he?

5. Are you positive she played ROSALIND?

6. Robin, your posh collar needs washing.

---

[1] Stress falls on the first syllable of the word 'cannot' / ˈkænɒtʰ/ in classic texts.

7. Oliver spoke so softly, we lost his lines.

8. The clock is on top of the closet, Robert.

9. John will probably go to college in Boston.

10. The shocked mobster was throttled by a toddler.

11. What star is speaking the donkey's jolly dialogue?

12. Empty the contents of your pockets onto the table.

13. Doctor, stop drinking all the hospital's hot chocolate.

14. Bob stopped swallowing scotch after spotting a Hobbit.

15. What popular jockey is famous for his coffee commercial?

Honest Bob's Coffee Shop

If possible, I always stop by Honest Bob's Coffee Shop when on holiday in Boston. A constantly evolving menu offers a positively intoxicating array of entrees, like hot Macintosh omelets served in crock-pots, and roasted peacock simmered in a light butterscotch broth.

Grip Top Sock

Give me the gift of a grip-top-sock;
A clip-drape, ship-shape, tip-top sock.
Not your spiv-slick, slap-stick, slip-shod stock,
But a plastic, elastic grip-top sock.
None of your fantastic slack swap-slop
From a slapdash flash cash haberdasher shop!
Not a knick-knack, knock-kneed knickerbocker's sock
With a mock-shot, blob-mottled ticker-tocker clock.
Not a rucked-up puckered up flip-flop sock,
Not a super-sheer seersucker ruck-sack sock,
Not a spot-speckled, frog-freckled, cheap sheik's sock
Off a hodgepodge, moss-blotched botched Scotch block.
Nothing slip-slop, drip-drop,
Flip-flop or clip-clop:
Tip me to a tip-top grip-top sock.

(Anonymous)

WORDS comparing back vowels /ɔ/ /ɒ/ /ɑ/

Note: /ɔ/ and /ɑ/ are generally long, while /ɒ/ is short. The lips are relaxed and unrounded for /ɑ/. *Read across.*

	/ɔ/	/ɒ/	/ɑ/		/ɔ/	/ɒ/	/ɑ/
1.	awe	opt	ah	11.	hall	hot	hah
2.	saw	sop	saga	12.	Paul	pot	pa
3.	ball	box	Bach	13.	Shaw	shock	shah
4.	call	cost	calm	14.	draw	drop	drama
5.	fall	fog	father	15.	jaw	jot	java
6.	Saul	sot	saga	16.	slaw	slot	Slavic
7.	caw	cot	koala	17.	stall	stock	Stalin
8.	cause	cough	Kafka	18.	dawn	don	Dante
9.	paw	pop	papa	19.	talk	tock	taco
10.	mall	mop	macho	20.	call	cop	Kahn

           ɒ   ɒ ɒ   ɔ   ɒ   ɒ ɒ   ɔ

If a Hottentot tot taught a Hottentot tot to talk,

        ɒ   ɒ

Ere the tot could totter;

  ɔ   ɒ   ɒ ɒ   ɔ   ɔ

Ought the Hottentot tot be taught to say aught,

        ɒ ɔ   ɔ

Or what ought to be taught her?

(Edward Lear: Nonsense Rhymes)

SENTENCES comparing back vowels /ɔ/ /ɒ/ /ɑ/

/ɔ/   /ɒ/   /ɑ/

Call Tom at the spa.
Talk to honest father.
Water Molly's corsage.
Salt the rotten avocados.
Authors were honored in Tahoe.

/ɒ/   /ɔ/   /ɑ/

Stop calling father.
Watch Paul samba.
Officers are taught to be calm.
The tots fought in Palm Springs.
Holly's daughter is in the armada.

/ɔ/   /ɒ/   /ɑ/

Saul wants hot tacos.
Authors promise drama.
We bought Florida palms.
Australians wanted guava.
They sought dogs and koalas.

/ɒ/   /ɑ/   /ɔ/

Honestly, Bali's bawdy.
It's probably Sinatra calling.
The cost of pasta is awesome.
We got the hibachi in August.
An impossible scenario was drawn.

/ɑ/	/ɔ/	/ɒ/

The suave caller is a mobster.
IAGO is auditioning tomorrow.
Picasso's drawings are popular.
These debutants are a saucy lot.
The sonata's thought to be modern.

/ɑ/	/ɒ/	/ɔ/

The Mafia shot Paul.
Tanya shops at the mall.
Calamari with hot sauce.
Gandhi's moral thoughts.
That aria is often withdrawn.

CLASSICAL AMERICAN TEXT /ɒ/ (h<u>o</u>nest). *Mark the following and speak out loud.*

       ɒ   ɒ   ɒ   ɒ
Nay, m<u>o</u>ck n<u>o</u>t, m<u>o</u>ck n<u>o</u>t.

(Much Ado About Nothing: I, i, 285)

I speak French shockingly.

(Chekhov: The Cherry Orchard)

Now blessed be the great Apollo!

(The The Winter's Tale: III, ii, 137)

I love thee not; therefore pursue me not.

(A Midsummer Night's Dream: II, i, 188)

Mine honor is my life, both grow in one;
Take honor from me, and my life is done.

(Richard II: I, i, 182)

No; let him die, in that he is a fox,
By nature prov'd an enemy to the flock.

(2 Henry VI: III, i, 257)

And ah! what dialogue!
My prince, I do believe you've turned the frog!

(Rostand: Cyrano de Bergerac)

I am so fond of coffee, I drink it day and night.

(Chekhov: The Cherry Orchard)

What do you want? Stop where you are. You're positively dripping.

(Ibsen: Ghosts)

Come lead me, officers, to the block of shame;
Wrong hath but wrong, and blame the due of blame.

(Richard III: IV, v, 28)

Nay, then he is a conjurer.

(2 Henry VI: IV, ii, 92)

Plead what I will be, not what I have been;
Not my deserts, but what I will deserve.

(Richard III: IV, iv, 414)

Mars laid waste to the sweets of poor Apollo—
Wife, shop, and all in a single swallow!

(Rostand: Cyrano de Bergerac)

No, Titus, no, the Emperor needs her not,
Nor her, nor thee, nor any of thy stock.

(Titus Andronicus: I, I, 299)

Cancel his bond of life, dear God, I pray,
That I may live and say, "The dog is dead."

(Richard III: IV, iv, 77)

What shall be done with him? What is your plot?

(The Merry Wives of Windsor: IV, iv, 46)

You are not really happy—that is at the bottom of it.

(Ibsen: Hedda Gabler)

You have taken your hat off. Put it on or you will catch cold.

(Chekhov: The Sea Gull)

Loves me, loves me not; loves me, loves me not; loves me, loves
me not.

(Chekhov: The Seagull)

He is six-or seven-and-twenty, and has never had the opportunity
of learning what a well-ordered home really is.

(Ibsen: Ghosts)

Well, 'tis no matter, honor pricks me on. Yea, but how if honor
prick me off when I come on? How then? Can honor set to a leg?
No. Or an arm? No. Or take away the grief of a wound? No.
Honor hath no skill in surgery then? No. What is honor? A word.
What is in that word honor? What is that honor? Air. A trim
reckoning! Who hath it? He that died a' Wednesday.

(1 Henry IV: V, i, 129)

'Liquid' / ju / (you)

When the /u/ sound occurs after 't', 'd' or 'n' in the spelling, /j/ is added before /u/ so that **'liquid'** /ju/ (you) is spoken. This is optional after 's' or 'l'.

AUDIO 56▶ **'liquid'** /ju/ (you)

>   dju
> Women, you see—in certain matters, they have a <u>deu</u>cedly
>   tju
> keen in<u>tui</u>tion.
> (Ibsen: The Master Builder)
>
>   tju
> Like sweet bells jangled out of <u>tu</u>ne, and harsh.
> (Hamlet: III, i, 158)
>
>   dju
> The old fantastical <u>Du</u>ke of dark corners.
> (Measure for Measure: IV, iii, 156)

WORDS with liquid /ju/ (you)

after 't'   astute, attitude, beatitude, constitution, costume, destitute, gratitude, institute, institution, latitude, obtuse, opportunity, platitudes, servitude, stew, steward, Stewart, Stuart, student, studious, stupendous, stupid, tuba, tube, tuber, tuberculosis, tubular, Tudor, Tuesday, tufa, tuition, tulip, tumescence, tumor, tumult, tuna, tune, tunic, Tunisia, Turin, tutelage, tutor

after 'd'   adieu, conducive, dude, deduce, deuce, dew, duality, dubiety, dubious, dubitation, duel, duenna, dues, duet, duke, dukedom, duly, dune, duo, duped, duplex, duplicate, duplicity, dutiful, duty, indubitably, induce, introduce, reproduce, residue

after 'n'   annuity, avenue, enumerate, ingenuity, knew, minute *(adj.)*, minutiae, mononucleosis, neume, neuter, neutral, neutralize, neutron, Newark, newborn, newcomer, newel, news, newspaper, newt, nuance, nuclear, nucleus, nude, nuisance, numerous, nutriments, nutrition, renewal, retinue, revenue

346

after 's'	assume, consume, ensue, presume, pursuit, pursue, sucrose,
(optional)	sue, suet, suicide, suit, suitor, super, superficiality, superfluous, superintendent, superior, superlative, supine
after 'l'	absolute, allude, allusions, aluminum, delude, dissolute,
(optional)	eluded, elusive, evolution, illuminate, illusory, lewd, lieu, lieutenant, lubricate, lucency, lucerne, lucid, Lucifer, lucrative, lucubrate, ludicrous, lugubrious, lukewarm, luminous, lunacy, lunar, lunatic, lute, resolution, salubrious, salute, solution

Note: There are also a few words that add the 'liquid' /ju/ (you) after 'z' and voiceless 'th', including:

enthused, enthusiasm, enthusiastic, exhume, exude, exuberant, exuviate, presume, resume, Zeus

The 'liquid' /ju/ (you) is **not** used:

(a) when the /u/ sound is represented by 'o' in the spelling, as in:

to, too, two, toot, do, noose, soup, Lou, loom, balloon

(b) when consonant combinations of /l/ are involved, as in:

flew, slew, blue, fluent, and plume

PHRASES with liquid /ju/ (you)

1.	great stew	6.	singing duo
2.	happy news	7.	overdue dues
3.	salutes stupidity	8.	brand new suit
4.	stupendous tune	9.	another new student
5.	introducing the duke	10.	passed the resolution

SENTENCES with liquid /ju/ (you)

1. Is tuna nutritious?
2. The news was amusing.
3. What a stupendous duet.
4. Don't assume he's destitute.
5. Was Hugo's contract renewed?

6.   Students resume classes Tuesday.

7.   The scene was played in the nude.

8.   The price of costumes is ludicrous.

9.   Mr. Nugent felt the apology gratuitous.

10.   What's the intersecting longitude and latitude?

11.   The newscaster remains enthusiastically neutral.

12.   The lute of unpolluted silver was sold on Tuesday.

13.   Don't presume your positive new attitude is lunacy.

14.   The news that there are no new tumors is stupendous.

15.   Cigarette smoke left a thin residue on all the new tables.

Studious Stewart Dumaine

You could argue that the studious humanitarian, Stewart Dumaine, is quite a suitable suitor for the enthusiastic beauty from Tulane. Presumably, the opportunity to introduce the duo will ensue on Tuesday at the Numerological Institute.

> A tutor who tooted the flute,
> Tried to tutor two tooters to toot.
> Said the two to the tutor:
> "Is it harder to toot,
> Or to tutor two tooters to toot?"
>
> (Anonymous)

CLASSICAL AMERICAN TEXT **'liquid'** **/ju/** (**you**). *Mark the following and speak out loud.*

              tju
I seem likely to be a perpetual student.

                     (Chekhov: The Cherry Orchard)

I do perceive here a divided duty.

                     (Othello: I, iii, 181)

Ah, tutor, look where bloody Clifford comes!

                     (3 Henry VI: I, iii, 2)

348

If opportunity and humblest suit
Cannot attain it, why then hark you hither!

(The Merry Wives of Windsor: III, iv, 20)

That she was never yet that ever knew
Love got so sweet as when desire did sue.

(Troilus and Cressida: I, ii, 290)

A goodly lady, trust me, of the hue
That I would choose were I to choose anew.

(Titus Andronicus: I, i, 261)

Were I a man, a duke, and next of blood,
I would remove these tedious stumbling-blocks.

(2 Henry VI: I, ii, 63)

Come now, which one of you will head the list?
You m'sieur? No? You? Or you? First duellist
Will meet with all grave honor can command.

(Rostand: Cyrano de Bergerac)

Never dropped mildew on a flower here till now.

(Webster: The White Devil)

Your honour, I stand ready for any duteous employment.

(Tourneur: The Revenger's Tragedy)

For strokes receiv'd and many blows repaid
Have robb'd my strong-knit sinews of their strength.

(3 Henry VI: II, iii, 3)

Tomorrow I shall have to speak to the whole assembled multitude.

(Ibsen: Ghosts)

This news is old enough, yet it is every day's news.

(Measure for Measure: III, ii, 229)

These clever fellows are all so stupid; there's not a creature for me
to speak to.

(Chekhov: The Cherry Orchard)

What difference is between the duke and I? No more than between
two bricks, all made of one clay: only't may be one is placed on the
top of a turret, the other in the bottom of a well, by mere chance.

(Webster: The White Devil)

/ æ / (th<u>a</u>t)

before 'm' 'n' 'g' 'ng' 'nk' spellings

In heightened[1] speech, the pure non-nasal vowel /æ/ is spoken before / m n g ŋ ŋk /. The back of the tongue remains relaxed and uninvolved.

AUDIO 57▶ /æ/ (th<u>a</u>t)

>   ae   ae   ae ae (or use weak forms)
> But I c<u>an</u>'t underst<u>and</u> how you c<u>an</u> h<u>a</u>ve made it go far
>
> enough for two.
> > (Ibsen: Hedda Gabler)
>
>   æ   æ   ə
> By heaven, I r<u>a</u>ther would have been his h<u>a</u>ng<u>ma</u>n.
> > (Othello: I, i, 34)
>
>   æ   ae (or ə)   æ
> You speak a l<u>a</u>nguage th<u>a</u>t I underst<u>a</u>nd not.
> > (The The Winter's Tale: III, ii, 80)

Tension, nasality, or variation in pronunciation of /æ/ sounds can be identified through the following exercise.

WORDS /æ/ **sounds in the following should 'rhyme'** *Read across.*

/æ/	apple	/æ/	am, amber, ambulance
/kæ/	cat	/kæ/	camp, camphor, camera
/dæ/	dash	/dæ/	damn, damp, damsel
/gæ/	gas	/gæ/	gamma, gamble, gamut
/hæ/	has	/hæ/	Hamlet, hammer, hamster

---

[1] The need for a slight relaxation of /æ/ before /m n g ŋ ŋk/ was addressed in NAS, since it is a tense sound in many North American dialects—but pure /æ/ is not required in NAS.

/hæ/	hat	/hæ/	hamper, hammock, hamstring
/stæ/	stack	/stæ/	stamp, stammer, stamina
/fæ/	fat	/fæ/	famished, family, famine
/læ/	lack	/læ/	land, landscape, landward
/hæ/	hat	/hæ/	hand, handsome, handbag

Assure that the vowel sound is releasing through the mouth by pinching the nose shut on the vowel. Be sure to release the pinching before the three consonant sounds that exit through the nose: / m n ŋ /.

/stæ/	stack	/stæ/	stand, standard, stand-in
/fæ/	fat	/fæ/	fan, fancy, fantasy, fantastic
/dæ/	dad	/dæ/	dang, dank, dangle, dangling
/ræ/	rack	/ræ/	rang, rank, rankle, ranked
/ʃæ/	shack	/ʃæ/	shank, Shanghai, Shangri-La

/ræ/	rack	/ræ/	rancor, rancorous, rancorously
/hæ/	hack	/hæ/	hang, Hank, hanker, hanger
/jæ/	yak	/jæ/	yang, yank, Yankee, Yangtze
/væ/	vat	/væ/	van, vanished, vanity, vantage
/æ/	at	/æ/	angry, angle, angular, anguished

/dʒæ/	Jack	/dʒæ/	jangle, jangly, jangling
/wæ/	wax	/wæ/	Wang, wangle, wangling
/stræ/	distract	/stræ/	strangle, strangler, strangling
/læ/	lack	/læ/	Lang, lank, languish, langley
/læ/	lap	/læ/	language, languid, languor

ae   ae ae *(or weak form)* ae   ae

I daresay you fancy that I am an extremely happy man.

(Ibsen: The Master Builder)

PHRASES /æ/ (that)

1.	pulling rank	6.	grand oat bran
2.	back to the bank	7.	Jackie, not Jan
3.	languidly fanned	8.	hamming it up
4.	trampled fantasies	9.	stacks of stamps
5.	not monogrammed	10.	thanks, but no thanks

SENTENCES /æ/ (th<u>a</u>t)

1. Yes, Lady Anne?

2. Thanks, but no thanks.

3. Who starred in *Champ*?

4. Terrific back-hand, Frank.

5. Nancy sent us a candygram.

6. That stage-gun shoots blanks.

7. What's the brand of champions?

8. Pam sang the Thanksgiving anthem.

9. Turn on a fan; it's so hot I can't stand it!

10. What's wrong, Francis? You look angry.

11. He sang his name, rank and serial number.

12. There's Hank, the family's favorite spaniel.

13. Mandy, you can't drink brandy on the left bank.

14. The jogger is stamping to stop muscle cramping.

15. I need a bigger tank for my brand new angle fish.

Lanky Frankie

L<u>a</u>nky Fr<u>a</u>nkie, P<u>a</u>mela's p<u>a</u>mpered sp<u>a</u>niel, r<u>a</u>n after a t<u>a</u>n afgh<u>an</u> r<u>a</u>mbling down Gr<u>a</u>nd <u>A</u>venue. Th<u>a</u>nkfully, Fr<u>a</u>nkie is b<u>a</u>ck with his f<u>a</u>mily, b<u>a</u>nqueting on h<u>a</u>m s<u>a</u>ndwiches. They are not <u>a</u>ngry, and Fr<u>a</u>nkie will h<u>a</u>ve no reprim<u>and</u>.

CLASSICAL AMERICAN TEXT /æ/ (th<u>a</u>t). *Mark the following and speak out loud.*

   ae   ae   ae
D<u>a</u>mn her, lewd minx! O, d<u>a</u>mn her, d<u>a</u>mn her!

(Othello: III, iii, 475)

Come, Hamlet, come, and take this hand from me.

(Hamlet: V, ii, 224)

Fate's a spaniel,
We cannot beat it from us.

(Webster: The White Devil)

I am your sorrow's nurse,
And I will pamper it with lamentation.

(Richard III: II, ii, 87)

The words would add more anguish than the wounds.

(3 Henry VI: II, i, 99)

You see me, Lord Bassanio, where I stand,
Such as I am. Though for myself alone
I would not be ambitious in my wish.

(The Merchant of Venice: III, ii, 149)

Look at me, my friend, and say what chance,
What hope have I, with this...protuberance?

(Rostand: Cyrano de Bergerac)

ROSALINE. Thou canst not hit it, hit it, hit it,
          Thou canst not hit it, my good man.
BOYET.   And I cannot, cannot, cannot[1],
          And I cannot, another can.

(Love's Labor's Lost: IV, i, 125)

BENEDICK. Fair Beatrice, I thank you for your pains.
BEATRICE. I took no more pains for those thanks than you take pains
          to thank me.

(Much Ado About Nothing: II, iii, 249)

Why, if thou never wast at court, thou never saw'st good manners;
if thou never saw'st good manners, then thy manners must be wicked,
and wickedness is sin, and sin is damnation.

(As You Like It: III, ii, 40)

The ring is on my hand,
And the wreath is on my brow;
Satins and jewels grand
Are all at my command,
And I am happy now.

(Poe: Bridal Ballad)

---

[1] Remember, stress usually falls on the first syllable of the word 'cannot' / ˈkænɒtʰ/ in classic texts.

/ aʊ̆ / (n<u>ow</u>)

/ aʊ̆ə̆/ (p<u>ower</u>)

This is an *optional,* subtle adjustment to the above sounds, which may be useful if they seem overly nasal or bright within the dialect. It is based on an older, more traditional Standard British pronunciation, which initiates these sounds with the relaxed back vowel /a/ (f<u>a</u>ther) rather than the brighter /a/ sound. The tongue arch gently flattens, dropping to the floor of the mouth for the first element, while the lips, cheeks, tongue, and throat muscles remain relaxed.

AUDIO 58▶ /aʊ̆/ (n<u>ow</u>) and /aʊ̆ə̆/ (p<u>ower</u>)

> aʊ̆
> It s<u>ou</u>nded like harps in the air.
> > (Ibsen: The Master Builder)
>
> aʊ̆ aʊ̆
> H<u>ow</u> n<u>ow</u>, you sec<u>r</u>et, black, and midnight hags?
> > (Macbeth: IV, i, 48)
>
> aʊ̆ aʊ̆ aʊ̆ aʊ̆
> Fl<u>out</u> 'em and sc<u>out</u> 'em and sc<u>out</u> 'em and fl<u>out</u> 'em!
>
> Th<u>ou</u>ght is free.
> > (The Tempest: III, ii, 121)

WORDS /aʊ/→/aʊ̆/

ouch	chow	vow	proud
allow	crowd	growl	prowl
down	count	mount	drown
flounce	astound	bounce	around
compound	paramount	surround	befouled

EXERCISE **relationship between /a/, /aʊ̆/, and /aʊ̆ə̆ /.** Relax the lips, cheeks, tongue, and throat, and flatten the tongue arch when initiating the following words, all of which begin with the most open back vowel /a/ (f<u>a</u>ther).

Read across.

/a/	/aŭ/	/aŭ/	/aŭə̆/[1]
Saga	sound	souse	sour
papa	pounce	pound	power
father	found	fountain	flower
tra-la-la	louse	loud	lower
bah	boughs	bounced	bower

PHRASES /aŭ/ (now)

1.	not allowed	6.	loud shouting
2.	bounced around	7.	town due south
3.	chow down now	8.	ounces and pounds
4.	soundless hound	9.	proud owls pouncing
5.	astounding house	10.	accountant floundered

aŭ   aŭ   aŭ
Thou thing of no bowels, thou!

(Troilus and Cressida: II, i, 49)

SENTENCES /aŭ/ (now) and /aŭə̆/ (power)

1. No kowtowing allowed.

2. Start the countdown now.

3. Sound all vowels out loud.

4. Do Girl Scouts sell sauerkraut?

5. Ever heard of 'surround sound'?

6. That sounded like a putdown, Howard.

7. The scoundrel impounded both houses.

8. What a well-pronounced announcement.

9. The guests caught trout and hunted grouse.

10. They found him cowering in the flowerbed.

11. I'm not so fond of that brown evening gown.

---

[1] Remember, the triphthong may also be rhythmically separated into a diphthong followed by the short, unstressed vowel of 'r' as in /aŭ ə̆/.

12.   Mr. Powell ran the endowment into the ground.

13.   He was fond of wandering around downtown.

14.   *Encounters* is playing at the Roundabout Theatre.

15.   After shopping for hours, she rested by the fountain.

CLASSICAL AMERICAN TEXT /aʊ̆/ (n<u>ow</u>) and /aʊ̆ə̆/ (p<u>ower</u>). *Mark the following and speak out loud.*

aʊ̆
For courage m<u>ou</u>nteth with occasion.

(King John: II, i, 82)

Or perhaps a wart adorns one jowl…?

(Rostand: Cyrano de Bergerac)

For God's sake let us sit upon the ground
And tell sad stories of the death of kings.

(Richard II: III, ii, 155)

Set down, set down your honorable load,
If honor may be shrouded in a hearse.

(Richard III: I, ii, 1)

How now, my pretty knave, how dost thou?

(King Lear: I, iv, 96)

Where art thou, proud Demetrius? Speak thou now.

(A Midsummer Night's Dream: III, ii, 401)

Even now we hous'd him in the abbey here.

(The Comedy of Errors: V, i, 188)

Enter Cyrano! saves the dangling grouse…
And I wake…as steward in his cousin's house!

(Rostand: Cyrano de Bergerac)

Drown thyself? drown cats and blind puppies!

(Othello: I, iii, 335)

I was afraid, partly on my own account. I was such a coward.

(Ibsen: Ghosts)

356

How now, thou core of envy?

(Troilus and Cressida: V i, 4)

A thousand crowns, or else lay down your head.

(2 Henry VI: IV, i, 16)

Beauford's red sparkling eyes blab his heart's malice,
And Suffolk's cloudy brow his stormy hate.

(2 Henry VI: III, i, 154)

I won't find peace till I'm down, won't rest till I'm down, down on
the ground! And once I'm down, I want to keep on going down
and down...

(Strindberg: Miss Julie)

Stay we no longer, dreaming of renown,
But sound the trumpets, and about our task.

(3 Henry VI: II, i, 199)

No one has any grounds to separate spirit from matter, seeing
that spirit itself may be a combination of material atoms.

(Chekhov: The Seagull)

Oh 'tis a brave thing for a man to sit by himself; he may stretch
himself in the stirrups, look about, and see the whole compass of
the hemisphere. You're now, my lord, i' th' saddle.

(Webster: The White Devil)

I would thou couldst stammer, that thou mightst pour this conceal'd
man out of thy mouth, as wine comes out of a narrow-mouth'd bottle,
either too much at once, or none at all.

(As You Like It: III, ii, 198)

As the bee hums communion with the flower...
A way to touch a heartbeat...and the power
As you taste a lingering instant of the soul!

(Rostand: Cyrano de Bergerac)

PURE VOWELS

before consonant / r /

When the consonant **/r/** (red) occurs in the middle of a word, it is preceded by a pure vowel sound, not by a diphthong of 'r'.

This element of Classical American is taken from Standard British pronunciation and can serve several purposes. This usage:

(a) affords a formality and an authenticity to the pronunciation of British-English proper names and places, especially in Shakespeare

(b) diminishes the amount of 'r' coloring, which helps encourage a release of the voice and speech forward through the mouth

(c) provides differentiation between words that would otherwise be pronounced the same, for example 'hairy' and 'Harry'

(d) helps to establish a time and place other than present-day America—as do the rest of the Classical American changes

This is an important body of work for students interested in studying other dialects. People with English as a second language often learn from British-English speakers. Therefore, the adjustments that follow are often required for speaking other dialects as well.

The vowel sounds and consonant **/r/** that follow are separated by a dash (–) throughout.

/ ɪ / (will)

before consonant / r /

Use pure **/ɪ/** (will), rather than the **/ɪə̆ /** (here) diphthong, before consonant **/r/** within a word. Words requiring this adjustment can often be recognized by an **/ɪ/** prefix (see page 97) and/or by the initial spellings: 'ir', 'irr'.

AUDIO 59▶ **/ɪ/ (wi̱ll) before consonant /r/**

I
You seem a bit low-spi̱-rited to-day, aren't you?

(Chekhov: Three Sisters)

I
The mi̱-rror of all courtesy.

(Henry VIII: II, i, 53)

I
O cruel, i̱-rreligious piety!

(Titus Andronicus: I, i, 130)

NAMES & PLACES /ɪ/ (wi̱ll) before consonant /r/

Be-rowne	Hispe-ria	I-ran	I-raq
I-roquois	Pi-randello	Sy-ria	Ty-rrel

WORDS /ɪ/ (wi̱ll) before consonant /r/

be-rate	be-reaved	be-reft	de-rision
de-rive	empi-rical	e-radicate	e-rase
e-rect	e-rogenous	e-rosion	e-rotic
e-rratic	e-rroneous	e-ruption	he-reditary
he-roic	i-rrational	i-rritable	i-rregular
i-rrelevant	i-rrespective	ly-rical	mi-racle
mi-rror	pre-rogative	py-ramid	se-rene
spi-rit	sy-rup	ty-ranny	vi-rile[1]

PHRASES /ɪ/ (wi̱ll) before consonant /r/

1.	i-rregular day	6.	clear mi-rror
2.	feeling be-reft	7.	tall py-ramid
3.	se-rene vacation	8.	trip to Sy-ria
4.	lovely pi-rouette	9.	e-rased pages
5.	floating di-rigible	10.	i-rreparable break

SENTENCES /ɪ/ (wi̱ll) before /r/

1. Change direction.

2. Who played BEROWNE?

---

[1] Standard British pronunciation of 'ile' endings is usually **/aïl/** (<u>aisle</u>) i.e., sterile, futile.

3. What remarkable lyrics.

4. The disease was hereditary.

5. How many lira for that mirror?

6. Do I see stirrups on that giraffe?

7. The tyrannical ruler was replaced.

8. They were bereaved and dispirited.

9. What spirited material he's written.

10. Rinaldo remains an imperious individual.

11. It was a pyrrhic victory, costing too much.

12. Imagine berating the delinquent instructor.

13. The irascible director erupted during rehearsal.

14. Challenge the satirical bully to a debate, sirrah!

15. Confidence in the relationship eventually eroded.

16. That was a heroic portrayal of the Iroquois Indians.

17. How miraculous: a serene vacation in a secluded spot.

18. We were explicitly advised to rely on empirical evidence.

19. We desire an innovative production, not a derivative one.

20. Two short, unstressed syllables? That's a pyrrhic rhythm.

Moose Mirage

Was it a mi̠-rage?

No, it was the largest stack of pancakes I had ever seen a gi̠-raffe eat.

Pouring on the sy̠-rup, the se̠-rene chewing of each little bite, it was both ly̠-rical

and he-roic. This tho-roughly e-rased the time I saw a moose preparing a

soufflé.

Exception: when /ɪɚ/ (here) diphthong ends the root of a word that is followed by a suffix, the diphthong is maintained and linking consonant /r/ is used to connect the suffix, including: 'age', 'ance', 'ence', 'eth', 'er', 'est', 'ing', 'y'. Therefore, 'hearing' is pronounced: /ˈhɪɚ-rɪŋ/.

ɪɚ-r   ɪɚ-r

My nea-rest and dea-rest enemy.

(1 Henry IV: III, ii, 123)

SOME EXCEPTION WORDS that keep /ɪɚ/ (here) before /r/

reareth	bleary	leery	wearier
fearing	gearing	cheery	peerage
appearance	smearing	queerer	clearance

CLASSICAL AMERICAN TEXT /ɪ/ (will) before /r/. *Mark the following and speak out loud.*

ɪ
Tell me, sirrah, what's my name?

(2 Henry VI: II, i, 115)

Now my spirit is going.

(Antony and Cleopatra: IV, xv, 58)

Poor rogue hereditary.

(Timon of Athens: IV, iii, 274)

The tyrannous and bloody act is done.

(Richard III: IV, iii,1)

Lord Bassianus lies beray'd in blood.

(Titus Andronicus: II, iii, 222)

Confirmed; this be the doom irrevocable.

(Tourneur: The Revenger's Tragedy)

Hast thou not spirit to curse thine enemy?

(2 Henry VI: III, ii, 308)

I have perhaps some shallow spirit of judgment.

(1 Henry VI: II, iv, 16)

In them I trust, for they are soldiers,
Witty, courteous, liberal, full of spirit.

(3 Henry VI:, I ii, 42)

Erroneous, mutinous, and unnatural,
This deadly quarrel daily doth beget!

(3 Henry VI: II, v, 90)

That all your interest in those territories
Is utterly bereft you: all is lost.

(2 Henry VI:, III i, 84)

And I, who at his hands receiv'd my life,
Have by my hands of life bereaved him.
Pardon me, God, I knew not what I did!

(3 Henry VI: II, v, 67)

Upon thy eyeballs murderous tyranny
Sits in grim majesty, to fright the world.

(2 Henry VI: III, ii, 49)

Lend your romantic looks, heroic stance –
And between us we'll make one *par excellence*!

(Rostand: Cyrano de Bergerac)

GLOUCESTER. Fellow, what miracle dost thou proclaim?
ONE.   A miracle, a miracle!
SUFFOLK.   Come to the King and tell him what miracle.

(2 Henry VI: II, i, 58)

The last is Berowne, the merry madcap lord. Not a word with
him but a jest.

(Love's Labor's Lost: II, i, 215)

Sirrah, your lord and master's married, there's news for you.
You have a new mistress.

(All's Well That Ends Well: II, iii, 242)

The girl with the irritating hair, that she was always showing off.

(Ibsen: Hedda Gabler)

/ e / (ge̱t)

before consonant / r /

Use pure **/e/** (ge̱t) before the consonant **/r/** rather than the **/eə̆ /** (the̱ir) diphthong. Use of pure **/e/** is often indicated by the spellings: 'er', 'err'.

AUDIO 60► **/e/** (ge̱t) before consonant **/r/**

>   e
> I often feel ready to sink under this te̱-rrible burden of debt.
> > (Ibsen: The Master Builder)
>
>   e
> Pleas'd you to do't at pe̱-ril of your soul.
> > (Measure for Measure: II, iv, 67)
>
>   e
> I am never me̱-rry when I hear sweet music.
> > (The Merchant of Venice: V, i, 69)

NAMES & PLACES **/e/** (ge̱t) before consonant **/r/**

Ame-rica	Be-resford	Be-ring	Che-ryl
De-rek	De-rry	E-rebus	E-ric
Fe-rris	Ge-rald	Ge-raldine	He-reford
He-rod	He-ron	He-rrick	Hespe-rides
Je-rry	Ke-rry	Me-rrill	Pe-rry
She-ridan	She-rry	Spe-rry	Te-rence

WORDS **/e/** (ge̱t) before consonant **/r/**

auste-rity	bu-ry	cele-rity	ce-remony
che-rish	che-rub	de-relect	de-rivation
de-rogate	e-rror	e-rrant	e-rrand
e-remite	fe-rry	fe-rrous	gene-ric
he-rald	he-resy	he-retic	he-roine

compa-rison	emba-rrass	ga-rish	ga-rret
gua-rantee	ga-rrison	ha-rass[1]	ha-rrowing
hila-rity	la-rynx	ma-rigold	ma-rry
ma-rriage	ma-rrow	ma-rathon	ma-riner
na-rrate	na-rrative	na-rrow	pa-rable
pa-rachute	pa-ragon	pa-ragraph	pa-rallel
pa-rasite	pa-rry	pa-rish	pa-rody
pa-rrot	pha-risee	singula-rity	spa-rrow
ta-rantella	ta-rragon	ta-rry	transpa-rent

PHRASES /æ/ (tha̲t) before consonant /r/

1.	such a cha-racter	6.	ca-rried on
2.	not emba-rrassed	7.	yes, Ha-rry
3.	decided to ma-rry	8.	overly a-rrogant
4.	sexual ha-rassment	9.	thinking na-rrowly
5.	straight as an a-rrow	10.	getting ca-rried away

MORE PHRASES /æ/ (tha̲t) before consonant /r/

1.	too emba-rrassing	6.	a-rid weather
2.	cha-racter building	7.	lovely pa-rrot
3.	na-rrating the book	8.	ta-rries awhile
4.	makes compa-risons	9.	especially ba-rren
5.	prepared a ga-rrison	10.	recounted pa-rables

SENTENCES /æ/ (tha̲t) before consonant /r/

1. They'll marry.

2. Carry it, Harriet.

3. Barry, tarry awhile.

4. Who's in the garrison, Garry?

5. I love playing arrogant characters.

6. She was harassed on Arrow Street.

7. I characterize him as a working barracuda.

---

[1] Accent the first syllable: 'ha-ra̲ss /'hæərəs/.

8.   *The Marriage Proposal* is playing in Paris.

9.   Darryl is playing the character of the Baron.

10.   Arid weather contributes to her harried look.

11.   The parish priest is a paragon of good health.

12.   Apparently, the garrison refused to eat carrion.

13.   The passage is too narrow for Harold's carriage.

14.   Harry and Larry were cast as the arrogant twins.

15.   The thought of running the marathon is hilarious.

16.   Mr. Farrell, the Barrister, disparaged the Saracens.

17.   Jarret proved a paragon in navigating the labyrinth.

18.   What garrulous baritone gets laryngitis with regularity?

19.   Harold Harris narrated the harrowing maritime parable.

20.   Barry Darrow is unparalleled in his charitable activities.

21.   Aragon was once its own Kingdom in Northeastern Spain.

22.   Ariadne guided Theseus through the maze without alarum.

23.   Ms. Farrow is known for her garish, claret-colored apparel.

24.   The Pharisee was carried through the barricade in a chariot.

25.   Harold wrote a comparative narrative from a garret in Paris.

Verily, Harry's Married

    eɚ   æ   æ   e   e   eɚ   æ
When hairy Ha-rry ma-rried ve-ry me-rry Mary in a ca-rriage,
         e   e   e
it was a pe-rilous and te-rrible e-rror.

CLASSICAL AMERICAN TEXT /æ/ (th<u>a</u>t) **before consonant** /r/. *Mark the following and speak out loud.*

    æ
M<u>a</u>rry, God forbid!

(Richard II: IV, i, 114)

Search the market narrowly.

'   (Pericles: IV, ii, 3)

I have a triple-barreled name.

(Chekhov: Three Sisters)

It is no sin at all, but charity.

(Measure for Measure: II, iv, 66)

That's a telegram from Paris.

(Chekhov: The Cherry Orchard)

How am I then a villain,
To counsel Cassio to this parallel course.

(Othello: II, iii, 348)

Sound, trumpets, alarum to the combatants!

(2 Henry VI: II, iii, 92)

Do you not follow the young Lord Paris?

(Troilus and Cressida: III, i, 1)

Fie! charity, for shame! speak not in spite,
For you shall sup with Jesu Christ to-night.

(2 Henry VI: V, i, 213)

But match to match I have encount'red him,
And made a prey for carrion kites and crows.

(2 Henry VI: V, ii, 10)

And after summer evermore succeeds
Barren winter, with his wrathful nipping cold.

(2 Henry VI: II, iv, 2)

That was not my most arrant cowardice—that evening.

(Ibsen: Hedda Gabler)

This was sometime a paradox, but now the time gives it proof.

(Hamlet: III, i, 113)

Call me Julie—there are no barriers between us now.

(Strindberg: Miss Julie)

Harry to Harry shall, hot horse to horse,
Meet and ne'er part till one drop down a corse.

(1 Henry IV: IV, i, 122)

She's not well married that lives married long,
But she's best married that dies married young.

(Romeo and Juliet: IV, v, 77)

Heat me these irons hot, and look thou stand
Within the arras.

(King John: IV, i, 1)

The fashion wears out more apparel than the man.

(Much Ado About Nothing: III, iii, 139)

Why, this is an arrant counterfeit rascal, I remember him now;
a bawd, a cutpurse.

(Henry V: III, vi, 61)

They circle round that thoughtful perch, seduced—
At last, you bring the sparrows home to roost!

(Rostand: Cyrano de Bergerac)

I learn in this letter that Don Pedro of Arragon comes this night
to Messina.

(Much Ado About Nothing: I, i, 1)

O peers of England, shameful is this league,
Fatal this marriage, cancelling your fame,
Blotting your names from books of memory,
Raising the characters of your renown,
Defacing monuments of conquer'd France.

(2 Henry VI: I, i, 98)

Not so, not so; his life is parallel'd
Even with the stroke and line of his great justice.

(Measure for Measure: IV, ii, 79)

Come, come, you paraquito, answer me
Directly unto this question that I ask.
In faith, I'll break thy little finger, Harry,
And if thou wilt not tell me all things true.

(I Henry IV: II, iii, 85)

Your father is not a man of strong character, Miss Engstrand.
He stands terribly in need of a guiding hand.

(Ibsen: Ghosts)

/ ʌ / (UH)

before consonant / r /

There are many words spoken with /ʌ/ (UH) before consonant /r/ rather than /ɝ/ (ER) in Classical American, which is derived from Standard British.

AUDIO 62▶ /ʌ/ (UH) before consonant /r/

        ʌ

Why do you keep w<u>o</u>-rrying me?

(Chekhov: Three Sisters)

       ʌ   o

I should like your conscience to be—to be th<u>o</u>-roughly ro'bust.

(Ibsen: The Master Builder)

      ʌ

And men sit down to that n<u>ou</u>-rishment which is called supper.

(Love's Labor's Lost: I, i, 236)

NAMES & PLACES /ʌ/ (UH) before consonant /r/

Cu-rrier	Cu-rran	Du-rham	Cu-rrer
Cu-rrie	Mu-rray	Mu-rrow	Su-rrey

WORDS /ʌ/ (UH) before consonant /r/

bo-rough	bu-rrow	cou-rage	cu-rrant
cu-rrency	cu-rrent	cu-rricle	cu-rry
discou-rage	encou-rage	discou-raged	flou-rish
flu-rry	fu-rrier	fu-rrow	hu-rricane
hu-rry	hu-rrying	mu-rrain	nou-rish
nou-rishment	occu-rrence	scu-rrilous	scu-rry
su-rrogate	tu-rret	tho-roughly	wo-rry

     ʌ

Lend me the fl<u>ou</u>-rish of all gentle tongues.

(Love's Labor's Lost: IV, iii, 234)

PHRASES /ʌ/ (UH) before consonant /r/

1.	hot cu-rry	6.	snow flu-rries
2.	too tho-rough	7.	not nou-rishing
3.	large fu-rrows	8.	fu-rrowed brow
4.	always hu-rrying	9.	changed cu-rrency
5.	very discou-raged	10.	needs encou-raging

SENTENCES /ʌ/ (UH) before consonant /r/

1. He has luck and courage!

2. Are there currants in curry?

3. Check the currency exchange.

4. Mother loved Currier and Ives.

5. No scurrilous language, please.

6. Can furriers flourish in summer?

7. Dudley needs a nourishing lunch.

8. They worried about murrains in Surrey.

9. The bulky gunner was stuck in the turret.

10. Your current assets are in what currency?

11. Murray was suddenly in no hurry to leave.

12. Children come running to see snow flurries.

13. Are there surrogate mothers in this borough?

14. You musn't furrow your brow so much, honey.

15. Murray is thoroughly discouraged by injustice.

16. The judge invoked the Durham Rule in sentencing.

17. Uncle Chuck worries compulsively about hurricanes.

18. He took his pulse before plunging into the swift current.

19. Humphrey was in a hurry to purchase *dhurries* from India.

20. Young Doug burrowed a tunnel under Durham just for fun.

CLASSICAL AMERICAN TEXT /ʌ/ (UH) before /r/. *Mark the following and speak out loud.*

          ʌ

Met him in b<u>o</u>roughs, cities, villages,
Attended him on bridges, stood in lanes.

(1 Henry IV: IV, iii, 69)

There is no answer, thou unfeeling man,
To excuse the current of thy cruelty.

(The Merchant of Venice: IV, i, 63)

A red murrion a' thy jade's tricks!

(Troilus and Cressida: II, i, 19)

You put sharp weapons in a madman's hands,
Whiles I in Ireland nourish a mighty band.

(2 Henry VI: III, i, 347)

A flourish, trumpets! strike alarum, drums!

(Richard III: IV, iv, 149)

Why do the Emperor's trumpets flourish thus?

(Titus Andronicus: IV, ii, 49)

Thanks, thanks, there is no hurry, my dear child.

(Ibsen: Ghosts)

Three times did Richard make a lane to me,
And thrice cried, "Courage, father! fight it out!"

(3 Henry VI: I, iv, 9)

No more, no more! worse than the sun in March,
This praise doth nourish agues. Let them come!

(1 Henry IV: IV, i, 111)

That island of England breeds very valiant creatures;
their mastiffs are of unmatchable courage.

(Henry V: III, vii, 140)

But Jean—give me courage—tell me that you love me!

(Strindberg: Miss Julie)

Now, if it were in a thoroughly nice house, with a real gentleman...

(Ibsen: Ghosts)

/ ɔ / (all)

before consonant / r /

Use pure /ɔ/ (all) before consonant /r/ rather than the /ɔɚ/ diphthong. Use of /ɔ/ (all) is often indicated by the spellings: 'or', 'aur'.

AUDIO 63▶ /ɔ/ (all) before consonant /r/

>   ɔ
> A frightful sto̱-ry. What am I to believe?
> > (Strindberg: Crimes and Crimes)
>
>   ɔ
> Now are our brows bound with victo̱-rious wreaths.
> > (Richard III: I, i, 5)
>
>   ɔ
> You may my glo̱-ries and my state depose,
>
> But not my griefs; still am I king of those.
> > (Richard II: IV, i, 192)

NAMES & PLACES /ɔ/ (all) before consonant /r/

Au-ro-ra	Isado-ra	Lau-ra	Mau-reen
O-rient	Tau-rus	To-ry	Victo-ria

WORDS /ɔ/ (all) before consonant /r/

au-ra	au-ral	au-ricle	au-riferous
cho-rus	cho-ral	deco-rum	eupho-ria
flo-ra	fo-rum	glo-ry	glo-rious
glo-rify	histo-rian[1]	labo-rious	lau-reate
memo-rial	merito-rious	mo-ron	noto-rious
o-ral	sto-ry	quo-rum	victo-rious

---

[1] histo̱ric, -al, -ally: pronounced with /ɒ/ (honest) rather than /ɔ/.

PHRASES /ɔ/ (all) before consonant /r/

1.	saw the To-ry	6.	Lau-ra's place
2.	quite an au-ra	7.	eupho-ric cho-rus
3.	a glo-rious day	8.	not quite a quo-rum
4.	mo-ronic sto-ry	9.	buying o-riental rugs
5.	noto-rious events	10.	cho-ral arrangements

SENTENCES /ɔ/ (all) before consonant /r/

1. Hello, Laura.

2. We're victorious!

3. What's the quorum?

4. Where is Laurel Canyon?

5. See you on Memorial Day.

6. That's a lovely Oriental rug.

7. What a glorious performance!

8. Victoria is a notorious Taurus.

9. Write the definition of 'moron'.

10. Saul's oral report was laborious.

11. Who is England's Poet Laureate?

12. He's sitting with the other Tories.

13. We saw you at the mall, Maureen.

14. What's the famous story of Aurora?

15. Paul, did you just call him a moron?

16. They thought he'd talk about the Orient.

17. There is a lack of decorum at Shoreham.

18. Maybe you'll be cast as QUEEN VICTORIA.

19. In our forum, a quorum isn't necessary for a vote.

20. The Orient is notorious for its floral arrangements.

Exception: When /ɔɚ/ (sp<u>or</u>ts) diphthong ends the root of a word that is followed by a suffix, the diphthong is maintained and linking consonant **/r/** is used to connect the suffix, including: 'age', 'eth', 'ic', 'ing', 'ous', 'y'. Therefore, 'pouring' and 'caloric' are pronounced **/'pɔɚ-rɪŋ/** and **/kə'lɔɚ-rɪk/**.

'pɔɚ-rɪŋ

When creeping murmur and the po<u>r</u>ing dark
Fills the wide vessel of the universe.

(Henry V: IV Chorus, 2)

SOME EXCEPTION WORDS that keep /ɔɚ/ (sp<u>or</u>ts) before consonant /r/

abhorreth	adoring	allegoric	boring
coring	exploring	gory	hoary
porous	soaring	storage	warring

CLASSICAL AMERICAN TEXT /ɔ/ (<u>a</u>ll) before /r/. *Mark the following and speak out loud.*

ɔ

Sir, make me not your st<u>o</u>ry.

(Measure for Measure: I, iv, 30)

Devils! Sharpen up your memory!
Here's that glorious opportunity—

(Rostand: Cyrano de Bergerac)

You are as good as a chorus, my lord.

(Hamlet: III, ii, 245)

O, bless me here with thy victorious hand,
Whose fortunes Rome's best citizens applaud!

(Titus Andronicus: I, i, 163)

But thinkst thou heaven is such a glorious thing?

(Marlowe: Doctor Faustus)

And by an auricular assurance have your satisfaction.

(King Lear: I, ii, 92)

That's the story I was loathe to tell you a moment ago.

(Strindberg: Miss Julie)

/ ɒ / (honest)

before consonant / r /

Use the pure **/ɒ/** (honest) sound, rather than the **/ɔɚ /** (sports) diphthong, before consonant **/r/**. The use of **/ɒ/** (honest) is often indicated by the spellings: 'or', 'ar', 'aur'.

AUDIO 64► /ɒ/ (honest) before consonant /r/

ɒ
But that's ho-rrible! And you did not suffer?

(Strindberg: Crimes and Crimes)

ɒ
We started qua-rreling at seven o'clock.

(Chekhov: Three Sisters)

ɒ
I will instruct my so-rrows to be proud,

For grief is proud and makes his owner stoop.

(King John: III, i, 68)

NAMES & PLACES /ɒ/ (honest) before consonant /r/

Bo-ris	Co-rin	Do-ris	Do-rothy
Flo-rida	Flo-rence	Flo-rizel	Go-rell
Ho-race	Ho-rowitz	Lau-rence	Mo-rris
No-rris	Wa-rwick	Yo-rick	Zo-rro

WORDS /ɒ/ (honest) before consonant /r/

abho-rrence	autho-rity	bo-rrow	co-ral
co-ronation	co-rrespond	flo-rid	flo-rist
fo-rage	fo-reign	fo-rest	histo-rical
ho-roscope	ho-rrible	ho-rrid	ho-rror
inco-rrigible	lau-rel	lo-rry	majo-rity

mino-rity	mo-ral	o-range	o-racle
o-rator	o-rigin	o-risons	o-rotund
po-rridge	qua-rantine	qua-rrel	qua-rry
rheto-rical	so-rry	tomo-rrow	to-rrent
to-rrid	wa-rrant	wa-rren	wa-rrior

PHRASES /ɒ/ (h<u>o</u>nest) before consonant /r/

1.	docile o-racle	6.	so so-rry
2.	reluctant wa-rrior	7.	a to-rrid affair
3.	so-rry for Mo-rris	8.	point of o-rigin
4.	very hot fo-rehead[1]	9.	not the mino-rity
5.	not another qua-rrel	10.	resist bo-rrowing

SENTENCES /ɒ/ (h<u>o</u>nest) before consonant /r/

1. What a horrible holiday!

2. Orangeade is popular in Potsdam.

3. It's too hot to play golf in Florida.

4. Gosh, Dorothy eats lots of porridge.

5. The forest filled with torrential rain.

6. Historical dramas are Oliver's favorite.

7. Robin, look at John and say you're sorry.

8. Norris, what's on the bottom of the lorry?

9. Laurence lives in a posh lodge in Oregon.

10. Florian was in the foreign release of *Zorro*.

11. Rob felt it immoral to pollute the coral reefs.

12. I'm fond of Laurence; he's my favorite florist.

13. Is it immoral to quarantine quarrelling warriors?

14. Doris found the orator's style horribly annoying.

15. The majority of Horace's employees have seniority.

---

[1] forehead: /ˈfɒ-rɪd/

16.   Boris borrowed from Corin to attend the coronation.

17.   Authorities presented a warrant to the somber mobster.

18.   Morris, Horowitz must remain quarantined in the forest.

19.   Is it possible the oracle's oratory will restore confidence?

20.   Sorry, but this correspondence won't go out until tomorrow.

CLASSICAL AMERICAN TEXT /ɒ/ (h<u>o</u>nest) before consonant /r/. *Mark the following and speak out loud.*

ɒ
What's the qu<u>a</u>rrel?
(Troilus and Cressida: II, i, 89)

No, I can better play the orator.
(3 Henry VI: I, ii, 2)

A sorry war—
We lay the siege, and starve ourselves!
(Rostand: Cyrano de Bergerac)

He receives comfort like cold porridge.
(The Tempest: II, i, 10)

On Wednesday next we solemnly proclaim
Our coronation. Lords, be ready all.
(Richard II: IV, i, 319)

I felt sorry, oh! So sorry for mamma all at once.
(Chekhov: The Cherry Orchard)

And have you changed your orisons?
(Middleton & Rowley: The Changeling)

Unlike young men, whom Aristotle thought
Unfit to hear moral philosophy.
(Troilus and Cressida: II, ii, 166)

Some foreign university has made him a doctor.
(Ibsen: Hedda Gabler)

I really must borrow of you just 180 roubles, only 180 roubles.
(Chekhov: The Cherry Orchard)

Present fears
Are less than horrible imaginings.

(Macbeth: I, iii, 137)

Sir, let me borrow of you but one kiss.

(Webster: The White Devil)

My brothers to bring a warrant for my death?

(Tourneur: The Revenger's Tragedy)

He'll be as full of quarrel and offense
As my young mistress' dog.

(Othello: II, iii, 50)

And when the hardiest warriors did retire,
Richard cried, "Charge! And give no foot of ground!"

(3 Henry VI: I, iv, 14)

Her hair is sprinkled with orris powder,
That makes her look as if she had sinned in the pastry.

(Webster: The White Devil)

Ah, you're naturally in great spirits to-day—what with to-morrow's
festival and Oswald's return.

(Ibsen: Ghosts)

1 MURDERER. What? art thou afraid?
2 MURDERER. Not to kill him, having a warrant, but to be damn'd for
killing him, from the which no warrant can defend me.

(Richard III I, iv, 109)

There's horror in my service, blood and danger.

(Middleton & Rowley: The Changeling)

My niece is horribly in love with a thing you have, sweet queen.

(Troilus and Cressida: III, i, 97)

'ary' 'berry' 'ory'
pure vowels before consonant / r /

Polysyllabic words are words of three or more syllables. Use a pure vowel sound before the consonant /r/ in the second to the last syllable of polysyllabic words ending spelled: 'ory', 'ary', and 'berry'. This adds formality without necessarily sounding British.

(a)   Words ending in 'ary' and 'berry' use pure /e/ before the consonant /r/

(b)   Words ending in 'ory' use pure /ɔ/ before the consonant /r/

AUDIO 65▶ **polysyllabic word endings pure vowel before /r/**

                ɔ

This goodly frame, the earth, seems to me a sterile promonto-ry.

(Hamlet: II, ii, 298)

         e   e

If it should ever be necessa-ry. But it will never be necessa-ry.

(Ibsen: Ghosts)

         e

If reasons were as plentiful as blackbe-rries, I would give no man

a reason on compulsion.

(1 Henry IV: II, iv, 239)

WORDS 'ary' endings pronounced /e-ri/

ˈactua-ry	ˈcapilla-ry	ˈordina-ry	ˈarbitra-ry
fiˈducia-ry	ˈnecessa-ry	ˈlegenda-ry	ˈFebrua-ry
ˈcustoma-ry	ˈadversa-ry	aˈpotheca-ry	ˈmercena-ry
beneˈficia-ry	ˈdictiona-ry	ˈcommenta-ry	reˈactiona-ry
ˈmomenta-ry	heˈredita-ry	evoˈlutiona-ry	conˈfectiona-ry

WORDS 'berry' endings pronounced /e-ri/

ˈbarbe-rry	ˈbaybe-rry	ˈdogbe-rry	ˈchinabe-rry
ˈcranbe-rry	ˈdewbe-rry	ˈblackbe-rry	ˈgoosebe-rry
ˈhackbe-rry	ˈmulbe-rry	ˈsnowbe-rry	ˈwinterbe-rry

WORDS 'ory' endings pronounced /ɔ-ri/

ˈorato-ry	ˈaudito-ry	ˈmandato-ry	ˈpurgato-ry
ˈminato-ry	ˈlaudato-ry	deˈrogato-ry	aˈccusato-ry
ˈpredato-ry	deˈposito-ry	ˈcirculato-ry	conˈciliato-ry
conˈtributo-ry	oˈbligato-ry	ˈpromisso-ry	exˈclamato-ry
interˈrogato-ry	preˈparato-ry	obˈservato-ry	maˈnipulato-ry

PHRASES polysyllabic word endings, pure vowel before /r/

1.	small invento-ry	6.	great libra-ry
2.	difficult reperto-ry	7.	not necessa-ry
3.	conservato-ry class	8.	hucklebe-rry bush
4.	elocutiona-ry expert	9.	tempora-ry position
5.	derogato-ry message	10.	unsanita-ry conditions

SENTENCES polysyllabic word endings, pure vowel before /r/

1. They requested sanctuary.

2. What a transitory itinerary.

3. That was forbidden territory.

4. Hallucinatory drugs were forbidden.

5. Improvisatory training is mandatory.

6. Oh, my favorite: brambleberry stew.

7. Not all migratory beasts are predatory.

8. There's no need for derogatory remarks.

9. She had coronary and auditory weakness.

10. Is it necessary to have a literary manager?

11. Actors need improved elocutionary skills.

12. The circus offered funambulatory training.

13. What an extraordinary vocabulary you have.

14. Monetary problems affected their inventory.

15. Intermediaries decide the compensatory amount.

16. She'll begin at the acting conservatory in January.

17. After secondary school he began veterinary training.

18. Boysenberry pie is made with special confectionaries.

19. He's in a quandary and will take a temporary position.

20. The missionary found sanctuary in religious ceremony.

CLASSICAL AMERICAN TEXT polysyllabic word endings, pure vowel before /r/. *Mark the following and speak out loud.*

e-ri
That was most extraordin<u>a</u>ry.

(Ibsen: Ghosts)

It were but necessary you were wak'd.

(2 Henry VI: III, ii, 261)

My mind was never yet more mercenary.

(The Merchant of Venice: IV, i, 418)

Like one that stands upon a promontory
And spies a far-off shore where he would tread.

(3 Henry VI: III, ii, 135)

Come, come, my boy, we will to sanctuary.

(Richard III, II, iv, 66)

And now again the same; what omen yet
Follows of that? None but imaginary.

(Middleton & Rowley: The Changeling)

I know him for a man divine and holy,
Not scurvy, nor a temporary meddler.

(Measure for Measure: V, i, 144)

Feed him with apricocks and dewberries;
With purple grapes, green figs, and mulberries.

(A Midsummer Night's Dream: III, i, 166)

But myself,
Who had the world as my confectionary.

(Timon of Athens: IV, iii, 259)

Made you my guardians, my depositaries.

(King Lear: II, iv, 251)

But nor the time nor place
Will serve our long interrogatories.

(Cymbeline: V, v, 392)

Oh, those horrible, revolutionary, free-thinking books!

(Ibsen: Ghosts)

You are full of heavenly stuff, and bear the inventory
Of your best graces in your mind.

(Henry VIII: III, ii, 137)

I'll prove the contrary, if you'll hear me speak.

(3 Henry VI: I, ii, 20)

The strawberry grows underneath the nettle,
And wholesome berries thrive and ripen best
Neighbor'd by fruit of baser quality.

(Henry V: I, i, 60)

Forgive the comment that my passion made
Upon thy feature, for my rage was blind,
And foul imaginary eyes of blood
Presented thee more hideous than thou art.

(King John: IV, ii, 263)

Whatsoever you may hear to the contrary, let Claudio be executed
by four of the clock, and in the afternoon Barnardine.

(Measure for Measure: IV, ii, 120)

PRACTICE TEXT: Front vowels before consonant /r/

Cheryl's Peril

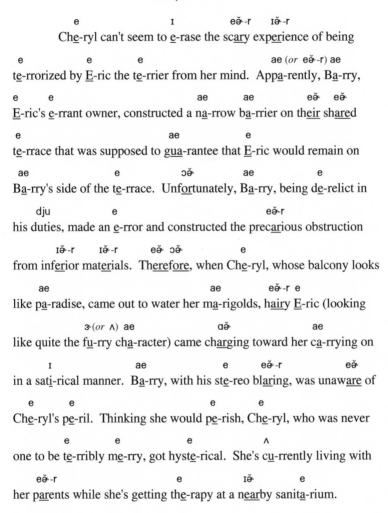

   e   ɪ   eə̆-r ɪə̆-r
Che̱-ryl can't seem to e̱-rase the sca̱ry expe̱rience of being

e   e   e   ae (*or* eə̆-r) ae
te̱-rrorized by E̱-ric the te̱-rrier from her mind. Appa̱-rently, Ba̱-rry,

e e   ae   ae   eə̆ eə̆
E̱-ric's e̱-rrant owner, constructed a na̱-rrow ba̱-rrier on the̱ir sha̱red

e   ae   e
te̱-rrace that was supposed to gua̱-rantee that E̱-ric would remain on

 ae   e   ɔə̆   ae   e
Ba̱-rry's side of the te̱-rrace. Unfo̱rtunately, Ba̱-rry, being de̱-relict in

  dju   e   eə̆-r
his duties, made an e̱-rror and constructed the preca̱rious obstruction

   ɪə̆-r ɪə̆-r   eə̆ ɔə̆   e
from infe̱rior mate̱rials. The̱refo̱re, when Che̱-ryl, whose balcony looks

   ae   ae eə̆-r e
like pa̱-radise, came out to water her ma̱-rigolds, ha̱iry E̱-ric (looking

     ɝ(*or* ʌ) ae   αə̆   ae
like quite the fu̱-rry cha̱-racter) came cha̱rging toward her ca̱-rrying on

   ɪ   ae   e eə̆-r   eə̆
in a sati̱-rical manner. Ba̱-rry, with his ste̱-reo bla̱ring, was unawa̱re of

  e   e   e   e
Che̱-ryl's pe̱-ril. Thinking she would pe̱-rish, Che̱-ryl, who was never

    e   e   e   ʌ
one to be te̱-rribly me̱-rry, got hyste̱-rical. She's cu̱-rrently living with

 eə̆-r   e   ɪə̆   e
her pa̱rents while she's getting the̱-rapy at a nea̱rby sanita̱-rium.

    eə̆-r   eə̆-r ae *or* eə̆-r
Note: pa̱rent, preca̱rious, appa̱-rent.

386

PRACTICE TEXT: Back vowels before consonant /r/

Isadora's Story

ɑɚ-r   ɒ   ɒ   ɒ
Cesario, in his co-rrespondence, requested my next composition be

ɑ   ɒ   ɒ
an a-ria of histo-rical significance: something with a mo-ral, but nothing too

ɒ   ɒ
ho-rrible. (He's inco-rrigible!)

                             ɔ   ɔ   ɔ
Finally, I came up with something authentic, memo-rializing Isado-ra

ɔ   ɒ   ɒ   ɑɚ-r   ɒ
the noto-rious fo-reign wa-rrior from some faraway place like Flo-rence or the

ɔ   ɒ
O-rient. (No one is really certain of her o-rigin.)

         ɔ   ɔ   ɒ   ɔɚ   ɔɚ   ɑ
This saucy Tau-rus lost her fortune while at war in the Saha-ra, and

ɔ   ɒ   ɔ   ɔ   ɔ
flaunted her to-rrid affairs; all of which makes for an enthralling sto-ry. It's

           ɔ   ɒ
finished, except the cho-rus, which should be completed by tomo-rrow, and—

ɑɚ-r   ɒ   ɔ   ɒ   ɔ
barring any qua-rrel with the autho-rities'—it will be playing in Australia to

ɒ   ɔ   ɔ   ɔɚ-r
an onslaught of applause. . . forever!

ɔɚ   ɒ
Note: war, wa-rrior

RHYTHM HIGHLIGHTER ADJUSTMENTS

Two more adjustments to NAS may be incorporated, if slightly more formality is desired. The rhythm of certain words is modified by speaking:

(a) slightly shorter /i/ (w<u>e</u>) sound in unstressed word endings

(b) slightly less 'r' coloring in vowels, diphthongs and triphthongs of 'r'

Unstressed / i / (w<u>e</u>) endings

The /i/ (w<u>e</u>) sound can be slightly shorter in length when in an unstressed position at or near the end of a word. These endings are usually spelled with a 'y', and occasionally with an 'i', as in 'marr<u>i</u>ed'. This is a subtle rhythmic adjustment, not a sound adjustment, and can be facilitated by emphasizing the vowel in the stressed syllable.

AUDIO 66▶ **slightly shorter /i/ (w<u>e</u>) endings**

The air bites **'shrewd**l<u>y</u>.

(Hamlet: I, iv, 1)

Why do we get **'laz**<u>y</u>, indifferent, useless, un**'happ**<u>y</u>?

(Chekhov: Three Sisters)

Ad**'ver**s<u>ity</u>'s sweet milk, phi**'los**oph<u>y</u>.

(Romeo and Juliet: III, iii, 55)

WORDS slightly shorter /i/ (w<u>e</u>) endings

'an<u>y</u>	'witt<u>y</u>	'eleg<u>y</u>	'ratt<u>y</u>
'Ital<u>y</u>	'prett<u>y</u>	'reall<u>y</u>	'amit<u>y</u>
'parit<u>y</u>	'rand<u>y</u>	'salar<u>y</u>	'man<u>y</u>
'vanit<u>y</u>	'sanit<u>y</u>	**'fair**l<u>y</u>	'hone<u>y</u>
'water<u>y</u>	'notar<u>y</u>	'cavit<u>y</u>	'chatt<u>y</u>

'pantry	'felony	'battery	'eighty
'faculty	'sweaty	'nightly	a'cidity
'regency	'brevity	di'vinity	'charity
'amnesty	a'trocity	curi'osity	a'ffinity
'certainly	'carefully	ca'lamity	bru'tality

PHRASES slightly shorter /i/ (we) endings. These can be notated with an underline or strikethrough, whichever marking works as a better reminder.

1.	some money	6.	just barely
2.	out of brandy	7.	real artistry
3.	the understudy	8.	has elasticity
4.	shines brightly	9.	a bit too drafty
5.	very very tricky	10.	fond domesticity

Days of the week can also be spoken with a short /i/ (we) ending rather than the Neutral American /eɪ/ (hey).

SENTENCES slightly shorter /i/ (we) ending:

1. See you Tuesday.

2. Bradley loves old movies.

3. The baby is due in January.

4. I saw her at a party on Friday.

5. Can I borrow a twenty, Mary?

6. Cathy's character is very fussy.

7. Actually, he's wary of investing.

8. Sorry I missed the charity event.

9. Gary visited Sally in the infirmary.

10. He's happily and hopelessly in love.

11. It can be especially cold in February.

12. I thought there would be reciprocity.

CLASSICAL AMERICAN slightly less 'r' coloring. *If marking text with an underline or strikethrough helps you to adjust this sound slightly, do so. Then practice out loud.*

Infirm of purpose!

(Macbeth: II, ii, 49)

Words, words, words.

(Hamlet: II, ii, 192)

I have no further with you.

(Coriolanus: II, iii, 173)

Surrender, musketeers!

(Rostand: Cyrano de Bergerac)

Where's my serpent of old Nile?

(Antony and Cleopatra: I, v, 25)

I do not much dislike the matter, but
The manner of his speech.

(Antony and Cleopatra: II, ii, 111)

Good Doctor Pinch, you are a conjurer.

(The Comedy of Errors: IV, iv, 47)

And therefore by His majesty I swear,
Whose far-unworthy deputy I am,
He shall not breathe infection in this air
But three days longer, on the pain of death.

(2 Henry VI: III, ii, 285)

Bring him his confessor, let him be prepar'd.

(Measure for Measure: II, i, 35)

And like an eagle o'er his aery tow'rs,
To souse annoyance that comes near his nest.

(King John: V, ii, 149)

Zounds, I was never so bethump'd with words
Since I first call'd my brother's father dad.

(King John: II, i, 466)

A woman would run through fire and water for such a kind heart.

(The Merry Wives of Winsor: III, iv, 102)

Against my heart, his letter, paled with years—
And still the faintest trace of blood, his tears.

(Rostand: Cyrano de Bergerac)

Look you how his sword is bloodied, and his helm more hack'd
than Hector's.

(Troilus and Cressida: I, ii, 232)

Ah, wretched man, would I had died a maid
And never seen thee, never borne thee son,
Seeing thou hast prov'd so unnatural a father!
Hath he deserv'd to lose his birthright thus?

(3 Henry VI: I, i, 216)

O, pardon me, thou bleeding piece of earth,
That I am meek and gentle with these butchers!

(Julius Caesar: III, i, 254)

Fetch hither the swain, he must carry me a letter.

(Love's Labor's Lost: III, I, 49)

I'll cull thee out the fairest courtesans
And bring them every morning to thy bed.

(Marlowe: Doctor Faustus)

We have no right whatever to give offence to the weaker brethren.

(Ibsen: Ghosts)

What glory our Achilles shares from Hector,
Were he not proud, we all should share with him.

(Troilus and Cressida: I, iii, 366)

A bloody deed! Almost as bad, good mother,
As kill a king, and marry with his brother.

(Hamlet: III, iv, 28)

To be a well-favor'd man is the gift of fortune, but to write and
read comes by nature.

(Much Ado About Nothing: III, iii, 14)

PRACTICE TEXT

IPA TRANSCRIPTION WORDS

Transcribe the following for Classical American.

1. cough	_____	21. story	_____
2. whining	_____	22. arrows	_____
3. cannot	_____	23. hurry	_____
4. duke	_____	24. dubious	_____
5. belong	_____	25. spirited	_____
6. student	_____	26. horrible	_____
7. within	_____	27. mirage	_____
8. whinny	_____	28. current	_____
9. renew	_____	29. terrible	_____
10. ominous	_____	30. voluntary	_____
11. anywhere	_____	31. glorious	_____
12. tomorrow	_____	32. secretary	_____
13. nuclear	_____	33. ludicrous	_____
14. monstrous	_____	34. minority	_____
15. detective	_____	35. character	_____
16. lieutenant	_____	36. promissory	_____
17. knowledge	_____	37. ceremony	_____
18. institute	_____	38. perilously	_____
19. tentative	_____	39. strawberry	_____
20. Washington	_____	40. supervision	_____

PRACTICE TEXT

Fill in the blank lines with the appropriate phonetic marking for Classical American pronunciation, then speak aloud. If slightly less 'r' coloring or shorter 'y' endings are being used, mark those with a strikethrough, too. Voiced endings before a (possible) pause have been double-underlined, syllabics and consonant combinations have been marked. See key page 410.

1.   I saw but I never let on I saw.

(Strindberg: Miss Julie)

2.   I beg the law, the law, upon his head.

(A Midsummer Night's Dream: IV, i, 155)

3.   Alack, thou dost usurp authority.

(King John: II, i, 118)

4.   It strook mine ear most terribly.

(The Tempest: II, i, 313)

5.   I have a king's oath to the contrary.

(King John: III, i, 10)

6.   Who dares not stir by day must walk by night.

(King John: I, i, 172)

7.   Oh! An endless summer of oranges, evergreens...

(Strindberg: Miss Julie)

8.   But I will remedy this gear ere long,

Or sell my title for a glorious grave.

(2 Henry VI: III, i, 91)

9.   The King is not himself, but basely led

By flatterers, and what they will inform.

(Richard II: II, i, 241)

10.   In wrongful quarrel you have slain your son.

(Titus Andronicus: I, i, 293)

MY CATHEDRAL
Henry Wadsworth Longfellow

Like two cathedral towers these stately pines
      Uplift their fretted summits tipped with cones;
      The arch beneath them is not built with stones,
      Not Art but Nature traced these lovely lines,
And carved this graceful arabesque of vines;
      No organ but the wind here sighs and moans,
      No sepulcher conceals a martyr's bones,
      No marble bishop on his tomb reclines.
Enter! the pavement, carpeted with leaves,
      Gives back a softened echo to thy tread!
      Listen! the choir is singing; all the birds,
In leafy galleries beneath the eaves,
      Are singing! listen, ere the sound be fled,
      And learn there may be worship without words.

From **MOBY-DICK**
Herman Melville

There is, one knows not what sweet mystery about this sea, whose gently awful stirrings seem to speak of some hidden soul beneath; like those fabled undulations of the Ephesian sod over the buried Evangelist St. John. And meet it is, that over the sea-pastures, wide-rolling watery prairies and Potters' Fields of all four continents, the waves should rise and fall, and ebb and flow unceasingly; for here, millions of mixed shades and shadows, drowned dreams, somnambulisms, reveries, all that we call lives and souls, lie dreaming, dreaming, still; tossing like slumberers in their beds; the ever-rolling waves but made so by their restlessness.

To any meditative Magian rover, this serene Pacific, once beheld, must ever after be the sea of his adoption.

From **CYRANO DE BERGERAC**

Edmond Rostand

CYRANO.

No, no, no, my friend—too short!

Why, one could have, in the end, *mon Dieu*! such sport

By variation on the theme—suppose:

Aggressive: If I, m'sieur, had such a nose,

I'd amputate at once, without a thought!

Friendly: A nuisance when you drink? You ought

To have a special tankard fit to shape!

Descriptive: Why, 'tis a rock, a bluff...a cape!

Did I say cape? Nay! a peninsula!

Curious: What is that oblong capsule? a...

What? An ink-stand, hm...? A scissors-box?

Gracious: Ah, your love of birds—in flocks

They circle round that thoughtful perch, seduced—

At last, you bring the sparrows home to roost!

Truculent: When you light up to smoke,

Do the clouds, m'sieur, come billowing out to choke

Those near, who cry: "your chimney is on fire"?

Prudent: I'd take care—such a weight could tire,

And send you headlong, in a nasty fall!

Effete: It wants a tiny parasol—

To shield its fragile colors from the sun!

Pedantic: Aristophanes writes of one

Such Hippo-camp-elephanto-camelos—

The extent of flesh and bone, so...grandiose!

Cavalier: A-la-mode, my friend, eh, what?

Why, all the rage, this hook to hang one's hat!

Absolute: No wind, I say, but *le Mistral*

Could blow catarrh so cold through that canal!

Dramatic: When it bleeds, the Red Sea looms!
Admiring: What a clever sign—! Perfumes!
Lyric: A conch? Hark thee to Neptune's roar!
Naïve: That monument, now…what is it for?
Respectful: Oh! the envious elite!
Now this—what I'd call 'fronting on the street'!
Rustic: Eh? what say? a nose—? No tellin'!
Could be a turnip—or a Spanish melon!
Military: Train it on the Cavalry!
Practical: Why not a lottery—
With this, m'sieur, you're sure to win first prize!
And, last—the tragic *Pyramus* gives rise
To travesty: "O nose! O night so black!
O nose! O nose—! Alack! alack! alack!"
Voila—!

These, but a sampling of the quips,
That, with wit or letters, might have graced your lips—
But of wit, alas, my cretin, have you not
One single atom! And of letters, what—?
You need but three to write you down an ass!
Yet, had you the inventiveness to pass
For quick, before these galleries that stay
Your serving me in clever repartée—
Be sure, that you would not have held the floor
One demi-quarter of a syllable, for…
I serve these up myself, m'sieur, with flair,
But allow none else to even venture there.

(English version: Christopher Martin)

SONNET 18

William Shakespeare

Shall I compare thee to a summer's day?
Thou art more lovely and more temperate:
Rough winds do shake the darling buds of May,
And summer's lease hath all too short a date;
Sometime too hot the eye of heaven shines,
And often is his gold complexion dimm'd,
And every fair from fair sometime declines,
By chance or Nature's changing course, untrimm'd:
But thy eternal summer shall not fade,
Nor lose possession of that fair thou ow'st,
Nor shall Death brag thou wand'rest in his shade,
When in eternal lines to time thou grow'st.
    So long as men can breathe or eyes can see,
    So long lives this, and this give life to thee.

SONNET 74

William Shakespeare

But be contented when that fell arrest
Without all bail shall carry me away,
My life hath in this line some interest,
Which for memorial still with thee shall stay.
When thou reviewest this, thou dost review
The very part was consecrate to thee:
The earth can have but earth, which is his due,
My spirit is thine, the better part of me.
So then thou hast but lost the dregs of life,
The prey of worms, my body being dead,
The coward conquest of a wretch's knife,
Too base of thee to be remembered.
    The worth of that is that which it contains,
    And that is this, and this with thee remains.

ɒ

Ro<u>me</u>, thou hast lost the breed‿of ꞌnob<u>l</u>e bloo<u>ds</u>!

hwen e

When went there by‿an‿age since the great floo<u>d</u>

ð   ð   æ

But[h] it was famꞌd with more than with one ma<u>n</u>?

hwen   aʊ   ɔ t[h]

When could they say, till now, that talkꞌd‿of Ro<u>me</u>,

ɔ   ɪ ʌ   æ

That her wide walks enꞌ**com**passꞌd but one ma<u>n</u>?

aʊ   ɪ

Now is‿it Rome‿inꞌ**deed** and room‿eꞌ**nough**,

hwen   æ

When there‿is‿in‿it but one ꞌ**on**ly ma<u>n</u>.

O! you‿and‿I have heard‿our ꞌ**fa**thers say

ɒ ə

There was‿a ꞌ**Brut**[h]us once that would have brookꞌd

ɪ

Th' eꞌ**ter**na<u>l</u> ꞌ**dev**i<u>l</u> to keep his state[h] in Ro<u>me</u>

ə

As ꞌ**ea**sily as‿a ki<u>ng</u>.

(Julius Caesar: I, ii, 135)

Polysyllabic[1] word endings

The short schwa sound with no 'r' coloring, /ə/ (<u>uh</u>), is used in the second to the last syllable of polysyllabic words ending in 'ary', 'ory', 'ony', and 'berry'. The final 'y' is spoken with the short /ɪ/ (w<u>i</u>ll) suffix, so the word endings are pronounced: /ə-rɪ/

AUDIO 73▶ **polysyllabic word endings**

ə-rɪ
I ran like the devil, plunging through the 'raspbe-rry canes,

ə-rɪ
across the 'strawbe-rry beds, and came up on the rose garden.

(Strindberg: Miss Julie)

pə'pɑ   ə-rɪ
Papa was a 'milita-ry man.

(Chekhov: Three Sisters)

ə-rɪ
O true a'potheca-ry! Thy drugs are quick.

(Romeo and Juliet: V, iii, 119)

PRACTICE see Standard British section, pages 464-467.

MID-ATLANTIC TEXT polysyllabic word endings. *Mark the following and speak out loud.*

LAFEW.   You have it from his own deliverance.
BERTRAM. And by other warranted testimony.

(All's Well That Ends Well: II, v, 4)

Shall we desire to raze the sanctuary
And pitch our evils there?

(Measure for Measure: II, ii, 170)

But (heav'n be thank'd!) it is but voluntary.

(King John: V, i, 29)

---

[1] Polysyllabic words are words of three or more syllables.

'Ask' List

The 'ask' list of words is spoken with the intermediate /a/ sound in Mid-Atlantic, not /æ/ (th<u>a</u>t) as in Neutral and Classical American, or /ɑ/ (f<u>a</u>ther) as in Standard British.

AUDIO 74▶ **ask list words spoken with /a/**

                           a

To which boarding school, might I <u>ask</u>?

(Strindberg: The Father)

                 a

I am not fit for the t<u>ask</u>.

(Ibsen: A Doll's House)

          a   a

For you and I are p<u>ast</u> our d<u>a</u>ncing days.

(Romeo and Juliet: I, v, 31)

Which words are included in the 'ask' list? There is no distinct rule for inclusion, but spellings can offer a fairly reliable indication.

<u>**aft**</u>	abaft, aft, after, aftermath, afternoon, afterward, behalf, craft, daft, draft, graft, raft, shaft, Shaftesbury, Taft, waft, witchcraft
<u>**ampl**</u>	ample, example, sample
<u>**ance**</u> /<u>**ans**</u>	advance, answer, chance, chancellor, chancery, dance, enhance, France, freelance, glance, lance, prance, trance
<u>**anch**</u>	avalanche, blanch(e), branch, ranch, stanch
<u>**and**</u>	Chandler, command(o), countermand, demand, reprimand, slander
<u>**ant**</u>[1] /<u>**aunt**</u>	advantage, aunt, can't, chant, chantry, enchant, grant, implant, plant, shan't, slant, supplant, transpl<u>a</u>nt, vantage

---

[1] Though 'ant' spelling can indicate inclusion on the 'ask' list of words, the word 'ant' (the insect) is pronounced /**ænt**/.

as(s)	alas, brass, class, Glasgow, glass, grass, pass, Passover, trespass
ask	ask, bask, basket, cask, flask, mask, task, rascal, vast
asp	clasp, gasp, grasp, hasp, rasp, raspberry
ast	aghast, alabaster, avast, blast, broadcast, cast, caste, castle, contrast, disaster, fast, ghastly, last, mast, master, nasty, past, pastor, pasture, plaster, repast, telecast, vast, vasty
ath	bath, lath, lather, path, rather, wrath
aff /affe	chaff, distaff, Falstaff, gaff, giraffe, quaff, staff
alf /aph	autograph, behalf, calf, half, epitaph, graph, telegraph
augh	laugh, laughter, draught

In the previous three lines above, all the consonant spellings listed are pronounced **/f/** (af, aff, affe, alf, aph, augh).

Finding the Mid-Atlantic /a/ sound: This vowel sound is not used on its own in Neutral American speech, but is spoken as the first element of the **/aɪ/** (my) diphthong.[1] Begin as if saying the pronoun "I", but do not pronounce the second element, so that only the first element **/a/** is spoken.

> *   a*
> *For 'twas your heaven she should be advanc'd,*
> *   a*
> *And weep ye now, seeing she is advanc'd*
>
> *Above the clouds, as high as heaven itself?*
> (Romeo and Juliet IV: v, 72)

The American Southern dialect often uses the vowel sound **/a/** rather than the diphthong **/aɪ/**. It may help you to just think of pronouncing the word 'hi' using the Southern dialect, written phonetically: **/ha/**. Pronounce this same vowel sound in the word 'half' for the Mid-Atlantic pronunciation of that word.

---

[1] The **/a/** sound, is also an important sound in many other dialects, including Northern England, Ireland and Boston.

ercise that follows, isolate the **/a/** sound on the word listed in
y using a slightly exaggerated Southern pronunciation. Then
ound to words listed in the second column. *Read across.*

WORDS /a/ (l<u>augh</u>) in Mid-Atlantic

'I'	**/a/** in southern	**/ask/**	ask, after
'bye'	**/ba/** in southern	**/bask/**	bask, bath
'die'	**/da/** in southern	**/daft/**	daft, dance
'pie'	**/pa/** in southern	**/past/**	past, path
'lie'	**/la/** in southern	**/laf/**	laugh, lather
'my'	**/ma/** in southern	**/mask/**	mask, master
'rye'	**/ra/** in southern	**/raft/**	raft, rascal
'tie'	**/ta/** in southern	**/taft/**	Taft, task
'sigh'	**/sa/** in southern	**/sav/**	salve, sample
'dry'	**/dra/** in southern	**/draft/**	draft, drafted
'fie'	**/fa/** in southern	**/fast/**	fast, fasting, faster
'guy'	**/ga/** in southern	**/gasp/**	gasp, ghastly
'sly'	**/sla/** in southern	**/slant/**	slant, slander

If you are familiar with the Boston dialect, think of the phrase: "Park
the car in Harvard Yard"—**'r'** coloring is dropped, and the remaining vowel
sound is the shorter, brighter **/a/**, as in:

> *"Pahk the cah in Hahvahd yahd."*

PHRASES /a/ (l<u>augh</u>)

1.	on his beh<u>al</u>f	6.	Na<u>s</u>ty Fr<u>a</u>nce<u>s</u>
2.	good ra<u>s</u>pberries	7.	just h<u>al</u>f a gl<u>ass</u>
3.	holds steadf<u>a</u>stly	8.	adv<u>a</u>nced at l<u>ast</u>
4.	cutting the gr<u>ass</u>	9.	filling empty fl<u>a</u>sks
5.	a p<u>ath</u> in Fl<u>a</u>nders	10.	entr<u>a</u>ncing s<u>a</u>mpling

    ɪ   hw   e ɪ

And speaking thick^h (which natuɾe made his blemish)

  ɪ   e (ə or syllabic) ə

Became the accents of the valiant^h;

                          ɑə ɪ

For those that could speak low and taɾdil̲y̲

          eə̆

Would tuɾn theiɾ own peɾfection̯ to abuse

       aĭ

To seem like hi̲m̲; so that^h in speech, in gait^h,

                ɪ aĭ

In diet^h, in affection̯s of delight^h,

      ə-ɾ̩ɪ

In military ru̲l̲e̲s̲, humoɾs of bloo̲d̲,

     ɒ   ɑə̆   a ˈkɒpɪ

He was the maɾk^h and glass, copy and book^h,

That fashion̯'d otheɾ̲s̲.

(2 Henry IV: II, iii, 9)

STANDARD BRITISH DIALECT (RP)

AUDIO SELECTIONS▶
James Anderson

SUMMARY CHECKLIST

When switching from Classical American to Standard British,[1] the following adjustments and sound changes are necessary:

The jaw is slightly more closed, the point of resonance is more forward on the upper gum ridge, consonants are spoken with increased vocal energy, and there is increased vocal range and variation in pitch and inflection.

---

[1] The *English Pronouncing Dictionary* by Daniel Jones, Cambridge University Press, is a valuable resource for Standard British pronunciation, especially the older fourteenth edition.

WORDS /i→ɪ / endings

ˈearly	ˈhoney	ˈsecrecy	ˈbarely
ˈitchy	ˈwintery	ˈbrutally	fuˈtility
ˈsunny	ˈintimacy	veˈlocity	ˈTuesday
ˈsanity	ˈshadowy	versaˈtility	ˈdefinitely
vulˈgarity	suˈpremacy	aˈppealingly	maˈliciously

PHRASES /i→ɪ / **endings** These can be notated with a phonetic symbol, underline, or strikethrough, whichever marking works as a better reminder.

1. very weary
2. lacks unity
3. reading daily
4. rainy and snowy
5. amazingly angry
6. such a bully
7. weekly party
8. terribly funny
9. going on Friday
10. especially fancy

SENTENCES /i→ɪ / endings

1. Mr. Whitney's tipsy.

2. Let's watch *The Mummy*.

3. Someone committed perjury.

4. Luckily, they saved the tapestry.

5. Actually, he's wary of investing.

6. The producer's policy: no nudity.

7. He's happily and hopelessly in love.

8. It can be especially cold in February.

9. There has been no scarcity of publicity.

10. I really thought there would be reciprocity.

11. After winning the lottery they lived in luxury.

12. She spoke loathingly of their cowardly behavior.

13. It was clearly amusingly and alluringly performed.

14. Gary reviewed *The Caine Mutiny* for *The Daily News*.

15. *Merrily We Roll Along* was carefully and lavishly staged.

STANDARD BRITISH TEXT / i→ɪ / endings. *Mark the following and speak out loud.*

        ɪ   ɪ
How frightfully, horribly true!

(Shaw: Man and Superman)

Surely it's not customary.

(Shaw: Man and Superman)

The man is perfectly a pretty fellow.

(Farquhar: The Beaux Stratagem)

The old man will be here immediately.

(Etherege: The Man of Mode)

Its sympathies are with misery, with poverty, with starvation
of the body, and of the heart.

(Shaw: Man and Superman)

So my vanity has deceiv'd me, and my ambition has made me uneasy.

(Vanbrugh: The Provok'd Wife)

I have dared to love you wildly, passionately, devotedly, hopelessly.

(Wilde: The Importance of Being Earnest)

I thank you heartily, heartily.

(Congreve: The Way of the World)

Yes, I think the good lady would marry anything that resembled
a man.

(Congreve: The Way of the World)

Come, sir, we don't mind ceremonies in the country.

(Farquhar: The Beaux Stratagem)

Pray, out of pity to ourselves, let us find a better subject, for I am
weary of this. Do you think your husband inclin'd to jealousy?

(Vanbrugh: The Provok'd Wife)

Master Horner, will you never keep civil company?

(Wycherley: The Country Wife)

My dear Lady Sneerwell, how have you been this century?

(Sheridan: The School for Scandal)

How strong is fancy!

(Vanbrugh: The Provok'd Wife)

I am in love with her already.

(Farquhar: The Beaux Stratagem)

Come, for my part, I will have only those glorious manly pleasures
of being very drunk and very slovenly.

(Wycherley: The Country Wife)

Authority! No, to be sure! If you wanted authority over me, you
should have adopted me and not married me.

(Sheridan: The School for Scandal)

To think of a whirlwind, though 'twere in a whirlwind, were a case
of more steady contemplation; a very tranquility of mind and mansion.

(Congreve: Way of the World)

Happy, happy sister! your angel has been watchful for your happiness,
whilst mine hast slept.

(Farquhar: Beaux Stratagem)

Thy peace being made with heaven, death's already vanquished;
bear a little longer the pains that attend this transitory life.

(Lillo: The London Merchant)

I'll say he died in Paris of apoplexy. Lots of people die of apoplexy,
quite suddenly, don't they?

(Wilde: The Importance of Being Earnest)

I suppose you really think you're getting on famously with me.

(Shaw: Mrs. Warren's Profession)

Charity, dear Miss Prism, charity! None of us is perfect.

(Wilde: The Importance of Being Earnest)

So, carry him off, carry him off; we shall have him prate himself
into a fever by and by; carry him off.

(Vanbrugh: The Relapse)

444

'r' Coloring

vowels, diphthongs, triphthongs

Completely eliminate **'r'** coloring from vowels, diphthongs and triphthongs of 'r', by allowing the tip of the tongue to gently rest touching the back of the lower teeth for the duration of the vowel, diphthong, or triphthong.

AUDIO 80▶ **no 'r' coloring**

$\underset{\text{ɔ̞}}{}$ $\quad\quad\quad\quad\quad\underset{\text{ɑ}}{}$

Good morning, fellow guardian.

(Shaw: Man and Superman)

He's gone to order the dog cart for me.

(Wilde: The Importance of Being Earnest)

Your eyes are better firearms than your pistol; they never miss.

(Farquhar: The Beaux Stratagem)

WORDS stressed vowel of 'r' /ɝ → ɜ/

her	girl	pert	curt
fern	turn	bird	first
burnt	curse	blurt	burst
worth	turnip	dearth	churn
church	Gertrude	hernia	hermit

When speaking key words of more than one syllable, highlight the vowel in the stressed syllable, making the rhythmic difference between stressed and unstressed syllables noticeable. This attention to rhythm will facilitate eliminating 'r' coloring in the unstressed syllable of the word.

Also, remember to rest the tip of the tongue down behind the lower front teeth for the duration of the final vowel when eliminating 'r' coloring.

VOWEL ADJUSTMENTS

/ əŭ / (go)

Use the diphthong sound represented by the symbol /əŭ/ rather than the Neutral and Classical American /oŭ/. Begin with the short, neutral schwa sound /ə/ (uh), then blend into a rounded /u/ (who).

AUDIO 81 ▶ /oŭ→əŭ/ (go)

   əŭ   əŭ
So you are Hamlet, I suppose.

         (Shaw: Man and Superman)

   əŭ   əŭ   ʊ əŭ
I really don't see anything romantic in proposing.

    (Wilde: The Importance of Being Earnest)

   əŭ   əŭ   əŭ
A young widow, a handsome widow and would be again a widow.

    (Congreve: The Way of the World)

WORDS /oŭ→əŭ/ (go)

oboe	slope	ocean	phony
home	elbow	Roman	loaning
loaves	stroked	moment	bloated
throated	disrobe	rainbow	devoted
probation	enclosure	foreshadow	overdraw

If producing this sound change is troublesome, it may be helpful to think of the first element as a bit brighter. The sound change is sometimes notated /oŭ→eŭ/, though I prefer /oŭ→əŭ/.

   ə əŭ   əŭ
Drown husbands! For yours is a provoking fellow.

   (Vanbrugh: The Provok'd Wife)

PHRASES /oŭ→əŭ/ (go)

1.	old soldiers	6.	golden holder
2.	ozone layer	7.	always stone cold
3.	owns toasters	8.	another stow away
4.	large explosion	9.	getting a sore throat
5.	newly betrothed	10.	waiting to be noticed

SENTENCES /oŭ→əŭ/ (go)

1. Go vote.

2. He loathes boasting.

3. Did you see *Frozen*?

4. Jonas was misquoted.

5. They filed in row by row.

6. Who is composing the music?

7. Everyone noticed his devotion.

8. I'd like a cozy evening at home.

9. Stop your moaning and groaning.

10. Don't sign a non-disclosure agreement.

11. She's playing in *The Marriage Proposal*.

12. He's chosen not to move to the west coast.

13. Lois, won't you show me your new photos?

14. She lost her composure when she won the Tony.

15. His home was in foreclosure, and then he got the part!

STANDARD BRITISH TEXT /oŭ→əŭ/ (go). *Mark the following and speak out loud.*

    əŭ   əŭ
A low paltry set of fellows.

                              (Goldsmith: She Stoops to Conquer)

No, no, hang him, the rogue has no manners at all.

                              (Congreve: The Way of the World)

I'll go into the army.

(Vanbrugh: The Relapse)

Oh no! I hope you do not know him!

(Etherege: The Man of Mode)

Oh, that stupid old joke of yours about me!

(Shaw: Man and Superman)

What, leave us with a filthy man alone in his lodgings?

(Wycherley: The Country Wife)

Go, go! You are a couple of provoking toads.

(Sheridan: The School for Scandal)

I won't, won't, won't, won't, WON'T marry you.

(Shaw: Man and Superman)

I have a perfect passion for listening through keyholes.

(Wilde: An Ideal Husband)

Disclose it to your wife; own what has past between us.

(Congreve: The Way of the World)

I suppose a man may eat his own muffins in his own garden.

(Wilde: The Importance of Being Earnest)

Excuse me; but I am so lonely; and this place is so awful.

(Shaw: Man and Superman)

What conceited ass has been impertinent enough to dare to propose
to you before I had proposed to you?

(Wilde: An Ideal Husband)

Oh, you can pronounce the word, then; I thought it would have
choked you.

(Vanbrugh: The Relapse)

Well, the only small satisfaction I have in the whole of this wretched
business is that your friend Bunbury is quite exploded.

(Wilde: The Importance of Being Earnest)

So, gentlemen, I hope you have all taken pains to show yourselves
masters in your professions.

(Vanbrugh: The Relapse)

452

Oh, to be sure—the most whimsical circumstance.
(Sheridan: School for Scandal)

If she cannot make her husband a cuckold, she'll make him jealous
and pass for one.
(Wycherley: The Country Wife)

You have no right to say such things, Jack.
(Shaw: Man and Superman)

But first bring me a pipe; I'll smoke.
(Vanbrugh: The Provok'd Wife)

You said his secretaries open his letters.
(Wilde: An Ideal Husband)

My life has been mostly spent in the service of the ladies.
(Farquhar: The Beaux Stratagem)

But she's cold, my friend, still cold as the northern star.
(Vanbrugh: The Provok'd Wife)

I find high birth and titles don't recommend the man who owns them,
to my affections.
(Lillo: The London Merchant)

You wrote to me as one of your oldest friends, one of your husband's
oldest friends. Mrs. Cheveley stole that letter from my rooms.
(Wilde: An Ideal Husband)

When an old bachelor takes a young wife, what is he to expect?
(Sheridan: School for Scandal)

No, no, hang him, the rogue has no manners at all, that I must own—
no more breeding than a bum-baily.
(Congreve: The Way of the World)

DON JUAN. I was of noble birth and rich; and when my person did
           not please, my conversation flattered, though I generally
           found myself fortunate in both.
STATUE.   Coxcomb!
DON JUAN. Yes, but even my coxcombry pleased.
(Shaw: Man and Superman)

/ ɔ̩ / (a̱ll)

This back vowel sound is made with the jaw slightly more closed, the lips more rounded, and the back of the tongue arched slightly higher in the mouth than in Neutral or Classical. This is represented in the IPA symbol by the vertical line underneath: /ɔ̩/. This sound tends to be energized and long.

AUDIO 82 ▶ /ɔ → ɔ̩/ (a̱ll)

>   ɔ̩   ɔ̩   ɒ̩
> This so̱rt of ta̱lk is no̱t kind to me, Jack.
>
>   (Shaw: Man and Superman)
>
>   ɒ̩   i   ɔ̩   ɔ̩
> I have no̱t been ca̱lled back to town at a̱ll.
>
>   (Wilde: The Importance of Being Earnest)
>
>   ɒ̩   ɔ̩   ɔ̩
> Nobo̱dy observes the la̱w for the la̱w's sake.
>
>   (Farquhar: The Beaux Stratagem)

Remember: common /ɔ̩/ spellings include: au, aw, alk, all, ought.

WORDS /ɔ → ɔ̩/ (a̱ll)

law	tall	chalk	fall
wall	saw	bawd	stalk
walk	balk	small	dawn
ought	sauce	sought	fought
flaunt	bought	audition	daughter

PRACTICE /ɔ → ɔ̩/ (a̱ll)

1. bo̱ught cha̱lk
2. ta̱ll da̱ughters
3. Da̱wn's ca̱use
4. tho̱ughtful Pa̱ula
5. beca̱use it's the la̱w
6. small ta̱lk
7. la̱wn party
8. doing la̱undry
9. wa̱lking in a̱utumn
10. a̱ltogether exha̱usting

SENTENCES /ɔ → ǫ/ (all)

1. Loosen your jaw.

2. Well, that was awkward.

3. The production was awful.

4. Return that horse to its stall.

5. They taught class on the lawn.

6. Is anyone in the drawing room?

7. Let's walk towards the waterfall.

8. Layer the sausages in the saucepan.

9. They called out, but Saul didn't hear.

10. The children are drawing with chalk.

11. We haven't met your daughter-in-law.

12. I understand the auditorium is haunted.

13. What did Shaun order? He's inaudible.

14. She auditioned to an onslaught of applause.

15. The exhausted author called off his scheduled talk.

STANDARD BRITISH TEXT /ɔ → ǫ/ (all). *Mark the following and speak out loud.*

        ǫ
I am more than usually ta̲ll for my age.
(Wilde: The Importance of Being Earnest)

How, you saucy fellow!
(Wycherley: The Country Wife)

I mean, he never speaks truth at all—that's all.
(Congreve: The Way of the World)

Run, I say; call him again. I will have him called.
(Etherege: The Man of Mode)

He talks Latin—it does me good to hear him talk Latin.
(Farquhar: The Beaux Stratagem)

Audacious villain!

(Congreve: The Way of the World)

Thought does not become a young woman.

(Sheridan: The Rivals)

Because I always had an aversion to being us'd like a dog.

(Vanbrugh: The Provok'd Wife)

Not to detain you then with longer pause
In short; my heart to this conclusion draws,
I yield it to the hand, that's loudest in applause.

(Sheridan: The School for Scandal, Epilogue)

I have brought over not so much as a bawdy picture.

(Wycherley: The Country Wife)

A cup, save thee, and what a cup hast thou brought!

(Congreve: The Way of the World)

CECILY.   Uncle Jack is sending you to Australia.
ALGERNON. Australia! I'd sooner die.

(Wilde: The Importance of Being Earnest)

Nothing but love could make me capable of so much falsehood.

(Etherege: The Man of Mode)

But who would have thought a woman could have been false to me?
I could not have thought it.

(Wycherley: The Country Wife)

You must not be so talkative, Diggory. You must be all attention
to the guests. You must hear us talk, and not think of talking.

(Goldsmith: She Stoops to Conquer)

If he has fallen from his altar, do not thrust him into the mire.

(Wilde: An Ideal Husband)

I was more than once nearly choked with gall during the honeymoon.

(Sheridan: The School for Scandal, Epilogue)

/ ɒ̞ / (honest)

This back vowel sound is similar to that spoken in Classical American, except that it is formed with the jaw slightly more closed, the lips more energized, and the back of the tongue arched slightly higher in the mouth. This is represented in the IPA symbol by the vertical line underneath: /ɒ̞/.

In addition, the sound can be expressed in a slightly more clipped manner in Standard British than in Classical American.

AUDIO 83 ▶ /ɒ → ɒ̞/ (honest)

>   ɒ̞   ɒ̞
> Life is n<u>o</u>t all plays and poems, <u>O</u>ctavius.
>
>   (Shaw: Man and Superman)
>
>   ɒ̞   ɒ̞   ɒ̞   ɒ̞   ɒ̞
> Wh<u>a</u>t? Wh<u>a</u>t is it n<u>o</u>t? Wh<u>a</u>t is it n<u>o</u>t yet? Is it n<u>o</u>t yet too late.
>
>   (Congreve: The Way of the World)
>
>   ɒ̞
> A p<u>o</u>x! They are come too soon!
>
>   (Wycherley: The Country Wife)

Remember: the /ɒ̞/ (h<u>o</u>nest) sound is used:

(a)   in words spelled with 'o' and pronounced with the /ɑ/ (f<u>a</u>ther) sound in Neutral American, as in:

              not, hot, on, box, top, stop, job, shopping, probably, Tom

(b)   in words spelled with 'qua' or 'wa' and pronounced with the /ɑ/ (f<u>a</u>ther) sound in Neutral American including:

              kumquat, quad, quaff, squab, squad, squalid, squalor, squash, squat, swaddling, swallow, swamp, wad, wallet, wallow, Wally, wan, wand, wander, want, wash, wasp, wast, wassail, watch, watt, yacht

(c)   in words spelled with 'o' and pronounced with the /ɔ/ (<u>a</u>ll) sound in Neutral American, as in:

cloth, moth, cross, boss, dog, office, often, song, belong

Exception: words spelled 'ought' as in bought, fought, and sought, are spoken with /ɔ/ in Standard British.

(d)   in strong forms of a few words pronounced with the /ʌ/ (<u>UH</u>) sound in Neutral American, including:

from, of, 'twas, was, wasn't, what, whatnot, whereof

WORDS /ɒ → ọ/ (h<u>o</u>nest)

topic	dogs	moth	boss
coffee	slosh	across	shop
strong	prompt	belong	Robin

PHRASES /ɒ → ọ/ (h<u>o</u>nest)

1.	l<u>o</u>st pr<u>o</u>perty	6.	h<u>o</u>t c<u>o</u>ffee
2.	wh<u>a</u>t sch<u>o</u>lars	7.	B<u>o</u>xing Day
3.	n<u>o</u>t pr<u>o</u>blematic	8.	J<u>o</u>hn's c<u>o</u>ttage
4.	Robert's d<u>o</u>ssier	9.	l<u>o</u>ts of m<u>o</u>nol<u>o</u>gues
5.	w<u>a</u>sn't w<u>a</u>tching	10.	interesting sh<u>o</u>pping

SENTENCES /ɒ → ọ/ (h<u>o</u>nest)

1.   It's not abolished.

2.   Is peroxide toxic?

3.   Economics can be problematic.

4.   Robin's fond of Moroccan food.

5.   Disc jockeys can be terribly cocky.

6.   Who's playing PROSPERO? I'm not!

7.   Stop looking at your watch, Thomas.

8.   Donald handed out copies of the play.

9.   It was shot in Hong Kong last October.

458

10.   John has such wonderful comic timing.

11.   The actor spoke of his 'process' over coffee.

12.   Doris is very cosmopolitan and knowledgeable.

13.   I need a summer cottage in the tropics, that's obvious.

14.   Who dropped his wallet in Washington, Joshua or Joffrey?

STANDARD BRITISH TEXT   /ɒ → ǫ̣/ (h<u>o</u>nest).   *Mark the following and speak out loud.*

ǫ̣
Their malice is int<u>o</u>lerable!
(Sheridan: The School for Scandal)

Eternal blockhead! Hey, sot.
(Vanbrugh: The Provok'd Wife)

That's my dear little scholar, kiss me again.
(Farquhar: The Beaux Stratagem)

Lord Foppington! I know him not.
(Vanbrugh: The Relapse)

Here, sirrah, reach me the strong-box.
(Farquhar: The Beaux Stratagem)

Cannot repentance wipe out an act of folly?
(Wilde: The Importance of Being Earnest)

She's gone, but she has left a pleasing image of herself behind that wanders in my soul.
(Etherege: The Man of Mode)

Succeed or no, still victory's my lot;
If I subdue his heart, 'tis well; if not,
I shall subdue my conscience to my plot.
(Vanbrugh: The Relapse)

What, invite your wife to kiss men? Monstrous!
(Wycherley: The Country Wife)

Stop a bit. I want to take you into my confidence.
(Shaw: Mrs. Warren's Profession)

A pox on him and his smile!

(Wycherley: The Country Wife)

See who that is. Set down the bottle first.

(Congreve: The Way of the World)

The strongest vessels, if they put to sea,
May possibly be lost.

(Vanbrugh: The Relapse)

'Tis for the honour of England, that all Europe should know we
have blockheads of all ages.

(Congreve: The Way of the World)

You astonish me! I thought you did not expect him this month.

(Sheridan: School for Scandal)

I do know your wife, sir; she's a woman, sir, and consequently
a monster, sir, a greater monster than a husband, sir.

(Wycherley: The Country Wife)

I have been the miserablest dog ever since that ever committed
wedlock!

(Sheridan: The School for Scandal)

'Tis the best plot in the world: your mother, you know, will be
gone to church.

(Farquhar: The Beaux Stratagem)

Odds whips and wheels! I've traveled like a comet, with a tail
of dust all the way as long as the Mall.

(Sheridan: The Rivals)

Yes, Juan, we know the libertine's philosophy. Always ignore
the consequences to the woman.

(Shaw: Man and Superman)

What would those modern psychological novelists, of whom we
hear so much, say to such a theory as that?

(Wilde: An Ideal Husband)

460

'Ask' List

This is a list of words that have alternate pronunciations depending on the dialect being spoken: Neutral American, Classical American, Mid-Atlantic[1] or Standard British.

Neutral American and Classical American: there is no change, the /æ/ (th<u>a</u>t) sound is maintained on the 'ask' list of words.

Standard British: the 'ask' list of words is spoken with the /ɑ/ (f<u>a</u>ther) sound.

AUDIO 84▶ /ɑ/ (f<u>a</u>ther) on 'ask' list words

ɑ
There is a r<u>a</u>scal in our midst.

(Shaw: Man and Superman)

ɑ
Don't play that gh<u>a</u>stly tune, Algy!

(Wilde: The Importance of Being Earnest)

ɑ   ɑ
My <u>aunt</u>, sir, yes, my <u>aunt</u>, sir, and your lady, sir; your lady

ɑ
is my <u>aunt</u>.

(Congreve: The Way of the World)

Which words are included in the 'ask' list?

There is not a distinct rule for inclusion, but spellings can offer a fairly reliable indication. For example:

<u>aft</u>   abaft, aft, after, aftermath, afternoon, afterward, behalf, craft, daft, draft, graft, raft, shaft, Shaftesbury, Taft, waft, witchcraft

<u>ampl</u>   ample, example, sample

---

[1] Mid-Atlantic dialect uses /a/ on ask list words. See pages 422-426.

ance /ans	advance, answer, chance, chancellor, chancery, dance, enhance, France, freelance, glance, lance, prance, trance
anch	avalanche, blanch(e), branch, ranch, stanch
and	Chandler, command(o), countermand, demand, reprimand, slander
ant[1] **/aunt**	advantage, aunt, can't, chant, chantry, enchant, grant, implant, plant, shan't, slant, supplant, transpl<u>a</u>nt, vantage
as(s)	alas, brass, class, Glasgow, glass, grass, pass, Passover, trespass
ask	ask, bask, basket, cask, flask, mask, task, rascal, vast
asp	clasp, gasp, grasp, hasp, rasp, raspberry
ast	aghast, alabaster, avast, blast, broadcast, cast, caste, castle, contrast, disaster, fast, ghastly, last, mast, master, nasty, past, pastor, pasture, plaster, repast, telecast, vast, vasty
ath	bath, lath, lather, path, rather, wrath
aff /affe	chaff, distaff, Falstaff, gaff, giraffe, quaff, staff
alf /aph	autograph, behalf, calf, half, epitaph, graph, telegraph
augh	laugh, laughter, draught

In the previous three lines above, all the consonant spellings listed are pronounced /**f**/ (af, aff, affe, alf, aph, augh).

There are a few words one might expect to find on the 'ask' list, which are actually pronounced with /æ/, for example: c<u>a</u>n, cl<u>a</u>ssicist, g<u>a</u>ther, cr<u>a</u>ss. If you question pronunciation, consult a *British-English* pronouncing dictionary.

PHRASES /ɑ/ (f<u>a</u>ther) on 'ask' list words

1.	on his beh<u>al</u>f	6	Nasty Fr<u>a</u>nce<u>s</u>
2.	hold steadf<u>a</u>stly	7.	just h<u>al</u>f a gl<u>a</u>ss
3.	cutting the gr<u>a</u>ss	8.	adv<u>a</u>ncing at l<u>a</u>st
4.	good r<u>a</u>spberries	9.	filling empty fl<u>a</u>sks
5.	a p<u>a</u>th in Fl<u>a</u>nders	10.	entr<u>a</u>ncing s<u>a</u>mpling

---

[1] Though 'ant' spelling can indicate inclusion on the 'ask' list of words, the word 'ant' (the insect) is pronounced /**æ**nt/.

462

SENTENCES /ɑ/ (f**a**ther) on 'ask' list words

1. It's very drafty.

2. Ask me after class.

3. Fasten your seatbelts.

4. Mr. Branch is a taskmaster.

5. Chandler demanded an answer.

6. That casting call was a disaster.

7. My aunt chants every afternoon.

8. They looked aghast at the avalanche.

9. There was no answer from the bathroom.

10. The paragraph was engraved in alabaster.

11. A ghastly smell wafted through the room.

12. They're casting *Dancin'* in the next classroom.

13. Give me an example of an artistic masterpiece.

14. Look how fast the glass-blowers made that sample.

15. The school master made him write, "I shan't slander."

STANDARD BRITISH TEXT /ɑ/ (f**a**ther) on 'ask' list words. *Mark the following and speak out loud.*

ɑ
She made me l**a**ugh yesterday.

(Vanbrugh: The Provok'd Wife)

I am more advanced than ever I was. I grow more advanced every day.

(Shaw: Man and Superman)

I think wit as necessary at dinner as a glass of good wine.
(Wycherley: The Country Wife)

I can't abide you; go, I can't abide you.

(Etherege: The Man of Mode)

Why, first she's an heiress, vastly rich.

(Vanbrugh: The Provok'd Wife)

Ay, ay, let that pass—there are other throats to be cut.

(Congreve: The Way of the World)

'Tis, let me see, a quarter and half quarter of a minute past eleven.

(Wycherley: The Country Wife)

They seem as a class, to have absolutely no sense of moral responsibility.

(Wilde: The Importance of Being Earnest)

Half the pretty women in London smoke cigarettes. Personally I prefer the other half.

(Wilde: An Ideal Husband)

When her folly makes 'em laugh, she thinks they are pleas'd with her wit.

(Vanbrugh: The Provok'd Wife)

There's something in that which may turn to advantage.

(Farquhar: The Beaux Stratagem)

The paragraphs, you say, Mr. Snake, were all inserted?

(Sheridan: The School for Scandal)

May I ask if you are engaged to be married to this young lady?

(Wilde: The Importance of Being Earnest)

And men, I suppose, never throw off the mask when their bird is in the net.

(Shaw: Man and Superman)

I'gad, if thou canst bring this about, I'll have thy statue cast in brass.

(Vanbrugh: The Relapse)

I take care never to come into a married family! The commands of the master and mistress are always so contrary, that 'tis impossible to please both.

(Farquhar: The Beaux Stratagem)

Polysyllabic word endings

There are two options for polysyllabic words (words of three or more syllables) ending in 'ary', 'ory', or 'berry' spellings:

(a)   The short schwa sound with no 'r' coloring /ə/ (uh) is used in the second to the last syllable. The final 'y' takes an /ɪ/ (wi**ll**) suffix, so the word endings are pronounced: /ə-rɪ/

(b)   The schwa that was in the second to the last syllable is dropped, making the word ending shorter and more clipped. So, 'purgatory' could be spoken: /'pɜgətə-rɪ/ or /'pɜgətrɪ/

Polysyllabic words ending in 'ony' are pronounced /ə-nɪ/.

AUDIO 85▶ polysyllabic word endings

(drop the schwa altogether, or speak: ə-rɪ)
Your caution may be **'ne**cess<u>a</u>-ry.

(Farquhar: The Beaux Stratagem)

(drop the schwa altogether, or speak: ə-rɪ)
That is satis**'fac**t<u>o</u>-ry.

(Wilde: The Importance of Being Earnest)

(drop the schwa altogether, or speak: ə-rɪ)
He promises to be an ex**'traor**din<u>a</u>-ry person.

(Congreve: The Way of the World)

WORDS 'ony' endings pronounced /ənɪ/

'acrimony	'agrimony	'alimony	'antimony
'ceremony	cere'monious	'matrimony	'patrimony
'parsimony	parsi'monious	'sanctimony	'testimony

mənɪ
At what hour would you wish the cere<u>mony</u> performed?

(Wilde: The Importance of Being Earnest)

VOWELS BEFORE / r /

In Standard British as in Classical American, when the consonant /r/ occurs in the middle of a word, it should be preceded by a pure vowel sound, not a diphthong.

In Standard British only, when the consonant /r/ occurs between two vowel sounds, the tongue tip can 'tap' the alveolar ridge, resulting in a sound similar to a soft /d/, and often associated with the word 'very' (ve_dy).

The vowel and the consonant /r/ that follows it are separated by a dash throughout, for clarity.

/ ɪ / (wi̱ll)

before consonant / r /

Use the pure /ɪ/ (wi̱ll) sound, rather than the /ɪɚ / (he̱re) diphthong, before consonant /r/. Words requiring this adjustment can often be recognized by the presence of an /ɪ/ prefix and/or by the initial spelling 'irr'.

AUDIO 86▶ /ɪ/ (wi̱ll) before /r/

                                          ɪ   ɑ
I always hoped it would be something really he-roic, at last.
                                          (Shaw: Man and Superman)

                              ɪ
For me you have always had an i-rresistible fascination.
                              (Wilde: The Importance of Being Earnest)

     'sɪrə
Here, si-rrah, light me to my chamber.
                              (Farquhar: The Beaux Stratagem)

PRACTICE WORDS, PHRASES, SENTENCES   page 357-361.

STANDARD BRITISH TEXT /ɪ/ (w**i**ll) **before** /r/. *Mark the following and speak out loud.*

I

Here you escape this t**y**ranny of the flesh.

(Shaw: Man and Superman)

I'll aid you with such arms for their destruction,
They never shall erect their heads again.

(Vanbrugh: The Relapse)

Here they talk of nothing else but love: its beauty, its holiness, its spirituality, it's the devil knows what!

(Shaw: Man and Superman)

Your decision on the subject of my name is irrevocable, I suppose?

(Wilde: The Importance of Being Earnest)

I suppose you will go in seriously for politics some day, Jack.

(Shaw: Man and Superman)

Though the renewing my visit may seem a little irregular, I hope
I shall obtain your pardon for it.

(Vanbrugh: The Provok'd Wife)

It needs a brain, this irresistible force, lest in its ignorance it should resist itself.

(Shaw: Man and Superman)

I little thought, madam, to see your spirit tamed to this degree.

(Etherege: The Man of Mode)

Marriage is honourable, as you say; and if so, wherefore should cuckoldom be a discredit, being derived from so honourable a root?

(Congreve: The Way of the World)

/ e / (g<u>e</u>t)

before consonant /r/

Use the pure **/e/** (g<u>e</u>t) sound, rather than the **/eə̆/** (th<u>eir</u>) diphthong, before consonant **/r/**. Words requiring this adjustment can often be recognized by 'er' or 'err' in the spelling.

AUDIO 87▶ **/e/** (g<u>e</u>t) before **/r/**

              e

With Ann as the he-roine?

(Shaw: Man and Superman)

           e

We are knight e-rrants, and so Fortune be our guide.

(Farquhar: The Beaux Stratagem)

                e

A pox take you both; fetch me the che-rry brandy then.

(Congreve: The Way of the World)

PRACTICE WORDS, PHRASES, SENTENCES   **page 362-365.**

STANDARD BRITISH TEXT   **/e/** (g<u>e</u>t) **before /r/**. *Mark the following and speak out loud.*

                   e

I don't mean to defend Charles's <u>e</u>rrors.

(Sheridan: The School for Scandal)

Why, I ask you nothing but what you may very well spare.

(Vanbrugh: The Provok'd Wife)

If he should marry and have a child, you may be disinherited, ha?

(Congreve: The Way of the World)

Yes, he has told me all about poor Mr. Bunbury, and his terrible state of health.

(Wilde: The Importance of Being Earnest)

/ æ / (th<u>a</u>t)

before consonant / r /

Use /æ/ (th<u>a</u>t) (rather than /eə̆/ (th<u>ei</u>r)) before /r/. These words can often be recognized by their 'ar' or 'arr' spelling.

AUDIO 88▶ /æ/ (th<u>a</u>t) before /r/

'næ-rəŭnɪs
I scorn its n<u>a</u>-rrowness.

(Shaw: Man and Superman)

æ   æ
Ah, nowadays that is no g<u>ua</u>-rantee of respectability of character.

(Wilde: The Importance of Being Earnest)

æ   ə
O, he c<u>a</u>-rries poison in his tongue that would c<u>o</u>-rrupt integrity itself.

(Congreve: The Way of the World)

PRACTICE WORDS, PHRASES, SENTENCES   page 366-370.

STANDARD BRITISH TEXT /æ/ (th<u>a</u>t) before /r/. *Mark the following and speak out loud.*

æ
What do you think of your p<u>a</u>ragon now?

(Shaw: Man and Superman)

Harry, take this, and let your man carry it for me to Mrs. Fourbes's chamber.

(Etherege: The Man of Mode)

He's firm in his resolution, tells me I must marry Mrs. Harriet, or swears he'll marry himself and disinherit me.

(Etherege: The Man of Mode)

Very Upper-Class Characters

Such characters may be played with a slightly slurred, whiny, nasal sound accomplished, in part, by the jaw's remaining mostly closed while under-utilizing the articulators.

The following may also be incorporated:

* especially short, clipped /ɪ/ (w<u>i</u>ll) endings

* /æ/ (th<u>a</u>t) sounds spoken as /e/ (g<u>e</u>t)

* brighter, longer /ʌ/ (<u>UH</u>) sounds that almost sound like the front vowel /a/

* more precisely 'formed' /əŭ/ (g<u>o</u>) diphthongs

* /aĭə/ (fire) and /aŭə/ (power) triphthongs blending their three elements to sound like one long vowel

* use of voiceless /hw/ on /w/ sounds spelled 'wh'

* more frequent tapping, rolling, or trilling of the consonant /r/ when it occurs between two vowels

This can be heard on Audio 97, a section of which is notated below:

> a   djuĕrɪŋ   'tempərɪ   ə   ʌ   ɒ
> *This aft^hernoo<u>n</u>, during my temporary absence in London on an*
> ɔ *(or ə)*   əŭ æ *(or e)*   haĭs
> *impo<u>r</u>ta<u>n</u>t questio<u>n</u> of romance[1], he obtained admissio<u>n</u> to my house[2]*
> ɒ   ɔ   ɒ
> *by means of the false pret^hence[3] of being my brothe<u>r</u>.*

(Wilde: The Importance of Being Earnest)

Note: Technically, the tapped /r/ is represented phonetically by the symbol /ɾ/ which is almost identical to the usual consonant symbol /r/. So the tapped **'r'** is notated by /d/ in the monologues on pages 493-497 to avoid confusion.

---

[1] Also commonly pronounced: /rəŭ'mæns/, even when used as a noun.

[2] Very upper class pronunciation of 'house' can be: /haĭs/.

[3] Also commonly pronounced: /prɪ'tens/.

COMMON BRITISH-ENGLISH WORDS
WITH AMERICAN-ENGLISH MEANING

Brit. word	Am. equiv.	Brit. word	Am. equiv.
aubergine	eggplant	mousse pudding	pudding
barrister	trial lawyer	nappy	diaper
biscuit	cookie	oven cloth	pot holder
bobby	policeman	pence	penny
bonnet	hood (car)	petrol	gasoline
boot	trunk (car)	pram	baby carriage
braces	suspenders	public school	private school
caravan	trailer	queue	line
caretaker	janitor	roundabout	traffic circle
chemist	druggist	shire	county
cloak room	toilet, bathroom	solicitor	lawyer
constable	police officer	stalls	orchestra seats
crisps	chips	stand for office	run for office
dressing gown	bathrobe	sticking plaster	band aid
dust	garbage	sweets	candy
flat	apartment	swimming	
fish slice	spatula	costume	swimsuit
form, class	grade	surgery	doctor's office
fringe	bangs	torch	flashlight
go on holiday	take a vacation	trunk call	long distance
hair grip	bobby pin	underground	
interval	intermission	(or) tube	subway, metro
jumper	sweater	waistcoat	vest
legal holiday	bank holiday	WC, (or) loo,	restroom, toilet,
lift	elevator	(or) lavatory	bathroom
lodger	roomer	windscreen	windshield
lorry	truck	wireless	radio
mackintosh	raincoat	zed	'Z'

COMMON AMERICAN-ENGLISH WORDS WITH
STANDARD BRITISH PRONUNCIATION
(transcribed without aspiration markings)

again	/əˈgen/	leisure	/ˈleʒə/
	or /əˈgeĭn/	lever	/ˈlivə/
against	/əˈgeĭnst/	lieutenant	/lefˈtenənt/
aluminum	/æljuˈmɪnɪəm/	massage	/ˈmæsɑʒ/
anti	/ˈæntɪ/	missile	/ˈmɪsaĭl/
baptize	/bæpˈtaĭz/	neither	/ˈnaĭðə/
barrage	/ˈbæraʒ/	nephew	/ˈnevju/
been	/bin/, /bɪn/	omega	/ˈəŭmɪgə/
borough	/ˈbʌrə/	patent	/ˈpeĭtənt/
clerk	/klɑk/	patriot	/ˈpætrɪət/
constable	/ˈkʌnstəbl̩/	potato	/pəˈtɑtəŭ/
depot	/ˈdepəŭ/		or /pəˈteĭtəu/
derby	/ˈdabɪ/	premature	/ˈpremətjŭə/
either	/ˈaĭðə/	privacy	/ˈprɪvəsɪ/
erase	/ɪˈreɪz/	process	/ˈprəŭses/
figure	/ˈfɪgə/	quinine	/kwɪˈnin/
frustrated	/frʌˈstreĭtɪd/	record	/ˈrekǫd/
futile	/ˈfjutaĭl/	schedule	/ˈʃedjul/
garage	/ˈgæraʒ/	sensual	/ˈsensjuəl/
glacier	/ˈgleɪsjə/	sexual	/ˈseksjuəl/
herb	/hɜb/	suggest	/səˈdʒest/
hostile	/ˈhɒstaĭl/	tissue	/ˈtɪsju/
inquiry	/ɪŋˈkwaĭɚɪ/	tomato	/təˈmatəŭ/
iodine	/ˈaĭədin/	vermouth	/ˈvɜməθ/
issue	/ˈɪsju/ or /ˈɪʃu/	weekend	/wiˈkend/
laboratory	/ləˈbǫrətrɪ/	'Z'	/zed/

PRACTICE TEXT

Mark the following selections from Mother Goose for Standard British and speak out loud.

1. **/i → ɪ/**

   Solomon Grundy,
   Born on a Monday…

2. **no 'r' color**

   Peter, Peter, pumpkin eater,
   Had a wife and couldn't keep her.

3. **consonants**
   esp. **/pʰ, tʰ, kʰ/**

   A farmer went a trotting upon his gray mare
   Bumpety, bumpety, bump!

4. **/oŭ → əŭ/**

   Old King Cole was a merry old soul,
   And a merry old soul was he!

5. **/ɒ → ọ/**

   Hickory, dickory, dock,
   The mouse ran up the clock.

6. **/ɔ → ọ/**

   Jerry Hall, he is so small
   A rat could eat him, hat and all.

7. **ask list /ɑ/**

   If the diamond ring turns to brass,
   Papa's going to buy you a looking-glass.

8. **polysyllabics**

   A man in the wilderness said to me,
   How many strawberries grow in the sea?

9. **pure vowels**
   before **/r/**

   Pease porridge hot,
   Pease porridge cold…

10. **tapped /r/**

    Pease porridge in the pot
    Nine days old.

11. **liquid /ju/**
    (& days of week)

    Monday's child is fair of face,
    Tuesday's child is full of grace.

12. **pure /aɪ̆/**

    Star light, star bright,
    First star I see tonight…

13. **pure /æ/**

    Pat-a-cake, pat-a-cake, baker's man,
    Bake me a cake as fast as you can.

14. **/ɑŭ/** (relaxed)

    Wee Willie Winkie runs through the town
    Upstairs and downstairs in his nightgown.

PRACTICE TEXT

Mark Standard British sound changes, then speak out loud.

1.   Oh! is it a proposal?

(Wilde: An Ideal Husband)

2.   I'll send for't tomorrow.

(Vanbrugh: The Relapse)

3.   Well, Tom, I find you're a marksman.

(Farquhar: The Beaux Stratagem)

4.   How pertinently the jade answers me!

(Congreve: The Way of the World)

5.   No; but seriously, I hate to do a rude thing.

(Wycherley: The Plain Dealer)

6.   I will not be seen in women's company in public again for the world.

(Wycherley: The Country Wife)

7.   I think your frankness does you great credit, Earnest.

(Wilde: The Importance of Being Earnest)

8.   The liberty you take abroad makes her hanker after it.

(Wycherley: The Country Wife)

9.   Well, my own dear, sweet, loving little darling, I really can't see
     why you should object to the name of Algernon.

(Wilde: The Importance of Being Earnest)

10. He's reckoning his money—my money it was—I have no luck today.

(Congreve: Way of the World)

11. I know nobody sings so near a cherubim as your ladyship.

(Vanbrugh: The Provok'd Wife)

12. I could hear but a word here and there; but I remembered they
     mentioned a Count, a closet, a back-door, and a key.

(Farquhar: The Beaux Stratagem)

13. I was obliged to call on dear Lady Harbury. I hadn't been there since
her poor husband's death. I never saw a woman so altered; she looks
quite twenty years younger.

(Wilde: The Importance of Being Earnest)

14. Here, take away the things; I expect company. But first bring me
a pipe; I'll smoke.

(Vanbrugh: The Provok'd Wife)

15. His master spends his money so freely, and is so much a gentleman
every manner of way, he must be a highwayman.

(Farquhar: The Beaux Stratagem)

16. Though I am a young rake-hell, and have played many a roguish
trick, this is so full-grown a cheat, I find I must take pains to come
up to't; I have scruples.

(Vanbrugh: The Relapse)

17. Wine gives you liberty, love takes it away.

(Wycherley: The Country Wife)

18. My courage should disperse your apprehensions.

(Vanbrugh: The Relapse)

19. I deposited the manuscript in the bassinette, and placed the baby
in the hand-bag.

(Wilde: The Importance of Being Earnest)

20. Where nights and days seemed all consumed in joy.

(Vanbrugh: The Relapse)

21. Ay; and what is very extraordinary, in all our disputes she is always
in the wrong.

(Sheridan: The School for Scandal)

22. Providence, thou seest at last, takes care of men of merit: we are in
a fair way to be great people.

(Vanbrugh: The Relapse)

23. People who don't keep their appointments in the Park are horrid.

(Wilde: An Ideal Husband)

24. Mrs. Clackitt assured me Mr. and Mrs. Honeymoon were at last become mere man and wife like the rest of their acquaintance.

(Sheridan: The School for Scandal)

25. You old bawd, how have you the impudence to be hobbling out of your grave twenty years after you are rotten!

(Vanbrugh: The Relapse)

26. He's but a half-brother, and I'm your entire friend.

(Farquhar: Beaux Stratagem)

27. Though I was born to servitude, I hate it.

(Farquhar: The Beaux Stratagem)

28. This pious charity to the afflicted well becomes your character.

(Lillo: The London Merchant)

29. Yet they seem to have a torrent of love to dispose of.

(Vanbrugh: The Relapse)

30. Were I that thing they call a slighted wife, somebody should run the risk of being that thing they call—a husband.

(Vanbrugh: The Relapse)

31. I have made you privy to my whole design, and put it in your power to ruin or advance my fortune.

(Congreve: The Way of the World)

32. O, ay, letters—I had letters—I am persecuted with letters— I hate letters—nobody knows how to write letters.

(Congreve: The Way of the World)

33. Well, I must leave you—and let me beg you, Mrs. Malaprop, to enforce this matter roundly to the girl;—take my advice—keep a tight hand—if she rejects this proposal—clap her under lock and key:—and if you were just to let the servants forget to bring her dinner for three or four days, you can't conceive how she'd come about!

(Sheridan: The Rivals)

PRACTICE TEXT

From **MAN AND SUPERMAN**

George Bernard Shaw

Mark Standard British sound changes, then speak out loud.

1. And who the deuce is the superman?

2. Dear lady: a parable must not be taken literally.

3. You are in good spirits today, Commander. You are positively brilliant. What's the matter?

4. I am not a man of honor: I am a man struck down by a dead hand.

5. But the English really do not seem to know when they are thoroughly miserable.

6. Never in my moments of superstitious terror on earth did I dream that Hell was so horrible.

7. You dare boast, before me and my father, that every woman found you irresistible.

8. And he came, sword in hand, to vindicate outraged honour and morality by murdering me.

9. Things immeasurably greater than man in every respect but brain have existed and perished.

10. Sincerity! To be fool enough to believe a ramping, stamping, thumping lie: that is what you call sincerity!

11. You know perfectly well that I am as sober and honest a citizen as yourself. As truthful personally, and much more truthful politically and morally.

12. The confusion of marriage with morality has done more to destroy the conscience of the human race than any other single error.

13. Have you any canonical authority for assuming that there is any barrier between our circle and the other one?

14. The earth is a nursery where men and women play at being heroes and heroines, saints and sinners, but they are dragged down from their fool's paradise by their bodies.

15. But even as you enjoy the contemplation of such romantic mirages as beauty and pleasure; so would I enjoy the contemplation of that which interests me above all things: namely, Life.

16. It is natural that I should have a certain delicacy in talking to my old friend's daughter about her behind her back.

17. I haven't any money, nor the smallest turn for making it.

18. And will all the men call me their dear Ana?

19. You are incorrigible, Jack. But you should not jest about our affection for one another. Nobody could possibly misunderstand it. You do not misunderstand it, I hope.

20. His excellency the Commander puts it with military bluntness; but the strain of living in Heaven is intolerable.

From A TALE OF TWO CITIES

Charles Dickens

It was the best of times, it was the worst of times, it was the age of wisdom, it was the age of foolishness, it was the epoch of belief, it was the epoch of incredulity, it was the season of Light, it was the season of Darkness, it was the spring of hope, it was the winter of despair, we had everything before us, we had nothing before us, we were all going direct to Heaven, we were all going direct the other way —in short, the period was so far like the present period, that some of its noisiest authorities insisted on its being received, for good or for evil, in the superlative degree of comparison only.

There were a king with a large jaw and a queen with a plain face, on the throne of England; there were a king with a large jaw and a queen with a fair face, on the throne of France. In both countries it was clearer than crystal to the lords of the State preserves of loaves and fishes, that things in general were settled for ever.

From GREAT EXPECTATIONS

Charles Dickens

We were running too fast to admit of more being said, and we made no stop until we got into our kitchen. It was full of people; the whole village was there, or in the yard; and there was a surgeon, and there was Joe, and there was a group of women, all on the floor in the midst of the kitchen. The unemployed bystanders drew back when they saw me, and so I became aware of my sister—lying without sense or movement on the bare boards where she had been knocked down by a tremendous blow on the back of the head, dealt by some unknown hand when her face was turned towards the fire—destined never to be on the Rampage again, while she was wife of Joe.

From **QUEEN MAB**

Percy Bysshe Shelley

THE FAIRY

"The Present and the Past thou hast beheld:
It was a desolate sight. Now, Spirit, learn
        The secrets of the Future.—Time!
Unfold the brooding pinion of thy gloom,
        Render thou up thy half-devoured babes,
And from the cradles of eternity,
Where millions lie lulled to their portioned sleep
By the deep murmuring stream of passing things,
Tear thou that gloomy shroud.—Spirit, behold
        Thy glorious destiny!"

From **THREE SONNETS ON WOMAN**

John Keats

Woman! When I behold thee flippant, vain,
        Inconstant, childish, proud, and full of fancies;
        Without that modest softening that enhances
The downcast eye, repentant of the pain
That its mild light creates to heal again:
        E'en then, elate, my spirit leaps, and prances,
        E'en then my soul with exultation dances
For that to love, so long, I've dormant lain:
But when I see thee meek, and kind, and tender,
        Heavens! How desperately do I adore
Thy winning graces;—to be thy defender
        I hotly burn—to be a Calidore—
A very Red Cross Knight—a stout Leander—
        Might I be loved by thee like these of yore.

KEY TO MARKING STANDARD BRITISH MONOLOGUES
(adjustments or changes from Classical American are shaded)

Rhythm Highlighters	Marking
Stressed syllables (not marked)	
Weak forms (not marked)	
/ɪ/ (wɪll) prefixes and suffixes	ɪ ɪ ɪ repeat, deny, closet
/ə/ (uh) schwa suffixes	ə ə statement, doorman
Syllabic endings marked /n̩ l̩ m̩/	wooden̩, little̩, prism̩
/i/→/ɪ/ unstressed endings (spelled 'y' or 'i')	ɪ ɪ ɪ pretty, tally, happiness
No 'r' coloring ('sports', 'car' diphthongs also drop the schwa)	here, father, short
Vowel Sound Considerations	**Marking**
Linking words (not marked)	
/e/ (get) before 'm', 'n' (in a stressed syllable)	e e e them, when, sent
/æ/ (that) before n, m, ng, nk (pure non-nasal vowel)	æ æ æ land, Hamlet, man
/ɔ/ (all) closed/longer, /ɒ/ (honest) closed/clipped	ɔ̞ ɔ̞ ɒ̞ ɒ̞ fall, ought, often, hot
/ʊə̆/ (poor) diphthong (more energized and no 'r' coloring)	ʊə̆ ʊə̆ assure, tour
/aɪ̆/ (my) diphthong (before voiceless consonant in the same word)	aɪ̆ aɪ̆ aɪ̆ bright, night, wife
Liquid /ju/ (you) (after 't', 'd', 'n', optional after 's', 'l')	tju dju nju tune, duke, news
/aʊ̆/ (now), /aʊ̆ə̆/ (power) (initial element changes)	aʊ̆ aʊ̆ə̆ mountain, sour
/oʊ̆/ (go) diphthong→/əu/	əʊ̆ əʊ̆ əʊ̆ go, don't, snow
'Ask' list of words spoken with /a/ (father) sound	a a a pass, craft, dance
Vowels before consonant /r/ (complete observation) (new change: the schwa with no 'r' coloring)	ə ə mutte-rer, flatte-rer, etc.
Polysyllabic endings: ary, ory, berry, ony spellings	trɪ (or) tə-rɪ secretary, secreta-ry
Consonant Sound Considerations	**Marking**
Consonants generally more vigorous and energized, Voiceless and voiced plosives more 'explosive'	hitʰ, tapʰ, packʰ
Voiced consonant endings (especially before a pause or silence)	dead, found
Consonant /r/ combinations (tr, dr, str)	tread, drive, street
Voiceless /hw/ (optional, used occasionally)	very upper class only

əʊ   æ   e   aʊ   'wɪə̆-dɪd
old as I am; when you have a thousand times wea-ried

        aɪ   ɑ
of heaven, like myself and the Commander, and a

   aʊ   dɪ   ɑ   ɪ
thousand times wea-ried of hell, as you are wea-ried

  aʊ   əʊ ɒ   ɪ   ɪ
now, you will no longer imagine that^h every swing

   ɒ   ɪ æ   ɪ
from heaven to hell is an emancipation, every swing

                 ivə'ljuʃn̩   aʊ
from hell to heaven an evolution. Where you now see

  ɪ ɔ   əʊ   ə   e   ɪ
reform, progress, fulfillment^h of upward tendencies,

          e   æ ɒ   ɪ   əʊ
continual ascent by Man on the stepping stones of

                           ɪ
his dead selves to higher things, you will see nothing

        ɒ   ɪ   ju
but^h an infinite comedy of illusions. You will discover

   əʊ aʊ   ɪ   dʒ   ɪ
the profound truth of the saying... that there is nothing
nju

new under the sun. Vanitas vanitatum.

(Shaw: Man and Superman / Don Juan in Hell)

APPENDIX

Short list of useful, indispensable books

A Treasury of Mother Goose. illustrated by Hilda Offen. New York: Simon & Schuster Books for Young Readers, 1984.

Barton, John. *Playing Shakespeare*: London: Methuen London Ltd., 1984.

Berry, Cicely. *The Actor and the Text*. London: Virginia Books, 1992.

Cambridge International Dictionary of English. Cambridge: Cambridge University Press, 2001.

Jones, Daniel. *English Pronouncing Dictionary*. Fourteenth Edition. London: Cambridge University Press, 1991.

Kenyon, John Samuel and Knott, Thomas Albert. *A Pronouncing Dictionary of American English*. Springfield, MA: Merriam-Webster Inc., 1953.

Linklater, Kristin. *Freeing Shakespeare's Voice*. New York: Theatre Communications Group, 1992.

Linklater, Kristin. *Freeing the Natural Voice*. Hollywood: Drama Publishers, 2006.

Onions, Charles Talbut. *A Shakespeare Glossary*. Edited by Robert D. Eagleson. New York: Oxford University Press, 1995.

Parkins, Ken. *Anthology of British Tongue Twisters*: New York: Samuel French, 1969.

Shakespeare, William. *The Riverside Shakespeare*. Boston: Houghlin Mifflin Co., 1997.

Skinner, Edith. *Speak With Distinction*. New York: Applause Theatre Books, 1990.

The Complete Rhyming Dictionary, edited by Clement Wood, revised by Ronald Bogus. New York: Doubleday, a division of Bantam Doubleday Dell Publishing Group, Inc., 1991.

APPENDIX I: SKINNER SPEECH

ABOUT THE AUTHOR

Patricia Fletcher has served as a Voice, Speech, Dialogue, and Dialect Coach for Broadway, Television, and Feature Films and has worked as an actor on and off Broadway. She has taught Dialects, Voice and Speech in numerous professional acting programs including: The New School for Drama, MFA Acting Program/New School University, Actor's Studio Drama School, Mason Gross School of the Arts MFA Acting Program/Rutgers University, Brooklyn College Graduate Acting Program, William Esper Acting Studio, and New Actors Workshop. She is a Designated Linklater Voice Instructor, holds an MA in Voice and Speech from Antioch University, and does extensive private coaching. www.patriciafletcher.com